BEST REGRETS

VMI'S JOHN MCKENNA
AND THE LOST AGE
OF COLLEGE FOOTBALL

Foreword by BOBBY ROSS

BY ROLAND LAZENBY AND MIKE ASHLEY

VMI Keydet Club
P.O. Box 932
Lexington, VA 24450
kclub@vmiaa.org

First edition: October 2014

The publisher is not responsible for websites (or their content) that are not owned by the publisher.

ISBN 978-0-692-26946-6
LCCN: GV956.6 .L39 2014

Printed in the United States of America

Also by Roland Lazenby

Michael Jordan: The Life

Jerry West: The Life and Legend of a Basketball Icon

*The Show: The Inside Story of the Spectacular
Los Angeles Lakers in the Words of Those Who Lived It*

Mindgames: Phil Jackson's Strange Journey

Mad Game: The NBA Education of Kobe Bryant

*Blood on the Horns: The Long Strange Ride
of Michael Jordan's Chicago Bulls*

Bull Run! The Story of the 1995-96 Chicago Bulls

Air Balls! Notes from the NBA's Far Side

The Lakers: A Basketball Journey

The Golden Game (with Billy Packer)

The NBA Finals

*Fifty Years of the Final Four: Golden Moments of the
NCAA Basketball Tournament* (with Billy Packer)

TABLE OF CONTENTS

PREFACE

J. H. Binford Peay III '62

General, U.S. Army (Retired)
Superintendent, Virginia Military Institute

It has been over 50 years since I played football at VMI under Coach John McKenna. He was a magnificent coach, leader, and role model for not only his players but for all with whom he came in contact. In retrospect, it was often after our time at VMI that we players understood the sheer genius of his coaching ability and the direction he gave us as we moved forward with our lives.

The idea for this book was initiated by two of Coach McKenna's former players, both from the Class of 1960 and both retired United States Air Force Officers, Tom Daniel and Howard Moss. It has been in the making since 2006, and VMI is fortunate that one of its own, Roland Lazenby, Class of 1974 and a renowned sports journalist and author, undertook the assignment.

Coach McKenna's tenure at VMI (1953-1965) was a time of the true student athlete. Perhaps, one-platoon football contributed to that as players competed both ways and had to be capable across the spectrum. He demanded that you perform academically, militarily, and ethically as well as on the playing field.

After the text of the book was completed, finding a publisher was the next task. On behalf of the Institute, I thank the VMI Keydet Club, our intercollegiate fundraising organization, for financing this venture.

Athletics are integral to who we are and what we do at VMI. The Keydet Club provides funding for athletic scholarships and financial support for athletic operations as well as helping to maintain and enhance that great intangible, the "Spirit of VMI."

It is ironic that this book is being published in the year of VMI's return to the Southern Conference, the league in which Coach McKenna and his Keydet teams had so much success. Through this book, we take a look back at a legend in VMI sports history, as well as a unique era in NCAA football, and why this man meant so much to so many.

FOREWORD

By Bobby Ross

Editor's Note: Ross, a 1959 VMI graduate, who played for John McKenna, won three consecutive Atlantic Coast Conference Championships from 1983 to 1985 as head football coach at the University of Maryland. In 1990, he led the Georgia Tech Yellow Jackets to an 11-0-1 record and a share of the national championship by finishing first in the final Coaches' Poll. That season Ross won the Paul "Bear" Bryant Award and the Bobby Dodd Coach of the Year Award. Ross was also highly successful in the NFL with both the San Diego Chargers and Detroit Lions. He led the Chargers to their only Super Bowl appearance, in 1995 (Super Bowl XXIX).

Coach John McKenna was many things to me – a mentor, a friend, an advisor, a coach – and I am quite sure the same to any of us who ever played for him during his football coaching career at Virginia Military Institute. I am honored to have been asked to write this Foreword on this very special man. When I got my first head coaching job, I went to see Coach McKenna and asked him, "Coach, if you could give me one piece of advice, what would it be?" I will never forget that moment. He shook his hand and said, "Rule with an iron fist."

I had played for Coach McKenna at VMI, and I understood immediately what he meant. His belief in discipline was extraordinary, and years later, we'd find ourselves still under the spell of that discipline; and it was funny, yet it was the perfect example of his powerful approach to coaching and to life. However, there was a softer side to him that I saw as an assistant on his staff in 1965 and later on as I would turn to him for advice. All who played for him at one time or another feared him, but we all, to a man, respected him even more!

His won/loss record at VMI as its head coach from 1953 to 1965 will probably never be equaled:

1. A winning record of 62-60-8
2. Four Southern Conference Championships – The Southern Conference then included West Virginia, Virginia Tech, William & Mary, and Richmond.
3. Six Virginia State Championships
4. The 1957 team was at one point in the season ranked 13th in the nation.
5. His 1957 &1958 teams went 18 games without a loss.
6. From 1957 – 1960 his teams went 30-5-5.
7. He was Southern Conference Coach of the Year in 1957, 1959, and 1962.
8. He is a member of the Virginia Sports Hall of Fame, and a Hall of Fame member of VMI, Villanova, and Loyola, Los Angeles (now Loyola Marymount).
9. He is an Honorary Alumnus of both VMI and Georgia Tech.

His many accomplishments while at VMI occurred at a school whose enrollment slightly exceeded 1,000 students (cadets). There is not another coach in this country who can match these accomplishments at a school with such a small student body.

As you read the following pages by Roland Lazenby and Mike Ashley, you will begin to understand what a unique and challenging environment VMI is and what a great, great coach John McKenna was to be able to succeed there against unimaginable odds for a Division I football coach. He lifted VMI to a level that allowed a small military school to compete against bigger, stronger teams – Virginia Tech, the University of Virginia, Penn State – in games that were just about always on the road. We were playing against those teams and competing, and it was good. We saw his character in winning and losing, and he never wavered. My freshman year at VMI, we won just one game. Two years later we went undefeated and climbed into the Associated Press ranking of the top twenty major college teams. He led us to that accomplishment and to witness it as a young man was a very powerful thing for me and for all of my teammates.

The Class of 1959 dedicated the VMI yearbook to Coach McKenna, but it was for much more than what he accomplished as a football coach – no, it was more for what he was as a man. Below are segments from that dedication and my talk upon his induction into the Virginia Sports Hall of Fame in 2007:

A gentleman and leader of young men, Coach McKenna has won the friendship of all those with whom he has come in contact, the respect of his players with his thoroughness and strict discipline, and the admiration of fans and sportswriters throughout Virginia.

His attributes as a speaker and as a VMI ambassador make him an excellent advertisement for VMI and athletics in general.

Newspaper columnists have called McKenna...an articulate and entertaining speaker, a spirited competitor, a deep thinker....

Coach McKenna has aptly been described as erudite (extensive knowledge acquired chiefly from books; profound in bookish learning), a characterization rarely earned by a member of the coaching profession. He concentrated as much on development of character in young men as he did on producing character on the gridiron.

In short, the impact Coach McKenna had on people's lives far exceeds his tremendous accomplishments as a football coach. For all who were ever touched by Coach – they became better people.

He was first and foremost a family man. He took great pride in his family, and if you were ever around them, you saw a great love for Coach. His passing came just a few days short of the 62nd wedding anniversary of him and his wonderful wife Eileen. She was every bit as strong as Coach, but in a very quiet and subtle manner. They both had a wonderful sense of humor; hearing him and Eileen joke back and forth was a real joy. He was a man of great faith. Being a Catholic, he required all Catholic players to attend a game day Mass, if it were possible. I can still hear him saying, "The bus leaves at 6:55 for Mass – be on it." Tom Joynes, a member of the athletic administration at VMI for many years, once called Coach "The Tom Landry of College Football." Coach was a true gentleman.

Some will talk of life's principles, but Coach lived them – he walked the walk, and he lived what he said. You listened attentively when he spoke – he was very direct.

He was always supportive – anytime anyone ever contacted him, there was always that letter of response, with words of wisdom and advice – hand written.

He had a profound influence on my coaching career, not only how I coached, but even where I coached. He had a direct impact on my getting the job at Georgia Tech, just as he had a direct impact when The Citadel hired me for my first head coaching job in college.

And when we won the national championship at Georgia Tech, it was a personal moment that he could celebrate too, because my coaching life, my ideals and approach, began with the great mentor and model that he was for us all. Over the course of my career, I always went back to Coach McKenna when there was a move that I was going to consider. I would always confide in him on everything I ever did coaching-wise. I would seek his advice, first and foremost. He was very much a factor in my coaching approach. I never forgot what he had told me about ruling with the iron fist.

He was nicknamed (certainly not to his face) "The Eagle" by the players, and I never knew why until I looked up the definition – "a bird noted for strength, size, and keenness of vision and power." – quite appropriate for this great man.

Coach has left us for a better place, but his imprint on our lives and that of our families will be with us forever. He was a Father figure, a mentor and confidant to all of us. And, although I can't say it nearly as well, I know that his family is very proud that a book has been written about such a distinguished man as their Father.

He was demanding of his football players, off the field as well as on – academically, doing the right kind of things, living the right kind of life – those things were very important to him. When you look at what his graduates have done, it's really remarkable. It was very important to Coach to see his guys do very well, and he took great pride in their accomplishments. All of them would realize, no matter what their careers or how their personal lives evolved, what they learned from him in football while at VMI carried over into their lives outside competition. That was something of which he was very proud. Below is a listing of accomplishments by his players off the field - approximately 180 scholarship players plus walk-ons.

- Engineering graduates – 104
- Physics, chemistry, biology, and math graduates – 67
- Liberal arts graduates – 77
- Rhodes Scholars – 2
- The entire backfield of the 1961 team wore academic stars – 3.5+ GPA
- One graduate ran for Governor of Virginia.
- One became a college president.
- Doctors – 23
- Lawyers – 27
- A large number entered military service with several reaching the rank of General

God bless Coach and his wonderful family – God bless VMI !

Bobby Ross '59

The tumult and the shouting dies:

The Captains and the Kings depart:

Still stands Thine ancient sacrifice,

An humble and a contrite heart.

Lord of Hosts, be with us yet,

Lest we forget – lest we forget!

From "Recessional," by Rudyard Kipling

CHAPTER ONE

THE EAGLE

The acid in the air has gone to work on the old black and white photograph, burnishing the finish with its first hint of sepia that casts a bygone era as some sort of alternate reality, slightly yellowed and faded, shimmering out there somewhere just past the edges of sweet memory. That's only fitting, because the moment comes to us now as an echo, a mere wisp sliced from a long, uncommon life.

It forms a piece of the portrait of the coach as the masterful and clear-eyed realist, in an age before the sport lost its soul.

Wearing an overcoat to ward off the chill wind, John McKenna stands on the sidelines in the late fall of 1954, arms folded, his face offering a slight, somewhat bemused grin, as he takes in the sort of tragic-comic scene that only a coach can fully comprehend. He's peering out from beneath the brim of his black fedora into a harsh late afternoon sun, low on the horizon, as his Virginia Military Institute Keydets, perpetual underdogs that they are, battle valiantly through yet another long and challenging Saturday.

It's that McKenna gaze that still speaks to the souls of his players, lo these many decades later. It's the visage that forms the grip he has mysteriously held on their lives long after their time together ended, to the point that as grown, mature, successful men they often found themselves fretting over whether he might see them smoking or taking a drink. Years later, they would catch themselves in the state of panic that only his facial expressions could plunge them, and they would shake their heads and laugh.

That was life with The Eagle, they would say, acknowledging the mystery of a man they have loved for years without ever having a hope of fully comprehending him.

They called him The Eagle because nothing seemingly ever escaped his eye. He saw everything, they said again and again. And if that wasn't entirely true, it didn't matter, because they believed that he did, such was the power of the withering stare from the man in the fedora.

If the visage somehow wasn't enough, the coach could tighten his hold with a few words, a simple comment or phrase here or there that often weighed like a sledgehammer.

"It made no difference where he was or how many separate drills were being conducted on the practice field," recalled Tom Daniel, who began playing for McKenna in 1956. "He didn't miss a thing. One cringed to hear a resounding 'Yo!' followed by the offender's name and lowly IQ assessment. It was more than a moment of shame and embarrassment. To be singled out by The Eagle was to suffer his terrible wrath... No one escaped the eye of The Eagle."

The quick assumption is that McKenna operated largely on fear alone, but his hold was far more complex than that.

"I don't know what it was about him, but everybody wanted to please him," said his wife Eileen, who was married to him for 62 years and, having graduated from college at age 20, was every bit a match for his intellect and wit. "They hated him sometimes, but if they did something that he approved of, then he would say, 'Nice job.' That made a day for them, which included me. I don't understand it. I loved him, but I still wanted to please him. I don't know what it was."

Such power could have been set to devastating purpose in the hands of a lesser man, someone given even to the slightest corruptions. The ensuing decades of American sporting life would reveal that painful truth as entire generations of coaches would be distinguished by unbridled misbehavior of every sordid stripe. But John McKenna was a godsend to the profession and to VMI, uncommon both in his ability and in his disinclination to profit from it.

At the height of his success at the school, its athletic boosters built a house for the coach and his family. "He insisted on renting it," State Senator Elmon Gray, who headed up the effort for VMI's booster club, once recalled, shaking his head with a smile.

"He was an amazing man," Eddie Barrett, the former athletic director at Marshall University, observed of McKenna. "That will be news for a lot of people because he certainly didn't toot his own horn. He didn't have a big ego."

His rival coaches, who were likewise puzzled by his aura and mystery, were known to confide on occasion to newspaper reporters that John McKenna just might be the best coach who ever lived.

That seems like an odd assessment considering his career as a college head coach lasted just 13 years, all of it at VMI in the historic little city of Lexington, Virginia. To arrive at such a conclusion, one would have to acknowledge the staggering degree of difficulty he faced, an almost unfathomable set of circumstances.

First, he didn't become a full-time football coach until he was thirty years old, when he took charge of the high school program at Malvern Prep in Pennsylvania. The first year, his team failed to win a single game. The next year his team was undefeated and un-scored upon. The arc of his rise propelled him just eight years later in 1953 to become the head coach at VMI's Division I college program.

The situation he encountered there bordered on the absurd. The school offered just a half dozen scholarships in football. It was the smallest college competing at the NCAA's Division I level with a student body that numbered just over nine hundred cadets. Its home field in football, Alumni Memorial Field, was built in the 1920s. It was not serviceable for much more than practice which meant that the team played a majority of its games on the road or at neutral sites. If VMI did have occasion to play a game in Lexington, never more than two per year prior to 1962 when a new stadium was built, it occasionally used the town's recreation field or played on Wilson Field, at neighboring Washington & Lee University.

VMI had almost no budget for athletics in the early 1950s. McKenna had first come to the school in 1952 to serve as line coach. The man he replaced had resigned to take a job coaching high school football in low-paying Louisiana, which offered a substantial increase over VMI's paltry salary.

At the time, many rival coaches considered VMI's overall athletic program a laughingstock. West Virginia University basketball coach Fred Schaus, who competed regularly against VMI in the Southern Conference, used to tell his assistants that he would resign his position immediately and retire from coaching if one of his teams ever lost to the Keydets. Basketball was easily the weakest of the school's sports in the 1950s. The football program was better off, but not that much, considering that its players always lined up against larger, stronger, better-financed teams.

Perhaps the biggest handicap was the constant battle not to give in to the complex mind-set that losing was in any way honorable. From the time the school first began playing it in the 1870s, the game has always added a different dimension for VMI. The small, state-supported military college guards the southern end of Virginia's majestic Shenandoah Valley at that point where the broad green landscape narrows and rises into the Blue Ridge and Allegheny mountain ranges.

The school's imposing Gothic barracks and neatly trimmed grounds stand as something of a cathedral to a proud Southern military tradition. Lexington itself, a city of seven thousand with quaint brick sidewalks, has long been dominated by the specter of the Confederacy's most hallowed generals. For VMI, there's Stonewall Jackson, who taught physics at the school before the Civil War. Just down the block on Letcher Avenue, there is the presence of his old commander, General Robert E. Lee, hovering over the proceedings at nearby Washington & Lee University. The general is buried in the small chapel that bears his name on the sloping hillside of the school's front lawn. Lee Chapel serves as a poignant centerpiece to W&L's distinctive Victorian red brick architecture that's framed by rows of white columns. Lee had retired to Lexington after the Civil War to serve as president of what was then called Washington College. The school later incorporated his name into its own after his death there in 1870.

At VMI, Jackson is also remembered at the school's chapel which bears his name, where the flag-lined meeting hall is overpowered by an eighteen by twenty-three foot oil on canvass painting that depicts rows of young VMI cadets charging through the smoke and haze at the 1864 Battle of New Market. The hall memorializes the ten cadets who died and another forty-five who were wounded in delivering victory for the Confederacy that day. Just a few hundred feet away, the main entrance to VMI's fortress of a barracks is Jackson Arch, engraved with a quote from the general — "You May Be Whatever You Resolve To Be" — that is ever present for cadets as they come and go for their daily affairs. Outside the arch a statue of Jackson, erect and stiff as a stone wall, stands behind a battery of cannon and gazes across VMI's broad parade field. It is a tradition at the school that freshmen, or Rats as they are designated during their indoctrination into the military system, must pause upon exiting the arch and salute Jackson's posterior.

If the Rats are so inspired and can spare a few minutes in their hectic schedules, they can visit the museum on VMI's campus to see the stuffed, well preserved, and mounted carcass of Jackson's beloved horse, "Little Sorrel." That same rich vein of reverence runs just as strong at Washington & Lee, where the remains of Lee's horse, "Traveller," are interred not far from his chapel.

If there's anything that helps to relieve the place's overpowering connection with its Confederate past, it's the loop around the parade ground in front of the VMI barracks where the school memorializes yet another of its titans, General of the Army George C. Marshall, with yet another statue and archway. Marshall was the chief of staff of the U.S. Army in World War II who later became Secretary of State in President Harry Truman's cabinet and devised the Marshall Plan for rebuilding a devastated Europe after the war, an effort that earned him the Nobel Peace Prize in 1953.

In the spirit of Marshall, the school has long endeavored to turn out graduates who are "Citizen Soldiers," leaders in both military and civilian society, the success of which is marked by an unusually high portion of alumni who have gone on to serve as successful corporate executives or reach the pinnacle of their chosen professions. To that end, the school prizes its Spartan lifestyle that harries cadets through a physically and mentally demanding regimen of class work, physical training, and military drill.

When McKenna arrived there in 1952, cadets marched to classes six days a week, then stood for a Saturday noon military inspection. On Sunday mornings they were again out of the hay (the term used for beds by cadets) and on the march to mandatory church services. In between the long hours of classes and drill, the Corps of Cadets assembled in ranks three times daily to march down the hill to Crozet Hall for meals.

It all formed a dizzying pace of march, march, march, work, work, work for cadets. It was only in 1995 that VMI relented and cut its class schedule back to five days, but the school has shown fierce determination over the decades in maintaining an atmosphere of spare, nineteenth century military discipline, which the Corps of Cadets has enforced with an unflinching honor system. "A cadet will neither lie, cheat, steal, nor tolerate those who do," is the basic code that drives life at the Institute. Those accused of violating the code face secret, late-night trials. If convicted, they are dismissed immediately afterward with a "drumming out" ceremony in the wee hours witnessed by the Corps of Cadets. The names of those drummed out are never to be mentioned, and they are barred from returning to the Post. The rules have always been broadly applied to even the school's most popular figures, from class presidents to star quarterbacks right on down to the newest Rat. It hasn't mattered.

Another huge strength of the school has been the camaraderie classmates, or "Brother Rats," develop as they share the hardships and difficulties of the VMI system. Most college football programs have long engaged in the practice of offering special privileges and inducements for athletes, from elite dorms to sumptuous dining. That idea, however, was seen to violate the very nature of VMI, where the challenge was to make football as much an organic part of the school's unique system as possible. Thus, star football players occupy the same cramped quarters and lean lifestyle of every other cadet. As a result, the game itself has always taken a back seat to this honor-bound way of life. Winning at all costs, the *modus operandi* for many major colleges, has never been an option at VMI.

The school excelled in the early days of college football, when the teams were student-run clubs playing a game that had more in common with rugby. Even as the sport evolved to leather helmets and pads over the first decades of the twentieth century, VMI continued to prosper in its engagements with the University of Virginia, Virginia Polytechnic, the University of Richmond, and other traditional rivals. Its 1920 team, the Flying Squadron, went undefeated and set the standard for a series of quick, hard-hitting clubs, including the 1923 team which scored better than 200 points over the season.

In 1924 VMI joined the Southern Conference, a vast alignment of major schools that adhered to strict provisions that kept the game from being exploited commercially. It allowed no broadcasting of games and no athletic fundraising from alumni. For the next decade, the Keydets held their own in competition against the South's biggest schools, but the first quake of change came in 1932 when a group of schools, including Georgia, Alabama, Kentucky, and Tennessee, broke away from the Southern Conference to form the Southeastern Conference. They hungered for big-time college athletics that included revenue from broadcasting games and raising money from alums.

The Southern Conference again splintered in 1953 when North Carolina,

Virginia, N.C. State, Wake Forest, and other schools departed to form the Atlantic Coast Conference. Even as college faculties across Virginia were fighting to de-emphasize sports, the schools themselves had entered into partnerships in search of what they routinely called "the big time."

With each passing season, the growing commercialization began narrowing the possibilities for VMI, although the school's alums refused to acknowledge that. By the time McKenna took over the program in 1953, the chasm between the little military school and its major college opponents had widened dramatically. Yet many a son of Virginia still saw VMI and its football team as very much among the big time. For more than a decade, John McKenna somehow kept it that way.

As they reached new heights, his teams confirmed for VMI's fans and boosters that character, smarts, and spirit would keep the Keydets in the fight. In fact, their fight song, "The Spirit," sung vigorously by cadets and fans at games and gatherings, celebrated the belief that the underdog's character could overcome crippling disadvantages in athletics.

"For when our line starts to weaken, our backs fail to gain,
Our ends are so crippled; to win seems in vain;
The Corps roots the loudest; we'll yet win the day,
The team it will rally and fight – fight – fight! RAY!
We'll gain through the line and we'll circle the end,
Old Red, White and Yellow will triumph again;
The Keydets will fight 'em and never say die,
That's the Spirit of VMI."

McKenna was always appreciative of such fervor, but he wisely kept it at arm's length. "Look," he once told publicity assistant Dick Sessoms. "It isn't the VMI Spirit that wins games. It's the beef up front." When Sessoms once waxed poetic in a publicity brochure about a player who helped engineer a comeback victory, the coach told him to tone down the copy. "Yo, Dick, players like him are the reason we're behind at halftime."

Despite such bravado and McKenna's best efforts, the sixties and seventies would painfully reveal the inevitable truth that a small military school with a limited alumni base simply couldn't compete with major universities in football. The gap widened between VMI and its competition, even though one of McKenna's successors, Coach Bob Thalman, led his teams to Southern Conference championships in 1974 and 1977. With the swift rise of the modern college game as an entertainment industry and the professionalizing of the players, the school soon slipped into miserable circumstances, decade after decade of defeat, a state that VMI's alums and administration met with an unflinching determination. Week after week in recent decades, the school has doggedly continued to march its entire Corps of Cadets down the hill from its stately old barracks to Alumni Memorial Field on game days, never mind the win-loss record, usually to witness yet another 32-13 destruction at the hands of, say, Marshall or William and Mary or Wofford.

The circumstances would have long begged questions of credulity and sanity at any other institution. Even at VMI, the football experience has led the school's alums and supporters to suffer great bouts of hand-wringing over the years of 1-10 and 2-9 seasons. Ultimately, however, their commitment has not wavered.

Duty, honor, and perseverance are the place's deeply held values.

A football loss? "Bah. That's nothing," the Corps of Cadets and its alumni seem to have been saying Saturday after Saturday through each miserable fall for most of the last four decades. Hearts are laid on the line and promptly crushed nearly every single game day.

Katrina Waugh, who covered the team for years for *The Roanoke Times*, recalled being struck by the agony of VMI players weeping in the locker room after yet another loss, how deeply they cared, how willing they were to face huge odds each week, to endure the humiliation of each outcome, to lay their sacrifice on some unseen altar.

The circumstances might seem untenable elsewhere, but it is the effort, the unyielding nature of the approach, that matters deeply at VMI, because it is a place where every little thing matters.

"Never say die" is their motto.

Die they have not, which perhaps helps explain why John McKenna remains their football icon a half century after he coached there. For decades now, the school has celebrated every touchdown and field goal by discharging a cannon in the end zone. The artillery piece, which came into use during McKenna's tenure, is named "Little John," in deference to McKenna himself.

"That's because it made slightly less noise than Big John," his wife Eileen once noted with a knowing smile.

Indeed, McKenna made quite a noise. The brilliant but unassuming coach's smart, fast teams won four Southern Conference championships from 1957-62. And that was when the Southern Conference's ranks still included the likes of West Virginia and Virginia Tech.

His 1957 club went undefeated, finished 9-0-1, and rose as high as thirteenth in the Associated Press major college football poll before finishing the year at twentieth. The team scored better than 200 points that season, held opponents under 100 points, all with only eleven players on the roster weighing more than 200 pounds and only two weighing more than 207.

More impressive, McKenna's teams ran off an eighteen-game unbeaten streak from 1957 to 1958 against a schedule of Division I competition. They did so with basically no home field advantage, a scant budget and a roster of mostly what McKenna called "free boys" or walk-ons, all of it in and around a regimen that frightened away only the hardiest of souls among the available athletic talent.

In looking back at the school's records, longtime athletic director Donny White, who played for McKenna, pointed out that a few games after the unbeaten streak ended, VMI launched into another unbeaten streak that ran for another fourteen games. "Those two things to him really meant a lot," White said. "And when you think about it, it's awesome. It's incredible, the two streaks."

If there was little funding for McKenna's football team, there was even less time for practice, barely two hours per day after the players had tended to all their academic and military duties. How focused was the coach on time management? Years later his players delighted in telling the story of teammate, Kenny Scott, who was injured in practice. Worried about losing valuable time, McKenna told his charges to "move the drill ten yards" away from the injury and keep going while the trainers tended to Scott. Virtually nothing was going to stop him from running his team swiftly through conditioning and drills and plays and scrimmage before they hustled off to evening mess and a night of studying. The school's demanding curriculum offered no easy courses to keep athletes eligible.

Bobby Mitchell was typical of many VMI players in those days. He wanted to go to college to study science or engineering. In the spring of 1957, Mitchell's college options included Princeton, the University of Virginia, and VMI. He visited the University of Virginia in Charlottesville, where he met a square-jawed, steely-eyed young assistant coach named Don Shula. Having just finished his playing career in the NFL, Shula had landed his first coaching job at Virginia. On his way to a Hall of Fame career, Shula was all business about football and keenly aware of the game's demands, what it would require to compete at the highest level.

In the course of their meeting, Shula soon turned the subject to academics. He wanted to know Mitchell's plans for a major. Mitchell told him engineering.

"He said you can't play football and study engineering," Mitchell recalled.

Shula, of course, was a visionary even at that young age. He saw that big-time competition was driving the game toward professionalism. For college football players, the sport was by necessity eroding academic concerns. All across the game, coaches were beginning to advise recruits that their study options were limited, that their primary focus of an athletic scholarship was to play the game.

Yet, on his recruiting visit to VMI that spring, Mitchell found a place where the coaching staff had no thoughts of shoving players away from demanding academic majors. McKenna had more than two dozen engineering and science majors on his football roster. Having earned a degree in philosophy from Villanova, McKenna proudly maintained his own status as a man of letters. It never occurred to the coach to steer his players away from a strong academic commitment.

"He was so proper," recalled the late Tom Joynes, who worked as an athletic publicist for VMI and later became the school's athletic director. "John had a coat and a tie and a hat. I think he slept with the tie on. He was like Tom Landry on the sideline. He was just a perfect gentleman all the time and he was so smart. He had a great vocabulary. Oh Lord, we went up one time to play Villanova, and that summer somebody had recommended a hotel for the team's stay, and John was leery. I said, 'Why don't we go up and look at it?' He said, 'That's a good idea.' I was business manager as well as sports publicity then. And so we went up to look at it, and we went in and met the hotel manager. I told him we were from VMI and were thinking about coming up and staying there when we played Villanova. John got to talking to him, and said he wanted to see a room, and he wanted to see the menu, and he wanted to see the kitchen. The guy finally said to me, 'This is very unusual. You are in the athletic department aren't you?' I said, 'Yeah.' He said, 'This guy is a professor, isn't he?' I said, 'No, he's the head football coach.'"

On the practice field, his players had no trouble identifying their coach. The Eagle was in full command. He produced results with a style that was heavy on discipline and spare in reinforcement. This austere approach and his great power of memory and intellect kept his players on the alert, wary of not doing the right thing, of not meeting his high standards.

"I guess that is probably one of the results of his discipline," explained his son, Steve McKenna, who would play on VMI's football teams of the late 1970s. "He showed those guys a very strong face. They were pretty frightened by him. But that was simply his belief that you don't compliment the grass for being green. If your assignment was to block the guy and if you blocked him, then you did what you needed to do. You don't have to stand up and pound your chest like they do these days. When you get in the end zone you act like you have been there before. You act like you do it every day."

"He had that strong, dynamic personality, and you just believed what he said," explained Dick Willard, another of McKenna's stalwarts. "If he said it was going to happen, you just believed that it was going to happen. By believing I guess that is why we won a lot of our games."

Of his many players, star quarterback Howard Dyer had the type of relationship that allowed him to engage McKenna on occasion, but only on occasion. A walk-on from Greenville, Mississippi, the 6' 1" Dyer arrived at VMI in August of 1957, hitching a ride with a woman from his church, who was headed to Richmond. "We pulled up in front of the barracks at Jackson Arch, and I got out of the car, and Miss Rawls drove off," Dyer said.

"The first person I saw was Coach McKenna," Dyer remembered, "and I expected him to say, 'Good morning, welcome to VMI, how was your trip?' He didn't. He just glared at me, it seemed like forever. And then he said. 'Dyer, I thought you were a bigger boy than this.' I will never forget. I felt intimidated, and I remained equally as intimidated for the next fifty years. That was my introduction to Coach McKenna."

Dyer went on to lead some of VMI's most successful teams. "That didn't matter," he said. "I was constantly intimidated by him, but he instilled confidence in me. He told me one time, 'Howard, you've got the ability to put the ball in the end zone and go do it.' I just had this confidence that I received through him. He made me believe I could get the ball in the end zone. He could be pretty tough on you. He was firm, but he was fair. If you made a bad throw, you know, or if you made a bad decision and called the wrong play before a particular situation, he would pour it out to you, quickly and decisively. He could talk sharp with you, and when he got through correcting you, then he would be instructive. He never crossed the line though, and I never lost respect that I had for him for one second."

"Most remember him," recalled Tom Daniel, who played end for McKenna, "as the stoic, driven coach, a perfectionist, a disciplinarian intolerable of weakness or stupidity or lack of total commitment. Win or lose, we dreaded the Monday game films. He was quick to anger and even quicker to humble with a colorful vocabulary for any player who erred or failed to meet his standards on the practice field. He was harsh, he was abrasive, a stern disciplinarian, a self-driven taskmaster. He demanded precision, and he drove his teams relentlessly to a level of performance that stunned opponents, sportswriters, and fans."

Bill Brill, the longtime sports editor of *The Roanoke Times* known for his invective, began as a young reporter in 1956 and soon was drawing complaints about his harsh coverage. Virginia Tech coach and athletic director Frank Moseley sat down each year to write a letter to the newspaper's publisher fussing about Brill, who made no apologies for his approach. A Duke graduate, Brill seemed on a personal mission to puncture the balloons of any self-important coach he met. Yet from the very beginning he revered McKenna.

"In more than a half century of covering college athletics, I consider John McKenna to be one of the very finest people, as well as a super coach, that I have known," Brill wrote, looking back in 2006. "I am absolutely certain that he would have succeeded wherever he had worked, but it was his decision to coach at VMI for thirteen seasons."

As his success mounted, schools came courting McKenna one after another. Kansas State, Boston College, Maryland, Villanova, Holy Cross, Virginia, Colgate, all were among the suitors at one point or another, all offering substantial raises and perhaps better opportunities to win. He once admitted that Villanova, his alma mater, was the toughest to turn down, but ultimately he decided that he found life in Lexington the best place for wife Eileen and his five young children.

"Part of John McKenna that people should understand," explained Tom Daniel, "is the gentleman, the warm and generous father and husband, the friend, and the man with a deep and genuine faith and spiritual commitment to God."

Dick Sessoms, who followed Tom Joynes as the school's manager of athletic publicity, recalled that one of his tasks for the team's many road trips was to make sure he had determined the location of the nearest Catholic Church and the times for Mass.

McKenna did so not just for himself, but also for the Catholic players he had recruited, many of them from the Northeast. His undefeated 1957 team alone had fourteen players, many of them Catholic, from Pennsylvania, a state with a strong football culture.

The coach's faith perhaps helps to explain one of the little-discussed roles he played in a major moment of Virginia history. The 1950s was a roiling time across the South in terms of civil rights, following the U.S. Supreme Court's 1954 landmark Brown vs. The Board of Education decision that opened the way for integration of public schools. Virginia soon was caught up in the legislature's "Massive Resistance" to school integration led by the Democratic Party machine of U.S. Senator Harry Byrd, Jr., a prominent VMI alumnus. Also opposing the sweeping court decision was State Senator Elmon Gray, a leader of VMI's booster club. It was not a quiet fight. Virginia Governor J. Lindsay Almond was on the cover of *Time* magazine in 1958 as one of the figures leading the battle across the South against social change. There were plans across Virginia to close the public schools rather than integrate, and indeed Prince Edward County closed its system of public education for several years rather than comply. Nothing was overlooked as the state's leaders scoured the landscape for anything that smacked even remotely of integration.

The strict edict of the Byrd machine was that there was to be no cooperation with anything that opened the door to integration, thus the term "massive resistance." Yet at the height of this tumult McKenna chose to schedule a game against Penn State, which had been known far and wide for its integrated roster since 1947. In fact, two of pro football's big stars in that era — running back Lenny Moore of the Baltimore Colts and tackle Roosevelt Grier of the New York Giants—were both Penn State alums.

The 1959 game at Penn State proved a hard-fought battle that saw VMI finally defeated in the second half. But the event came off without a hitch. Surprisingly there was no media commentary about the fact that VMI was engaging an integrated team. The players, most of whom were aware of the situation well before the game, recalled no special instructions from their coach and no different approach to the competition. In fact, McKenna was personally quite comfortable with the integrated game, as he had both recruited and coached black players at Loyola, Los Angeles.

Only a coach of McKenna's stature and respect could have pulled off such a move in Virginia. Governor Almond himself that same year publicly broke from the Byrd machine, deserted massive resistance, and made concessions to the federal government, a move that opened the door for integration of the state's public schools in the 1960s. Almond was ostracized for much of the remainder of his life for the concession he made. Yet John McKenna continued to enjoy the esteem of the entire VMI community. More importantly, the coach's quiet but determined efforts to schedule and play an integrated opponent had sent a first reassuring message across the entire state: an integrated game could be played without incident.

Across America it had been the Catholic schools and universities that had embraced social change and integration well ahead of the public universities in both the North and South. McKenna's faith and his upbringing in a diverse Massachusetts mill town had clearly provided him the background for his quiet leadership in troubled times. As much as anything, it helps to explain how VMI came to field an integrated football team in 1968 and 1969, well ahead of both the University of Virginia and Virginia Tech. His scheduling of Penn State quietly defused the matter before it ever had an opportunity to become an issue in Lexington. His presence in so many ways had set change in motion. Yet it's likely that McKenna was far more interested in seeking the best competition for his team than he was in any sweeping social agenda. Whatever the unarticulated explanation, somehow in the midst of a chaotic time, McKenna quietly directed his program and the school itself in the right direction, one that it could later look back on with some sense of pride.

CHAPTER TWO

ONE-PLATOON FOOTBALL

McKenna's story at VMI is essential also in that it is almost perfectly emblematic of the "lost age" of college football, when the game paused in the face of a troubling future to try to regain its past.

In 1952 the rules committee for major college football made revolutionary and dramatic changes to the game. It voted to do away with most substitution by coaches and established for the sport a "one-platoon" system.

The new rules meant schools could have smaller rosters and thus save money for athletic departments at a time when costs were already beginning to spiral out of control.

More importantly perhaps, the "one-platoon" rules would remain in effect until 1965, which meant they slowed down the growth of college football as it was evolving into its highly commercialized modern identity.

No longer could one group of players play only defense and another group of players perform only as offensive specialists. No longer could coaches run players in and out of the game on a whim. Instead, coaches would have to substitute entire lineups, then allow them to play the game on both offense and defense.

At the time, the sport was moving full speed toward the age of specialization that modern fans know so well today, where the offensive linemen are huge, their bodies distended by diet and training practices that push them to sumo-style physiques in excess of 300 pounds, where the quarterbacks are prima donna passing specialists, where team rosters run to 100 players, where scholarship costs for major programs and coaching salaries have soared into the tens of millions of dollars.

The great percentage of major college programs today have little hope of covering their millions in expenses even though these teams generate millions in revenue from the fan bases of the major universities they represent. Yet perhaps the greatest indictment of the modern game is the long-running criticism that college teams have become professional sports organizations, ill-suited for the academic mission of the universities they represent.

This current state is a result of a trend that university presidents have railed against from the sport's earliest days on campuses in the nineteenth century. However, time has revealed that college administrators are almost powerless to effect change against the modern game's immense popularity with alumni, fans, and corporate interests.

McKenna's tenure at VMI calls to mind an era when colleges found the power to limit their football programs. Abruptly, as college football was moving toward this over-the-top modern identity, the rules committee voted to put the evolution of the game on hold. It opted to return football to its leaner, simpler past, beginning with the 1953 season, McKenna's first as the head coach at VMI.

The Associated Press announced the change in 1953 by reporting, "College football's costly two-platoon era, which introduced the gridiron specialist and bankrupted the football programs of many small colleges, came to a sudden end today."

McKenna had seen first-hand just how costly the sport had become when he lost his job as an assistant coach at Loyola, Los Angeles in 1951 after the school dropped football even though it had a successful team. Just up the California coast, the University of San Francisco had done the same thing that year despite its great undefeated team, the '51 Dons (which were memorialized decades later in an ESPN documentary). The expenses of more players and more scholarships had hit Catholic and other church-supported universities particularly hard in the 1940s.

Under the new rules, the players would have to think for themselves, to make a hundred different decisions that today are made by coaches and "coordinators," many of whom sit in the press box and communicate offensive plays, defensive formations on a play-by-play basis via radio headsets.

In essence, the rules committee for college football gave the game back to the players. As with so many rules enacted by the National Collegiate Athletic Association (NCAA), these were intended to create greater competitiveness and to hold down the rising costs of competition.

And that's exactly what they did.

"One-platoon football has proven its worth," the Harvard Crimson announced in December 1954 after two seasons under the new rules, adding that since the rule changes "football has regained the respect of educators."

Soon, small colleges came to realize that they could compete with big ones, because the game was no longer a matter of stacking up far more players than needed. And while money still mattered, for a time, it didn't matter as much.

What did matter was McKenna's supreme discipline, which allowed him far greater control over the playing environment than many of his contemporaries. The rules reshaped the game and enforced disappearing standards that had once been an accepted part of football. For example, before the 1953 season, the position of quarterback had been evolving rapidly into a specialized offensive player. The one-platoon rules halted that evolution and reinstated the traditional notion that the quarterback would also have to play defense, to make tackles and defend passes. The quarterback also stayed on the field often to punt the ball, just as quarterbacks had been doing for decades earlier in the century. Essentially, there were no special teams, no kickers and designated long snappers, just one unit at a time playing the complete game.

Almost overnight, the changes brought a renewed emphasis in the game on well-rounded players who were smart and versatile. Rosters were usually limited to not much more than forty players, or enough to fit on a single bus if the school's budget was squeezed.

The one-platoon rules changes would last for thirteen seasons, McKenna's exact tenure at VMI, and they would necessitate an age of smart, tough, creative coaching.

Today, this period of college football is largely lost to memory, its adjustments and eccentricities obscured by a modern game that has changed dramatically and exploded in popularity and pageantry. Douglas S. Looney revived that memory briefly with a 1990 article in *Sports Illustrated* that asked Chuck Bednarik, one of the last two-way players in both college and pro football, to discuss just how different modern, specialized players were from those of yesteryear.

"They couldn't do it. They'd run out of gas," Bednarik said when asked what would happen if college players from the nineties had to play both ways. "Before the half, they'd be suckin' and huffin' and puffin'. We keep hearing how great they are. One-platoon football would let us really find out how great they are."

Penn State coach Joe Paterno told Looney: "If it were up to me, I'd love to go back to one-platoon football right now. It would get us back to a lot of basic values."

Now, looking back at the game five decades after one-platoon football ended, it seems clear that behind the noise and façade of the grandly staged events of college football in the 21st century, something essential has been lost. And those losses may well be felt most by those who sacrifice the most, the players themselves, in terms of what they gain from the sport. McKenna and VMI stand as primary evidence of that, a small school that prospered in that era due to the efforts of an exceptional coach and his small, fiercely loyal staff. Considered in the scope of American football history, it was a brief moment, one treasured in retrospect by the scores of young men deeply affected by their experiences playing for McKenna, experiences that defined their lives long after their playing days ended.

His personal story is entwined with the larger picture of the game itself, because the changed rules allowed for a fairer competition, one in which arguably the players had a greater role and, as a result, received greater gains from the experience.

THE VOTE

In so many ways, John McKenna's time at VMI was rife with irony. His most cherished moment came at the end of a 1-9 disaster of a season when his team defeated The Citadel and received an emotional show of support from the Corps of Cadets upon their return to barracks. Meanwhile, his greatest achievement brought mostly enduring regret.

There were only about a half dozen bowl games in America in 1957 when McKenna's Keydets defeated Virginia Tech in Roanoke's Victory Stadium to complete their undefeated season. Representatives of several bowls were on hand for the game, and afterward the Sun Bowl offered a bid to the tiny school. As was typical of some teams in that era, McKenna decided to allow his players vote on the matter. After all, it was their time that would have to be sacrificed to prepare for the game and then play it during the upcoming holidays. He assumed they would jump at the honor and was stunned when a majority opted to turn down the invitation.

There were supposedly physical confrontations among the players in the locker room after the vote, and the members of the school's booster club were bitter with disappointment. McKenna himself was staggered by the outcome, but he never lost his composure and quietly emphasized his players' right to choose. Yet there's little question that the vote produced an anger and confusion among the players themselves that would remain largely unresolved for decades.

There were conflicting perspectives over the ensuing years as to how deeply the coach regretted his decision to allow his team to vote. Jim Sam Gillespie, one of his former players who later served on McKenna's staff, recalled the coach never forgot those who voted against the trip. But Steve McKenna said his father once confided that given the opportunity again, he would have made the same decision. It was the players' holiday from the school's strict regimen that was at stake as well as their right to choose.

Obviously then, if McKenna had regrets, they were the best regrets, the kind that the best of people harbor when they have remained true to their values and their discipline.

Perhaps his greatest satisfaction from coaching came with the ensuing decades as large numbers of his players went on to become doctors, lawyers, engineers, military commanders, and college faculty. In fact his teams spawned so many people of professional accomplishment that their reunions came to resemble more an honor fraternity than a football team.

"That success of his players, even more than his own success, is probably McKenna's greatest legacy," observed General Binford Peay, who played as a reserve quarterback for McKenna and later became VMI's 14th superintendent.

McKenna remained fully alert into his nineties with a full recall of the young men he had coached a half century earlier. "At age 92, he still knew everything about his former players," Steve McKenna explained. "He could tell you where the player was from, what his parents did, if he was on scholarship or – as he would say it – was a 'free boy,' a walk on. He could tell you what the player's wife's name was and if he had kids... He had a remarkable memory for those kinds of things."

His players had long understood that he remembered the things about them because, despite his toughness, McKenna cared deeply about those who played for him. The coach's career may have fallen within the confines of the sport's "lost decade," but the passing years have only confirmed that McKenna brought personal qualities to the task that should be a timeless measure of all coaches — how their charges view them decades after their playing days ended.

"He was my mentor, I'd have to say," said Bobby Ross, who played for McKenna at VMI before enjoying a college coaching career that included winning a national championship at Georgia Tech, where McKenna finished his career as an athletic administrator. "Other than my parents, he might be the most major influence in my career," Ross said, echoing an opinion expressed again and again by dozens of McKenna's former players. "If he wasn't there in person, he'd be sending me a handwritten note. I worked under a lot of good people, but whenever I was looking for advice, whether it was personal or professional or whatever, I'd always go back to 'Coach.'"

McKenna corresponded with an array of his former players over the years, checking in at key points in their lives and careers. Peay said he wasn't even sure how his first letter from McKenna found him. As a young U.S. Army officer in Vietnam faced with tremendously difficult challenges, he found the correspondence comforting and reassuring.

As a VMI player, Peay was among the smallest on the roster and had spent two years on the scout team before moving into position to play sparingly as a senior. Yet McKenna had reached out to him, as he did to so many of his other players at key points in their lives.

The letters would continue over forty years. "A couple of them were really long when I was in combat and particularly as a captain in Vietnam. Every one of the letters was handwritten. There are some I just cherish. He did this for so many of us; he had that unique ability to know how to reach you, what made you tick, whether on the football field, in the corporate world, on the battlefield, or in your personal life."

"He taught us so much," Peay explained. "And I carried that knowledge into all the commands I have had in war and peace, structure, hard work, that kind of quiet but important discipline, attention to detail, and more. We had some tough times in Vietnam, and he gave me strength."

This figure who would mean so much to a generation of young men had arrived at VMI in 1952 by an especially serendipitous route, something that neither the school's officials nor the coach himself had planned, or even given the slightest consideration. Neither had McKenna planned on some great coaching career. His meager circumstances had never allowed much in the way of grandiose career goals. But years later, as they all looked back at his arrival in Lexington and the events that followed, the mystery of it all gave those involved immense pleasure and a sense that they had encountered a singular greatness. Much like his wife Eileen, none of them could ever fully articulate exactly what it was, except they knew that it was real.

CHAPTER THREE

THE TENEMENT

It was in the winter of 1952 at the NCAA Football Convention that 38-year-old John McKenna was interviewed and hired for the job of line coach at VMI. When the school's athletic business manager heard that McKenna had been hired, he threw a fit over the relocation costs. "You couldn't find a coach on the East Coast?" he asked head coach Tom Nugent.

Indeed, there was little money for McKenna to return to California to retrieve his young family. Plus he had to get started right away in his new job. In fact he went to Lexington without his family for spring practice and lived in the Bachelor's Officer Quarters for the duration of spring ball.

When it was completed, he returned to Los Angeles to pick up his family, which at that time included his wife and three little girls, one of them a month old baby. John and Eileen made arrangements to drive in tandem with another family – good friends of the McKenna's – who were also driving back to the East Coast. It was the Easter season as Kathleen, the oldest daughter remembers, and the two families shared a Bible to read the Easter scriptures. Even so, it proved quite a trip in those days before the Interstate highway system.

Eileen McKenna had mixed feelings about leaving California. Originally from Pennsylvania, she was in favor of anything that would take her back to the East Coast and closer to her family. Still, she had liked the West Coast. The place held charm and beauty, and the people had been so nice to them. They had lived very close to Los Angeles International Airport, the infamous LAX. In those days it was far smaller. When her husband would return home from a scouting trip or some other coaching business, she would grab up their small daughters and walk over to the runway to greet him. He'd hop over a fence and they'd have a happy reunion right there in the grassy fields.

Her husband had enjoyed success helping to coach the team at Loyola, Los Angeles, which would later change its name to Loyola Marymount. Still, when the school dropped football after the 1951 season, he hadn't complained. He had felt somewhat isolated on the West Coast and jumped at the chance to head back east. And she clearly didn't mind making the trip to follow him.

The young couple from the North and West suddenly found themselves in a very Southern town that seemed quite different from the large cities in which they had lived. Lexington, in the early 1950s, was an initial culture shock. Some of the public water fountains were marked "Colored." Doug Chase, who would later become the sports editor of the *Lexington News Gazette*, was a small child in the city during that period. He recalled asking his parents why the water was colored, and just what color was it?

Southern culture was equally perplexing for Eileen McKenna. On the day she first arrived in Lexington, her husband invited her to walk downtown with him. "Washington & Lee happened to be having a parade," she recalled. "So, they are parading down the street. On Saturday morning many of the residents from Rockbridge County had come into town to buy and sell goods or whatever they did. The men had beards, full-length beards and boots. And I thought to myself, 'What has John brought us into?'"

"I couldn't believe it," she added. "I did not know what VMI was about… didn't know what Washington & Lee was about. That was my introduction." She and her husband also had trouble finding a place to rent. It seemed that McKenna's arrival in Lexington had been preceded by a visit from Kentucky coach Bear Bryant, who had stopped off at VMI to have a little fun with former VMI football coach Pooley Hubert, an old college pal from Alabama. Bryant had Frank Howard and Peahead Walker, two other prominent coaches with him. Apparently the group raised so much hell in Lexington, drinking, partying and driving wildly around the streets that landlords in town were leery of renting property to coaches.

Finally, McKenna was able to convince a landlord on Stonewall Street that he had not come to Lexington to throw wild parties, and the family found a place to settle down. Very quickly the faculty and coaching wives moved in to make her feel welcome. The moment sent a signal that Lexington may have been a place with a thick air of reverence for the past, but the people there freely offered up their personal warmth. Part of that had to do with McKenna himself. She marveled at how, no matter where they went, people were drawn to her husband. His bonding with VMI was almost seamless. They loved him, and he loved the place.

"The life that they had here, life with discipline, that was his life," she explained. "He was a very disciplined person. You know he was tough on his players. But as he said, 'Those kids welcome toughness if you're being fair to them and tough at the same time.' That was the way he worked."

If McKenna had been the kind of man who spent time talking about himself, his new coworkers might have understood how the discipline at the military college echoed the struggles of his early life. He talked little of his past, however, and offered almost nothing about his upbringing in the mill town of Lawrence, Massachusetts, where an array of immigrant and first-generation families—Russians, Poles, Italians, Germans, Irish, Middle Easterners—labored for long hours amidst the constant clatter and clacking of the textile factories. If residents grew weary of complaining about the noise, they could turn their attention to the soot from the smokestacks that lined the Merrimac River.

There was almost nothing about this polished, professorial football coach that suggested he had come of age on the streets of the gritty mill town, the only one of his circle of friends to make it out of the clutches of Lawrence during the Great Depression. He had been born in 1914, on the third floor of a tenement. He grew up the middle child and only son among five children, which led to the family joke: McKenna didn't learn to speak until age 5, if for no other reason than he couldn't get a word in edgewise, recalled his daughter, Margaret Houck.

For all of the challenges Lawrence offered, McKenna had fond memories of a childhood where one of the chief recreational delights was a swim in the dangerous, polluted waters of the Merrimac. Each week, his father or grandfather would count out a few pennies that allowed the purchase of a dollop of ice cream or a piece of candy. He won a spelling bee in fifth grade in the fall of 1924 at the Bruce School, which sat across the street from a fire station, which delighted young John each time the alarm rang and the horse-drawn fire wagon rolled out of the station.

His grandfather, John Cafferty, lived with the family in their cramped apartment on the third floor. He had once sailed the seas as an adventurer, and in his advancing years, he shoveled coal in a boiler room to make his living. McKenna loved listening to his grandfather's sea-faring stories, just as he loved the occasions when he and his parents had a few extra pennies to take in the silent picture shows at Lawrence's Colonial Theater where an orchestra played while the action rolled across the big screen.

There were hard times aplenty, but there was also much happiness until McKenna turned seven. His mother Anna died of breast cancer that year at age thirty-eight, leaving behind a struggling family and a grieving husband. McKenna's father became more and more detached during this time of personal loss and often turned to alcohol. His grandfather took on a larger role in the household in the wake of his daughter's death, but he too died a little more than a year later, plunging the family into further distress.

It would have been best for McKenna's younger sisters, indeed for all the family, if their father had remarried. He did not, however, which led to substantial hardship for all the children as the Great Depression wore on.

Young John stepped up to help his sisters and father by taking on a variety of jobs. One of his first was working on an ice truck, hauling one hundred pound blocks of ice up the steps of Lawrence's many tenement houses. That became a factor in building the great physical strength for which he would be known. He also worked on a bread truck, and he later gained employment in the mills with his father.

His sharp mind had long made him a favorite of his teachers, but with his family in need, McKenna dropped out of school to work. He later returned, then dropped out yet again. Records from the U.S. Census Bureau show that he had been out of school for more than a year in 1930 while working in the textile mills. The products of the mills included clothing and dress goods, fancy cashmeres, worsteds, French-spun yarns and ordinary worsted yarns.

McKenna and his father both worked with yarn as worsters. However, one of his biggest chores and concerns became trying to protect his father from doing harm to himself due to his alcohol problems. Young John would try to keep his father from slipping out of the house at night to find alcohol, but often to little avail.

"The difficult family life troubled my father," Margaret Houck explained. "The drinking influenced him growing up. He was a very responsible youth. He helped his sisters. He had a very high sense of what is good, what is right. He was strict. He was strict with himself first of all. He was strict with others. He was unyielding in many respects, because of his experience growing up. But it wasn't for self-gain and it wasn't self-aggrandizement. He was a real person, a real man. He was morally strong."

Finally the family stabilized enough that McKenna could return to school at seventeen to begin his junior year. Apparently he wasn't eligible for football that year, but an English teacher encouraged him to think of the impossible—that a poor boy from a Massachusetts mill town might actually go to college. "He had a love of grammar, a love of precision, a love of logic," Margaret explained. "Those things were all connected."

He would connect them to the game of football as well. He had begun playing the sport in the streets and on the sandlots as a boy of ten, McKenna once recalled. By his senior year he was again playing for his school team as his size and strength and athletic ability gained notice with his academic abilities. His priest likewise encouraged him, and soon the prize in young John McKenna's life became the possibility of playing football at Villanova.

Harry Stuhldreher, a three time All American, who had played at Notre Dame in the famed Four Horsemen of the Apocalypse backfield, was the head football coach at Villanova. He had inquired of a local friend if there were any good football prospects in Lawrence. McKenna was mentioned as a possibility. To earn a scholarship, he would have to take a train down from Massachusetts to the school in the Philadelphia suburbs, where he would have to try out for the football team. If he made it, he would be allowed to stay and attend classes. That was the harsh nature of opportunity during the Depression.

"Father took the train down. He arrived at night," Margaret Houck recalled. "He said the moon was shining above the twin towers of the chapel spires at Villanova. He had a suitcase with two pair of pajamas and two shirts. He was nineteen. If he made the team, he got to stay."

Because football had been so closely enmeshed with his own education, as a coach he would later consider it critical to the education of his players. McKenna stayed four years at Villanova. Each spring he had to try out again for the team. If he made it, his scholarship would be renewed. If he didn't, he would have to pack up and go home. "He loved Villanova, loved the religious atmosphere," his daughter explained. "He loved the football competition. He made friends on that football team that were friends for the rest of his life. He made the team. He had the grades. He had the foundation.

The opportunity to go to college changed his life."

His primary friend was Jordan Olivar who played guard for Villanova, on both offense and defense. McKenna played center on offense and linebacker on defense. They were obviously the two brightest on a smart Wildcats team. Even though Olivar was a guard, he was trusted to call the offensive plays, and McKenna called the defenses.

Villanova, ranked thirteenth in the Associated Press poll, went 7-2-1 for 1936 and played Auburn on New Year's Day 1937 in the Bacardi Bowl, in Havana, Cuba. It was the first time that two American universities played college football on foreign soil, and it almost didn't happen. Dictator Fulgencio Batista had just taken over the country, but the game's promoters failed to include his photo in the game program. Only a last-minute reprint cleared the way for kickoff.

Auburn struck in the first quarter, and Villanova scored on a blocked punt late in the game, to force a 7-7 tie.

Later that spring, at graduation, McKenna met Eileen Finucane. "He was waiting to get a ride home to Massachusetts after graduation, not his graduation but a friend's graduation," she recalled. "He was getting a ride. He usually hitch-hiked everywhere. I was going to graduation with my mother and family because we had friends that were graduating. There was John among the kids that were graduating. You know what graduation day is like, and by golly, he turned out to be a friend of the friend that we had gone to see graduate. John was a junior, and it wound up that everybody ended up at our house for dinner. Nine years later we were married - he was in and out of our lives."

She had been immediately attracted to him. "They used to tell him, 'John, those looks have taken you far.' People wanted to please him. How he got that way, I don't know. Again people appreciated what he stood for, even as a young man."

His senior leadership led the Villanova defense through an undefeated season in 1937, and McKenna was an honorable mention All American center. The Wildcats allowed only one touchdown the entire season. Against Loyola, Los Angeles, McKenna intercepted a pass and ran it back. Just as he was about to be tackled, he was able to lateral the ball to an open teammate, who carried the ball down to the goal line. On the next play, Villanova scored on the way to a big win on the road.

In the spring of 1938, McKenna graduated with a degree in philosophy, worked for a few months, then joined the Navy with the goal of becoming a pilot. The 1940 census found him in flight school in Florida, but he soon developed problems with his ears. Eileen McKenna recalled. "He went to Pensacola to be a flier. He was discharged because of ear problems. He could not stand the pressure on his ears. The Navy had their pick of people. They didn't want to bother with a guy with ear problems."

He returned to Philadelphia and went to work in the shipyards. Once World War II began, he tried to re-enlist, but his medical discharge precluded that.

"He couldn't get back into the Navy so he had to have a war job," his wife explained in a 2006 interview. "He became a foreman in the shipyards on a riveting crew building warships. It was hard work, but he was a strong fellow."

CHAPTER FOUR

MALVERN PREP TO VMI

It wasn't until 1945, at age 30, that he got into coaching, his wife recalled. "A priest whom he knew said, 'John they are looking for a football coach at Malvern Prep. What do you think?' He said sure. That was the beginning."

Her husband had no grand plan to be a coach, she explained, adding that the era really didn't allow for much in the way of big dreams. "It just happened. Life happens. I don't know if he ever wanted to be a coach, but it was natural for him. He was by nature a teacher."

In the wake of his second season at Malvern Prep, McKenna's undefeated, unscored-upon team, his old teammate, Jordan Olivar, was named the head coach at Villanova. He quickly asked McKenna to join him to coach the line and run the defense. In short time, they boosted the Wildcats back to national prominence, a top 20 ranking in the polls for 1948. Olivar's team finished 8-2-1 that year and walloped Nevada in the Harbor Bowl, 27-7. Supposedly, Olivar was on the train with his team heading back to the East Coast when he learned that Nevada's coach was about to take the head coaching job at Loyola, Los Angeles. Olivar got off the train in Los Angeles and phoned Loyola, where he spoke with the priest who headed up the athletic department. Olivar informed him of the score of the Harbor Bowl and asked if the school would rather hire the winner. He got the job over Nevada's coach.

McKenna arrived back in Philadelphia with the team and soon learned that he would be moving his family to Los Angeles. He and Olivar quickly revived Loyola's fortunes and pushed the Los Angeles school to national prominence for three years, only to learn at the close of the '51 season that the football program was being dropped to cut athletic department expenses and re-assert academics as Loyola's primary mission.

How profound was McKenna's impact at Loyola? Although he only coached there three years, and only as an assistant coach, the school's Sports Hall of Fame committee thought enough of McKenna to induct him more than five decades after he coached at the school.

McKenna's 1950 defense was ranked tenth nationally against the rush. He also had a hand in the offense that finished the season ranked fifth nationally. Loyola lost just one game that year. In short time, he had gained a reputation for teaching fundamentals, for showing his players exactly how he wanted them to play the position.

"He was a tough coach but a real leader," recalled Fred Snyder, who played for McKenna at Loyola. "He knew how to do everything."

Cut loose to look for a new job, McKenna ran into VMI coach Tom Nugent at a coaching clinic. They both hailed from Lawrence, Massachusetts. They had known of each other but had never met. Texas A&M and the Winnipeg Blue Bombers of the Canadian Football League had also inquired about his services, but he liked what Nugent had to say about VMI.

Nugent had first come to VMI in 1948, hired away from Hopewell High School, where he had been the head football coach. In Lexington he was given the titles of athletic director and head football coach, for which he was paid $7,500 a year, solid money for coaching at a time when the average worker made about $2,500 a year. Nugent's 1950 team finished 6-4, and his 1951 club won the Southern Conference championship outright with a 7-3 record, quite an accomplishment considering the 1951 Southern Conference still fielded North Carolina, Wake Forest, N.C. State, Virginia, Maryland, and Duke. The teams would leave two years later to form the Atlantic Coast Conference.

Nugent, credited with devising the famed I-Formation to counteract the opposing team's larger defensive linemen and linebackers, unveiled the new formation in the opening game of 1950 against William and Mary leading to a 25-19 VMI win over a team which had beaten the Keydets 54-6 the previous season. His record slipped to 3-6-1 in 1952, but the victory total included a lopsided win over Florida State in Tallahassee, a victory aided by a fumble from Seminole freshman running back Lee Corso, who would later gain fame as a college coach and ESPN analyst.

Florida State had a relatively new program and had just joined the Southeastern Conference. The athletic council was impressed enough with Nugent's team that they offered him their head coaching job for 1953 and lured him away with a raise—to eight thousand a year. Unhappy with VMI's lean athletic budget, Nugent had been looking around and jumped at the chance to move to Tallahassee.

Nugent had actually been frontrunner for the head job at N.C. State the previous season, but that deal fell through when State didn't want to buy out the contract of head coach Beattie Feathers. With 7,000 students and a new co-educational status, Florida State would provide "plenty of scholarship money," Nugent said and predicted that within a few years the Seminoles would hold their own in the SEC.

Roanoke World News columnist Roland Hughes echoed a popular opinion of the day. "Nugent is known to have had ambitions to go higher, and it was expected that he would get his opportunity. He's young, capable and popular. Just what the advantages Florida State offers over VMI aren't readily discernible. There must be some or he wouldn't make the move."

Back in Lexington, McKenna's promotion shared equal billing with Nugent's departure. VMI's decision to hire an assistant was part of a trend. Of the 30 odd coaching changes across the country since the end of the '52 season, promoted assistants filled most of the jobs.

"Along with the platoon system, the 'old guard' of the college football coaching profession is fading out, and a fresh batch of new names is moving in to fill the ranks," the Associated Press reported that January. "The big colleges no longer are going after the big names. To fill vacancies, they are dipping into their own reservoirs to bring up assistants or reaching out to pluck some little-known mentor from a minor institution."

Texas Christian had already replaced Dutch Meyer with Abe Martin, and former freshman coach John Cherberg took over at University of Washington for Howie Odell. George Barclay moved in for his old boss, Carl Snavely at North Carolina, and Tennessee took assistant Harvey Robinson to fill in for ailing General Bob Neyland.

A week after McKenna's ascension, Art Gueppe resigned at Virginia to move to Vanderbilt, and a week later, the Cavaliers tabbed line coach Ned McDonald as their head man.

The 38-year-old McKenna was given a two-year contract for an at-the-time undisclosed amount, believed to be about seven thousand. He was set to assume his duties on February 1.

"We are extremely pleased to have John McKenna take over the Head Coach duties here at VMI," Colonel Kenneth S. Purdie, chairman of VMI's athletic council, said at the time. "We are fortunate indeed to have such a capable and well qualified man already on our staff to assume the football coaching assignment."

McKenna was just part of a lot of changes in the old guard at VMI in the early 50s. The previous August, former General Electric Company executive, William H. Milton, Jr., VMI Class of 1920, had become the Institute's eighth Superintendent and the first from an exclusively non-military background. Milton had held a number of senior management positions at GE prior to his retirement in 1952. Upon his appointment at VMI, he was also appointed a Major General in the Virginia Militia.

When Nugent resigned, effective January 31, it left Milton to fill two positions, as the football coach had also been the athletic director the last two years. So, in addition to McKenna, Lieutenant Colonel Arthur Lipscomb, an associate professor of English, was named interim athletic director.

Milton later brought in a fellow businessman to serve as Graduate Manager of Athletics, Weir Goodwin, a VMI alumnus. Goodwin had worked 33 years at Standard Oil Company in New Jersey and had served as Standard's deputy coordinator of marketing activities.

That spring, Goodwin and McKenna would set about raising a new standard, one that Milton and the athletic council were trying to take in a different direction. They wanted to emphasize a better-rounded athletic program rather than get caught up in the growing national passion for college football.

Later that spring, Milton would release a formal statement of athletic policy that pointed to a more "well-balanced sports program," including expanded intramural activities. Still, the school's alums were no different than other places. They wanted football. Through its Alumni Educational Fund (athletic scholarship fund raising) and its growing Athletic Association, VMI had begun increasing its funding for football scholarships. Milton and the council were met with an increasing presence and pressure from boosters, something college football was experiencing across the country.

Milton moved to decrease the Athletic Association's hold and eventually hoped to eliminate their scholarship donations altogether. Additionally, VMI planned to reduce the number of "money games" in football where the school received guarantees to play bigger, richer programs.

The idea was, more monies would be funneled to athletics through "independent businesses," like the campus barber shop, pressing and repair shop, and Post Exchange. Those funds would be shared among all Keydet athletes, or so it was hoped.

VMI used the announcements of the coaching change to give the impression that it was taking firm control of its own athletic programs and turning away from trends that were breaking apart the Southern Conference. These same trends were lifting college football to unprecedented popularity while beginning to create a quagmire of off-the-field problems that would become a persistent familiar element on the landscape of college athletics.

In fact, there were already rampant rumors of a "Big Nine Conference" geographically along the mid-Atlantic coast that would include Southern Conference members Virginia, West Virginia, Maryland, South Carolina, Clemson, North Carolina, Duke, Wake Forest and N.C. State. "The purpose of the alignment," wrote *Roanoke World News* sports editor Roland Hughes, "would be primarily for more prestige in football. These stronger schools would schedule each other heavily."

VMI wanted to schedule more regional opponents while mostly seeking to avoid the blossoming football factories. Hughes also noted that in the new league, "the (Virginia Tech) Gobblers would be overlooked because of the limited plant facilities to go big-time. The same would go for Richmond." Quite simply, Virginia Tech had terribly outdated facilities, although they were still better than VMI's.

Some critics in the media offered that VMI was opting to "deemphasize football." Still, the ramifications over the next few seasons would have the opposite effect. The decision to cut those "money games" with trips to places like Georgia Tech and Texas A&M, and replace them with more "natural rivals," would stoke the school's competitive spirit and pave the way for a Golden Age for the Red, White, and Yellow. It only made alums hungrier for success.

"This is no new policy," Milton repeated in a speech to the Corps of Cadets and the VMI Sportsmen's Club prior to the Spring Game of McKenna's first year as head coach. "But it is stated firmly, and I believe the

Institute is setting a standard of leadership in intercollegiate athletics in the State of Virginia. It's about time we took the leadership."

AMONG FRIENDS

From Nugent's staff, McKenna retained Clark King as an assistant coach, 25-year veteran Herb Patchin as trainer, and young basketball and baseball coach Chuck Noe as a football scout and assistant, at least until he returned to basketball fulltime on November 1 each year. McKenna hired John DeLaurentis as line coach. The former Washington Redskins star had played center, guard and tackle at Waynesboro College in Pennsylvania and also played for the NFL's Brooklyn Dodgers.

However, King was clearly the major hire. He had joined the VMI staff in 1952 after a chance meeting with Nugent and was one of McKenna's first calls after he became head coach. King had been hired part-time and returned to his Blair, Nebraska, home after the season was over. That arrangement would change under McKenna, and King would go on to become a major figure at the school, serving VMI in many capacities for 39 years until his retirement in 1991.

A Marine officer in World War II, King was awarded the Silver Star for gallantry at Iwo Jima and received the Purple Heart and a Presidential Citation. He was coaching at Camp Lejeune (named for former VMI Superintendent Lieutenant General John Archer Lejeune) when he met Nugent and was offered his first job at VMI.

"Coach King was another wonderful man," said Bobby Ross looking back. "I guess, next to Coach McKenna, he would have been the guy I respected most. He was my backfield coach. He was everything that I think VMI was looking for. He was very soft-spoken, but boy, he was one of those that if he raised his voice, you better look out."

McKenna and King forged a strong bond in the good fight to elevate VMI football. McKenna told reporters that spring that he preferred a small staff. This made sense because he didn't hold athletic director's duties like Nugent had, and since players were now playing "both ways," squad sizes would be smaller. McKenna planned to continue doing much coaching of the line himself. King would handle the backs and John DeLaurentis the ends.

Despite his success, Nugent had not been overwhelmingly popular at the school, and McKenna's promotion made apparent the dramatic difference in approach of the two coaches.

Tom Joynes, then a young athletic publicist and business manager, was not particularly fond of the departing coach. "Nugent spent a lot of time at practice on how to come out of the huddle, how to look," Joynes once recalled dismissively. "Everything was showmanship. He invented the I-formation for showmanship really. He thought it looked good. He didn't realize it was going to be that effective, I don't think. He leveled with me several times about it. He said I didn't think anybody was going to pick that up. I just thought it was something to be different and to sell some pictures. Nugent was a pure salesman. His whole idea was to sell tickets."

"John was a football coach," Joynes recalled. "He was to the other extreme; practice focused on how to play football with fundamentals. He would take guys who were seniors and show them how to make a tackle. They had been playing for a showman, but we needed to reinforce fundamentals. We really did. John had a tough time for a few years."

Despite the challenges, McKenna bonded almost immediately with his staff. It wasn't just Clark King. He took an immediate liking to everyone involved. They all had a sense of humor, which was good, because there was plenty they just had to laugh at.

"The guys he worked with, he liked them all," recalled Eileen McKenna, "But one of his very favorite individuals at VMI was Julie Martin. She worked in public relations. She had all the information. She knew every cadet, every ball player, and they loved her. She was mother to all of them."

Martin became known for providing sweets for the players, until McKenna finally had to ask her not to bring any more cookies. He called donuts and cookies "colon cloggers" and believed they were bad for athletic training.

"When Coach McKenna was in his first decade as VMI's head football coach, I was in my first decade as an employee in the Institute's public relation's office," Martin recalled. "I am a Lexington native and was brought up as a fan of VMI football, and I adored the players, always baking goodies for my favorite players to have after a Saturday game. Once, when the team suffered a devastating loss, I made a special effort to see that there were brownies, banana bread, and even pies awaiting their return to barracks. Coach McKenna who wasn't dubbed old 'Eagle Eye' for nothing, chastised me for doing this after that loss. 'But I knew they felt bad and needed cheering up,' I replied. Coach McKenna's response: 'They need to feel bad!'"

Another highlight was young Chuck Noe, who coached both basketball and baseball. Each fall, until basketball practice opened the first of November, he served as a scout for McKenna.

"What a coach he was," Joynes said of Noe. "He coached basketball, baseball and was an assistant in football. He came over to John and said, 'I'm supposed to be an assistant. I'll do whatever you want me to do. I don't know much about football.' John said we'll see and told me sometime later, 'I'll bet if you give him a book on women's field hockey he would have a winning team. What a hell of a coach.' And he was."

One of Noe's biggest challenges was doing something about VMI's woeful baseball program, an effort followed with amusement by the school's longtime athletic trainer, Herb Patchin.

"When Chuck had his first baseball practice down on Alumni Field, Herb was sitting up in the training room in Cocke Hall watching," Joynes recalled. "So Chuck came up and said, 'Herb, you saw what I've got. What am I going to do?'

"Herb said, 'Hire two homers for umpires,'" Joynes recalled, laughing. "And he did. He hired two guys who had, let's say, VMI's best interest at heart. They were real homers."

Noe had once played basketball and baseball for the University of Virginia, which set up a dilemma when his alma mater came to Lexington to play baseball against the sketchy umpires.

"The Virginia baseball coach was old Augusta Bell," Joynes recalled. "He was famous. When they came here to play, he and Chuck got in an argument with the umpire. Finally the umpire told Chuck, 'You are out of here.' But Chuck and Augusta both sat down, and they started to bitch again. Finally, Augusta Bell said to the ump, 'You threw him out. Why is he still here? Why is he on the bench? He should be out of here.' The umpire turned to Chuck and said, 'Coach, you shouldn't be on the bench. You should be out of the park because I threw you out.' And Chuck said, 'Well, if I go, your check goes with me.' And the umpire let him stay. Augusta Bell got up and asked the ump, what happened? He said, 'I changed my mind.'"

Herb Patchin, the trainer, was even more of a character than Noe, always ready with a quip or a story.

One of Patchin's favorite players was future VMI Sports Hall of Fame running back Johnny Mapp. "They hit it off from Mapp's first day as a Rat player in 1950," Joynes recalled. "That Fall, Mapp was receiving an unusual amount of harassment from one particular sophomore corporal in the barracks. Patchin got wind of it around early October and sent a message for the cadet to come to his office. When the youngster reported, Herb, a giant of a man, minced no words, 'Look you little SOB, if you don't leave Johnny Mapp alone, I'll have you eating fish heads and rice for the remainder of your cadetship.' From that day forward, Mapp didn't have any more trouble with the corporal."

"After one upset victory, someone asked Herb what happened," said Joynes. He said, 'the Christians 'et' the lions.' Somebody said Herb went to the University of Illinois, but I don't think he ever graduated. He went into the boxing business as a trainer in Pittsburgh and a guy with a college degree wouldn't do that. There is not a lot of baccalaureate in boxing. After that, somehow through some alumni connection, he got the job at VMI as a trainer. This was in probably the mid-1940s. I think it was probably during the War. He was also director of physical education, in spite of weighing close to 400 pounds; he was huge. Under Herb, physical education for the Rats was to take a nap. He said they needed that worse than anything else."

"Patchin had a great sense of humor," said Joynes. "John McKenna loved it. John wanted to talk to him all the time, and Herb was a good trainer. He got people back up on their feet. We had a back who was always after the trainer, always complaining of something wrong. So finally, Herb got some paint, and labeled the back of the chair, where this guy sat with his foot in the whirlpool, the director's chair. There was always something to laugh about and Herb would keep you in stitches."

"There was another guy that Patchin was not particularly fond of, a great big kid, strong as an ox, but he was slow, and Herb thought he was lazy," recalled Joynes. "Herb would keep on him all the time about keeping moving. This kid played football and was the basketball center. Smoking his cigar, Herb would sit on the bench by Chuck Noe during basketball games. This big kid would be out on the floor, just standing there and loafing, by Herb's standards, so one night Herb told Chuck, 'Get that big son of bitch out of there.' So Chuck got to looking at the bench. He leaned over to Herb and said, 'Which one of these All Americans should I put in?' Herb shook his head and said, 'Leave that bastard in.'"

Most people didn't realize that Patchin paid for several cadets to go through VMI out of his own pocket, Bobby Ross remembered. "Herb was a great guy. He was an easy A when it came to physical education classes for Rats. He knew people needed a break."

Ross recalled his time in the training room waiting for Patchin to tape his ankles. "I used to love to sit in there," Ross said. "He just had so many stories to tell."

THE FIRST SPRING

His coworkers may have kept him chuckling, but McKenna had plenty to worry about that spring. The NCAA had voted to end organized spring football as part of its de-emphasis of the sport, but "volunteer" practices were still allowed. Apparently McKenna and VMI had encouraged the players to volunteer. The new coach had to quickly build a staff, shift his offense into a Split-T formation plan for the return of one-platoon football that fall, and replace 18 players from the previous season, including quarterback Bill Brehany, who was selected in the NFL Draft by the Chicago Bears that winter.

Brehany's favorite receiver, end Jim Byron was also graduating, and the personnel losses included transfers – tackles Warren Carpenter to Arkansas and Charlie Spaneas to Boston University and end Tom Smith to Illinois.

Forty-four players were on hand when workouts commenced that March, with McKenna trying to get in 20 days of practices around the Institute's demanding student schedule and a rainy and snowy month in Lexington.

He fully expected the Southern Conference to reinstate the freshman rule meaning "yearlings" would have their own freshman squad separate from the varsity. McKenna reiterated that simplicity would be a key for both his squads. With VMI a military school first, the coach pointed to less actual practice time than at other colleges, which meant keeping the Xs and Os simple. After all, players would now have to learn both offensive and defensive assignments as part of one-platoon football.

Nugent's old style military huddle was gone, replaced by the Split-T and the popular oval huddle – though McKenna instituted more of a box design.

Some coaches, such as Michigan State's Clarence "Biggie" Munn, who had just stepped down to become the school's athletic director, hated the new rules. One-platoon football had begun to subside in the late 1930s, only to regain popularity during World War II, when it was much more difficult to find players. Legendary Michigan coach Fritz Crisler was one of the first to revive the two-platoon practice after the war in a game against Army. He split his team into two units in 1945, often employing eight players who played just offense and eight more just on defense, while three played both ways.

Army coach Earl "Red" Blaik, one of the most respected in the game, liked the strategy so much that he not only employed it but is credited with adding the military moniker "platoon" to the system. From 1946-50, Army had twice finished the season ranked No. 2 in the Associated Press poll, and other coaches, seeking to build on that idea, began adding platoons themselves.

The 1953 elimination of platoons meant a tightening of the substitution rules. The specific rule, long a thorn in the games' rules, was couched in tangled language and left more than a few coaches scratching their heads: "A player withdrawn from the game shall not return during the period from which he was withdrawn, except that a player withdrawn before the final four minutes of the second or fourth period may return during the final four minutes of the period from which he was withdrawn."

Former Tennessee football coach, General Bobby Neyland, who had become the athletic director for the Volunteers, was delighted and quipped that the outlawing of two platoons had brought the "end of chickenshit football."

McKenna sensed the new rules would be good for VMI. The Keydets could now focus on training a limited cadre of athletic, intelligent, adaptable players around whom he would build a program.

The new coach's acumen would become apparent later, but right then, national trends were bringing the game back to where VMI could really compete. Prior to 1953, some recent college teams had rosters with as many as 130 players. Now, the emphasis would have to be smaller and better focused.

"I feel that free substitution makes for a faster game and better football," McKenna observed at the time.

Babe Caccia, the coach at Idaho State, agreed: "The new rule is good for small schools. It gives us a better chance. With the elimination of the two-platoon we will be able to give a good account of ourselves and not be snowed under as in the past. We are going to hold our heads a little higher in football circles and talk a little bigger."

Bud Wilkinson, who was building a powerhouse at Oklahoma that would dominate the 1950s, liked the change, too, for a simple reason. "The statement that more boys play is erroneous because so many schools have given up football since the two-platoon system came into use. It's a big advantage only to a larger school."

Missouri coach Dan Faurot, who had pioneered the Split-T as an option offense, put his finger on what could make the new rules special, particularly for teams with smart, disciplined athletes. "It gives the game back to the players. They will have to be a little more resourceful on the field. Coaches no longer will be able to send information onto the field in a steady stream. It's a leveling factor, enabling more schools to have a chance to win against bigger, richer schools."

McKenna admitted that finding the right players to implement his system was a more difficult task than most other coaches faced. Because VMI athletes endured a more rigorous day-to-day regimen than players at other schools; they seemed to have a tendency to wear down at season's end under the grueling pressures of the military lifestyle and competing against larger teams week after week.

Roanoke Times sports columnist Harold Wimmer detailed some of VMI's obstacles as a football school, part of an intrinsic value the Institute offered to its students and of which it was proud:

Virginia Military Institute, the military half of Lexington's educational empire, has few of the appearances generally associated with American colleges. In fact, VMI resembles a military installation more than a place of learning.

However, like a book, you can't judge the value of VMI by outward appearance. All but babes in arms know that some of America's greatest men have come from the halls of the Institute. They have served the country well in civilian and military roles.

The young gentlemen who receive their education at VMI come out well-rounded men, capable of stepping into their place in society. In addition to an education, VMI men receive something that can't be learned anywhere but at the Institute – The VMI Spirit....Only the fellows who live the closely-knit life of a VMI Cadet can capture the spirit and even they can't define it.

Life at VMI is far from an easy one. Students must maintain passing grades in a stiff academic course. Then too, the military side of VMI is as strict as any in the land. There are many hardships, and the boys who live close together in barracks learn to share the good and the bad.

The *Roanoke World News* had a similar opinion:

A kid has to be attracted to the military life before he wants to go to VMI. And he has to have a yen for rigid discipline to make a good cadet.

"Competing with other schools that offer ROTC, here it means lights out *at 11 and bugle at 6:50 a.m. It means hours of drills. At other schools, these ROTC students have a life of freedom, as it were.*

On the plus side for McKenna, many freshmen came to practice that spring with playing experience. Nugent had been forced to play more and more of them – under the old rules – as the 1952 season had worn on. McKenna's new line looked strong among starters like Karl Klinar, Buck Boxley, and George Ramer, but depth, as always, would be an issue. Dave Woolwine looked like the starter at quarterback in what McKenna said would be a more freewheeling formation with the ends split, backs in motion and as "much aerial works as seems profitable." Mostly, however, he built the team on eleven solid defenders who could learn "the offensive patterns."

VMI suffered some injuries that spring, and by the spring game on March 21, McKenna joined the list, missing the contest in the hospital with a kidney infection. Woolwine led the Red Team to a 20-12 victory over the Whites on a beautiful spring afternoon. Johnny Mapp had two touchdowns despite the handicap of "a pair of pants which appeared to be three sizes too large," *The Roanoke Times* reported. "The practice pants fit the five-foot, ten-inch, 165-pound youngster so poorly that he could easily have been mistaken for a cow-pasture 'ringer.'"

Mapp had more than 200 yards from scrimmage and caught passes of 25 and 81 yards for scores. Those feats were even more impressive considering Mapp didn't practice regularly that spring due to his obligations with the track team. He scored 13 points for VMI in the Southern Conference Indoor (track) Games in Chapel Hill, N.C., winning the hurdles, the broad jump and placing second in the 70-yard dash.

"Boy, what an athlete he was," Tom Joynes recalled of Mapp in a 2006 interview. "He's probably the best athlete that ever went to VMI. He could do everything. He was the best swimmer we had. He was the best tennis player, the best golfer, the best sprinter, the best punter. He could do everything. He was a real athlete. He ran a 9.8 in the one hundred yard dash. He had tremendous speed. He fit what McKenna wanted to do. John's byword was speed."

"Fast guys could beat slow guys in checkers," McKenna liked to say.

Mapp wasn't the only track star on the team. Wendell Shay, the new fullback who had moved over from end, had won the 220-yard dash at the State Big Six Indoor Meet the previous winter. At that time the Big Six Schools were VMI, Virginia Tech, University of Virginia, William & Mary, University of Richmond, and Washington & Lee University.

The spring game was played under the new limited substitution rules that stipulated that once a player was removed for a replacement, he could not enter the lineup during that particular quarter of play, except during the final four minutes of the second and fourth periods. The impact on the players was immediately obvious. Assistant coach Clark King observed after the spring game that the players were starting to realize the conditioning challenge the change would bring. "They found out it's a long game under the new rules."

CHAPTER FIVE

THE STRUGGLES

The late summer of 1953 brought a searing sun that hung over Lexington and much of the Mid-Atlantic just as McKenna's first team labored to get ready for the season. Record high temperatures up to 100 degrees hampered VMI's early practices, so the new coach moved morning sessions to 6 a.m. and then brought his 45 Keydets back out in the afternoon from three to six. Junior quarterback Dave Woolwine of Abingdon lost nine pounds on the first day of workouts and had to sit out the next day. Woolwine was scheduled to battle sophomore Dick Fencel of Lancaster, Pennsylvania, as the starting quarterback.

McKenna drilled his squad in the fundamentals of tackling, blocking and positioning, hoping to maximize talent and hide what would be a consistent trouble spot throughout his tenure, a lack of size up front and throughout the squad.

McKenna's first VMI team had just 15 players who had any true varsity experience, something the new coach considered his biggest obstacle. Playing the new one-platoon system would help somewhat with that problem.

He was keenly aware of VMI's shortcomings. In addition to the inexperience, the Keydets were not very deep heading into the 1953 campaign. Center Karl Klinar and tackle Abney "Buck" Boxley were the foundation for the front wall. Woolwine and end Bill Ralph and steady George Ramer had some experience, too, as did backs Johnny Mapp, Mike Foley and Charlie Byrd. Everywhere else, though, VMI was as raw as a summer field onion. The loss of 197-pound junior Tim O'Neil, the team's fastest "big" man, further complicated matters. O'Neil had suffered a fractured left elbow in the spring, and the injury just hadn't healed properly. *The Roanoke Times* predicted that VMI would win three games that season.

Against that backdrop, three thousand fans turned out for the first collegiate football game ever under the lights in Rockbridge County at the Lexington Recreation Field on September 19, and they didn't have to wait long for something to celebrate besides the crisp Virginia night air. Just two minutes and 40 seconds into the proceedings, fullback Troy Carter went over the left side for four yards, and the first of many VMI scores against an overmatched Catawba squad.

Foley zipped 49 yards for another score on the next possession and a 44-0 rout was on to begin the McKenna Era at VMI. Team co-captain George Ramer blocked a punt to set up a Woolwine scoring pass to Mapp. It was the first of Mapp's four touchdowns on the evening, which helped explain his nickname, "The Norfolk Flyer."

The Keydets, operating out of their new T-Formation, piled up over 400 yards rushing. Bespectacled center "King" Karl Klinar earned much of the credit for the Keydets' dominance on both sides of the line, particularly on offense where he blasted open big holes for McKenna's "Blistering Backfield." (It was an age for alliteration and nicknames in sports writing.)

The enthusiasm of the fast start was dampened a bit the next week in the Southern Conference opener. The Keydets jumped on top of George Washington early when Foley intercepted a pass and then scored on a nifty catch-and-run pass from Woolwine.

The Colonials went up 14-7 early in the third quarter, then VMI's Fencel scored from the one. The failed conversion left VMI down a point.

In the fourth quarter, the Keydets drove to the GW 23, but powerful fullback Nick Servidio was stopped short on a fourth-and-one. In the final two minutes, VMI drove past midfield, but the Colonials sealed their win with an interception and a 14-13 final score.

McKenna and King hopped in a car following the game and drove off to scout "Big Six" rival Richmond, who hadn't given up a touchdown in two games. That next week, the Spiders scored a first quarter touchdown, but Karl Klinar crashed in to block the extra point attempt to hold it to 6-0.

Mapp soon returned a punt 50 yards to set up VMI's first touchdown and a 7-6 lead. Richmond struck on a long pass in the third quarter, which was good enough for the final 13-7 margin. VMI had been held to just 220 total yards and had lost two fumbles.

The bright spot for McKenna was obviously Mapp, a "whirlaway runner." Mapp held the VMI school record with a 9.8 time in the 100-yard dash. He now ranked eighth nationally in rushing and averaging 9.3 yards per carry. The 5'-11", 165-pound Mapp was also tied with Ohio State's Bob Watkins and Illinois' Mickey Bates for the national scoring lead with 48 points. He had been used exclusively on defense prior to this season, and was so solid on that side he had earned All-Southern Conference honors. Now his emergence on offense was the talk of the Southern Conference. After one of Mapp's long runs, *The Roanoke Times* reported a frustrated defender came off the field shaking his head, and muttered, "That guy's legs go one way and he goes the other."

The Keydets bounced back the following week in the battle of southern military schools by spoiling The Citadel's homecoming with a 14-0 victory.

The "eel-like" Mapp rushed for another 116 yards, including a 48-yard touchdown in the first quarter. Reserve halfback Charlie Lavery, subbing for an injured Foley, also played well, as the Keydets rolled up 402 yards on the ground.

Woolwine added a quarterback sneak for a score in the third quarter, and the defense never allowed the Bulldogs inside their 24-yard line.

"Many players on the Big Red team played exceptionally well, with Tom Dooley, Bill Miller, Buck Boxley, Bill Ralph, Freddy Poss, George Ramer and Joe Siler leading the attack on the front line," reported the VMI student newspaper, *The V.M.I. Cadet.*

The only negative as VMI snapped the two-game losing streak was the loss of Fencel, the "alternate" quarterback. He had suffered a broken collarbone while making a tackle, one of the obvious detriments of a one-platoon system – offensive skill players had to put their bodies in harm's way to play defense.

Preseason speculation had forecast the 19-year-old Fencel as a possible starter. He was known for his passing, in the tradition of VMI great Bobby Thomason, a 1949 graduate, who became a Pro Bowl quarterback in the NFL. But Fencel was now out for the season.

Next up was the University of Virginia, a team that had beaten VMI ten straight times. The Cavaliers were the defending "Big Six" champions. McKenna knew that Virginia's defense would be stacked to try to slow Mapp so he used him as a decoy while fullbacks Nick Servidio and Wendell Shay got the bulk of carries right up the gut. With VMI struggling in the first half, Virginia took the lead on a 40-yard touchdown pass. Conversions, however, had become an immediate victim of the new rules because limited substitution meant that getting a kicking specialist into the game was almost impossible. Virginia failed to convert and led, 6-0.

VMI faired no better in the kicking game. Royce Jones had gone 21 of 24 on extra point attempts the previous season, but VMI had been unable to get him in the game under the new rules and had missed six of the first 12 point-after kicks in the new season.

In the third quarter, the Keydets recovered a fumble at the Virginia 20, and moments later Mapp tied the score from six yards. Fortunately, McKenna had inserted Jones into the lineup before the score, and his extra point kick put VMI on top, 7-6.

The Cavaliers fumbled again when VMI's Freddy Poss and Bill Ralph broke through the line and tackled Virginia's Herbert Hartwell for a big loss. Poss recovered the loose ball at the four-yard line, moments later Mapp scored again. Ralph and VMI's defensive front put pressure on Virginia quarterback Rives Bailey all afternoon, especially in the fourth quarter. A late VMI touchdown secured a 21-6 victory.

It was VMI's first win over Virginia since 1942. A *Roanoke Times* headline proclaimed Mapp the "most feared player in (the) Southern Conference." He had an interception to go with his two touchdowns on offense.

With the win, McKenna equaled the previous season's victory total, but the following weekend, the Keydets came back down to earth a bit. They traveled to Morgantown, West Virginia, to meet the nation's eighth-ranked team and ran into a buzz saw. The Mountaineers added to their winning streak with a 52-20 homecoming victory before 23,000 fans. West Virginia's eleven consecutive victories represented the longest such streak in the country, and the Mountaineers did it in convincing fashion, running up a 26-0 lead before Woolwine scored on an eight-yard run.

Ralph fell on a Charlie Byrd fumble in the end zone for a later score to make it 46-14, and Woolwine added a 30-yard interception return for the Keydets' final points.

Mapp, the Southern Conference's leading scorer, was not only kept out of the end zone but had just 26 yards on five carries.

Faced with a short hand, McKenna had tried "stunting" his defense against the West Virginia mastodons. "Stunting throws the offense off their assignments and often times will enable you to do well against a team that has you out-classed. That didn't work for us so we reverted to our regular defenses which were also ineffectual."

The next week was even more disheartening, if possible. Playing their fifth straight game on the road, the Keydets fell behind their old coach, Tom Nugent, and Florida State, before a raucous Saturday night crowd in Tallahassee.

In a game filled with an "electric-charged-tension," the Seminoles went ahead in the second quarter on an eight-yard scoring run from Talmadge Metts. Klinar blocked the extra point. After a Woolwine fumble, FSU went 31 yards for another score, with Bob Graham powering in from the one. Again the Seminoles failed to convert the extra point.

Woolwine guided a 71-yard VMI scoring drive in the third quarter, with Mapp and Servidio playing key roles. Woolwine's one-yard sneak and his extra point kick put the Keydets back in the game, 12-7, but McKenna's team was uncharacteristically sloppy on the humid night, fumbling six times and losing the ball on four of those occasions. The Seminoles ground out 265 yards rushing to control the contest, and McKenna's disappointment was palpable. His team couldn't score again. It was just the second victory of the year for Nugent and the Seminoles.

"The boys waited until the game was 25 minutes old, and then it was too late," said the coach.

From their low in Tallahassee, the Keydets returned to Roanoke to play a traditional home game in Victory Stadium against a one-loss William and Mary team that was in the running for the Southern Conference championship. It proved to be a classic on a bitingly cold afternoon. Freezing temperatures limited the crowd to around 5,000 fans in the near-30,000-seat stadium.

Quarterback Charlie Sumner sneaked over from one yard to put the Indians on top early, but Mapp's five-yard run and Woolwine's kick gave VMI the lead. Woolwine got an interception and then fired a 36-yard pass to Ralph to set up his own sneak and a 14-6 lead just 45 seconds before the half.

McKenna used only 16 players in the game, and center Karl Klinar and guard Joe Siler both sat out the second half with leg injuries.

The Tribe scored two touchdowns in the first four minutes of the second half to take charge, and VMI trailed until Woolwine found Mapp for a 23-yard touchdown with just 56 seconds remaining to make the score 20-19. The Keydets had driven 70 yards for the final score, with Woolwine converting two fourth down passes to keep the march alive.

The game was touted as one of the best ever in the Roanoke stadium, as VMI upset the "Eleven Iron Indians and ended William & Mary's hopes for a Southern Conference title. It was just the second loss of the season for William & Mary and the team's first loss to a team from the state of Virginia.

Next up on November 14th in Cincinnati's Nippert Stadium, McKenna matched his team against the offensive genius of Coach Sid Gilman's Bearcats, who were leading the nation in total offense with 399.4 yards per game. It didn't help that the Keydets were playing without the benefit of a scouting report as the assistant coach who was sent to Cincinnati the week before became ill and was unable to attend the game.

The result was beyond ugly. Cincinnati rolled to a 67-0 win, picking up their eighth win in the process. For VMI, it was the team's worst defeat (a record that still stands). Cincinnati set a school scoring record in what McKenna labeled "a touchdown parade." The Bearcats rolled up a record 608 total yards and handed the Keydets their fifth loss of the year. VMI fumbled 10 times, lost six, and managed just 132 yards. The Keydets failed to score at least a touchdown for the first time in 17 games and along with the West Virginia loss, lent credence to the feeling that McKenna had serious recruiting work to do.

"A lot of guys that Nugent had recruited were not really that good," Tom Joynes remembered years later, stressing how much more selective McKenna would become during his tenure.

With a little time off to heal his thin squad, McKenna found no trouble in getting his players ready to face Virginia Tech in the annual Thanksgiving Day clash in Roanoke.

Mapp found his way into the end zone three times before a packed house of 26,000, but the Keydets had to come from behind. Tech jumped on top 7-0 in the second quarter, and led 13-7, before Mapp crashed over from five yards for his second score and a 14-13 advantage. He finished with 91 yards on 14 carries, while Servidio pounded out 87 yards on his 22 attempts.

Frank Moseley had begun building a team in Blacksburg, but McKenna's players kept their legs in the second half and took a surprising 28-13 win. The VMI defensive front – Siler, Klinar, Boxley and Bill Miller – controlled the action the rest of the way.

Servidio's five-yard scoring run made it 21-13 in the third quarter. Then Mapp's 70-yard, broken-field run in the fourth quarter put the game away. Jubilant alumni and fans mobbed the Keydets after the game for avenging a 26-7 loss to their rivals the previous season.

Woolwine played one of his best games ever, rushing for 68 yards, passing for 25 more. On defense, he recovered a fumble and intercepted a pass. Sportswriters on hand voted him the player of the game, awarding him a gold watch. He was one of five Keydets – Mapp, Klinar, Boxley and Siler the others – who played the full 60 minutes. Only 17 Keydets played.

"We certainly came out better than we hoped for," said McKenna. "We never did know if the boys could hold up. They were certainly patched and taped up."

"Patched up" is particularly appropriate. Beloved and long-time trainer Herb Patchin told writers after the game that he had used 24 rolls of tape – each 10 yards long – to get the Keydets ready for the game. Klinar used up six rolls himself to overcome his bumps and bruises, and winced after the game every time a portion was removed from his knees, thighs, shoulders, hips and ribs.

"I don't know how I stayed together for 60 minutes," he said.

It was a tremendously reaffirming moment for McKenna considering that it came in the wake of the crushing loss to Cincinnati. His up-and-down Keydets had finished 5-5 and laid claim to the Big Six state championship for the first time since 1939.

Mapp finished the season with 13 touchdowns and 78 points to lead the Southern Conference and the Big Six. His 656 yards rushing on the season helped land him on the All-Big Six and the All-Southern Conference First Teams, the only Keydet so honored.

McKenna revealed following the season that assistant coach John DeLaurentis had actually returned to his New Jersey home the last three weeks of the season with an undisclosed illness. With Chuck Noe moving over to basketball November 1, McKenna had just Clark King to assist him down the stretch.

"I refrained from making the matter public in order that no suspicion of seeking an alibi for a possible loss could be directed at us," he wrote in his weekly newsletter to Sportsmen's Club members. "A two man staff for a major college team is unheard of in these times."

McKenna also apologized for not responding to alumni letters, particularly regarding recruiting leads or booster "bird-dogging," as he called it. He cited the manpower problem in that regard. He was ready to set sail recruiting and build his program, which was already garnering support.

The VMI student newspaper praised McKenna's first team in a November 30 editorial:

It has been a truly refreshing sight to see a Fighting Squadron on the field once more, and to witness play by men who wanted to play the game to the hilt every time they walked on the field. A great deal of the praise for such a team is due John McKenna, working at the helm for his first time this year. Though not a debonair figure, who would immediately make a big splash with the press, McKenna's quiet manner and firm voice have earned him the respect of his players and of the Corps. Believing in fundamentals, striving to teach the spirit as well as the mechanics of the game, McKenna has contributed something far greater to the Corps than have others with more successful seasons – a renewal of the Corps' spirit and of his team's will to win.

1953 (5-5)

DATE	VMI	LOCATION	OPP
S 19	44	Catawba	0
S 26	13	George Washington	14
O 3	7	at Richmond	13
O 10	14	at The Citadel	0
O 17	21	at Virginia	6
O 24	20	at West Virginia	52
O 31	7	at Florida State	12
N 7	20	William & Mary (Roanoke)	19
N 14	0	at Cincinnati	67
N 26	28	Virginia Tech (Roanoke)	13

THE SECOND SEASON

If nothing else, McKenna's surprisingly successful first campaign gave the players, alumni, and fans a sense of the discipline he could bring to the program. "Coach McKenna was a 'natural' for VMI as well as its athletic program," longtime VMI publicist Julie Martin said, looking back. "He was, more than anyone I have ever known, a man of discipline. I don't mean the soldier who has learned to obey orders, or the cadet who has learned to use his time to best advantage. I'm thinking of the total man and his never-failing self-discipline, the self-control that was always evident in his behavior, the restraint with which he lived his life – although former players may not think of him as being necessarily restrained."

VMI had long established that it was a brutally difficult place for coaches, but McKenna had quickly proved it perfect. His wife Eileen recalled that her husband thought the discipline that went along with the military lifestyle, was a textbook fit to his style. "The life they had here, life with discipline; that was John," she said.

Yet McKenna's second season quickly became a reminder of how far he had to go in building a program. The campaign became one of steps forward and some missteps backward as he tried to bring more of his own style of players into the program. The cerebral coach preferred quick-thinking athletes who were also quick on their feet, a preference for speed over size, if that choice had to be made.

The loss of Mapp to graduation was a blow as 35 upperclassmen and 14 freshmen reported for the first day of practice.

An early trip to Fort Bragg, North Carolina, allowed VMI to scrimmage regimental teams. One highlight was a fantastic freshman, Sonny Randle, who caught two touchdown passes, though Randle wouldn't last at VMI. He left school and ended up at rival Virginia and was later an all-Pro in the National Football League (NFL), a development that highlighted the attrition that has plagued athletics at the school throughout its history. Players get there, realize the immense difficulty of the challenge, both personally and with the team, and elect to transfer. It was not an environment that produced a large amount of feel-good moments, especially for freshmen facing the intense Rat Line, which intentionally set out to leave cadets with a profound sense of being overwhelmed.

The loss of a talent like Randle would later loom large, but there were other factors that would cast a sense of foreboding almost immediately on the 1954 season.

The Roanoke Times reported that Dave Woolwine's throwing arm was improved, but the loss of Mapp and some veteran ends hurt on both sides of the ball. All factors considered, the *Times* said, VMI has "more rebuilding to do than any other Big Six outfit."

The Keydets lived down to that prediction in a startlingly unsuccessful opener at Davidson on September 18th. Davidson hadn't won a single Southern Conference game since 1952. Perhaps that contributed to a sense of overconfidence. Servidio had 86 yards rushing, many in the first quarter on a 59-yard drive to the Davidson 3-yard line. An illegal use of hands penalty stalled the march there, and the Keydets never seemed to recover. The Wildcats scored 20 seconds before the end of the half to break a scoreless tie and then held off the mistake-prone Keydets in the second half. Penalties and mental mistakes hurt VMI all day, including a Woolwine interception that was returned for a touchdown in the fourth quarter to seal the Keydets' fate, a 19-0 loss.

Penalties, especially crucial ones like the one early against Davidson, were an anomaly for McKenna-coached teams, drilled in the fundamentals so extensively that such errors were rarely a factor. Inexperience, though, was the natural enemy of such a style of football.

McKenna's luck seemed to turn worse the following week in practice when Woolwine, his veteran starting quarterback, was injured while practicing punting. Although Woolwine was still able to do some punting, the coaches turned to backup quarterback Royce Jones that next Saturday against favored George Washington. VMI was trailing 14-7 but tied the game in the fourth quarter after Jones engineered an 80-yard drive that allowed the Keydets one of the more unusual and dramatic victories in school history. Late in the game, Jimbo Thornton intercepted a pass in GW territory. But VMI couldn't move, and Woolwine's punt was downed at the 3-yard line with less than 30 seconds remaining. Two plays later, Charlie Byrd roared into the backfield to sack GW quarterback Arnie Trannen and produce a victory on the game's final play via a safety. Bill Miller, Buck Boxley and Jerry Kress ably assisted Byrd on the big play in the 16-14 victory.

"It was a team victory in every sense of the word and that includes the Corps of Cadets," *The V.M.I. Cadet* reported. "The Corps was behind the team every minute of the way and when the safety came it brought a roaring, screaming mass of gray out of the stands to carry the team off the field."

That momentum carried over the following week at Richmond in a 19-6 win. Charlie Lavery rushed for two scores and Royce Jones, in again for the injured Woolwine, scored another as VMI pulled off a road upset for the second straight week.

Jones, who hadn't been particularly accurate throwing in recent practices, stepped in and hit five of six passes for 80 yards. The Keydets led 7-0 at the half and got an emotional lift from McKenna during his halftime remarks. The coach waited until then to inform the team that co-captain and three-year letterman "Buck" Boxley had been drafted and would be reporting to Fort Jackson in South Carolina the following week.

"Let's win this one for Buck," the coach said before the team charged back on the field.

Boxley, who got his orders the day before the game, traveled with the team and played 60 minutes in his final contest. Afterward, teammates carried him off the field on their shoulders and presented him with the game ball.

Lavery scored on a 19-yard run in the fourth quarter to make it 19-0 against a Richmond defense that had dominated previous opponents. Tom Dooley also starred, keeping the Spiders at bay with several fine punts, including a 60-yarder.

The jubilant victory was quickly forgotten the following week at Boston College. Big, strong BC flexed its muscle and extended a five-game winning streak with a dominating 44-0 home win over VMI at Fenway Park. The Eagles, who would win eight games on the season, rushed for 352 yards and held the Keydets to just 99 total yards. VMI didn't get a first down against the Eagles' big, fast defense until the third quarter.

"The situation, in a nutshell," wrote McKenna to the Sportsmen's Club, "was that they controlled the line of scrimmage completely on offense and defense and our backs did little to alter the situation. When such conditions exist, you have had it, and the only question is 'how much?'"

The news wasn't any better at Virginia on October 16. The Cavaliers outweighed VMI almost 15 pounds per man up front, and VMI was shutout for the second straight week, 21-0. Johnny Morgan and Charlie Byrd were stellar on the line in defeat and reserve halfback Joe Moody of Raleigh, North Carolina, emerged as a "player," particularly on defense, on a chilly day in Charlottesville in front of 17,000 fans.

In the bigger picture, halfbacks Dale Vaughn and Bobby Jordan both went down with injuries, joining end Bobby Cooper, who had broken his arm at Boston College. Jordan's loss was a big blow. The talented back was leading the Southern Conference and ranked 13th nationally with a 39.6-yard punting average.

Things got worse when 10th-ranked West Virginia romped to a 40-6 victory in the fourth annual Coal Bowl festival in Bluefield. The powerful Mountaineers led 28-0 in the third quarter before VMI, which moved the ball well, finally cashed in for a score on Frank Boxley's one-yard run.

"Scrap Iron" Servidio led VMI with 65 yards on 14 rushes. The undermanned Keydets had 18 first downs against the Mountaineers. Surprisingly, McKenna said he thought his team played one of its best games.

"To give the Keydets their due, they never stopped trying against a line that out-weighed them twenty-five pounds per man and against backs that were bigger and much fleeter," McKenna wrote to the Sportsmen's Club.

The VMI losing streak reached four games the next week when Tom Nugent's Florida State team pulled away late for a 33-19 win in Lynchburg. Freshman FSU quarterback Vic Prinzi, whose name wasn't even in that day's "Jaycee Bowl" program, threw for three scores.

The game was tied at 13-13 after Woolwine hit Dooley for a 58-yard touchdown and Foley had a four-yard TD run. The Seminoles struck for three second half touchdowns while Foley added a three-yard score in the last three minutes for the final tally. The Keydets rolled up 407 yards (129 by Foley on the ground) but hurt their own cause with six turnovers. "That's how it goes some days," said McKenna, who again thought his team had played well, maybe the best of the season.

Unfortunately, the schedule got no easier. Next was the Shrine Crippled Children's Benefit game in Roanoke's Victory Stadium against William & Mary. The pageantry was thick with 23 high school and junior high marching bands in attendance.

VMI wasted little time jumping in front. Foley recovered a fumble in Indian territory, and seven plays later, he cashed in with a three-yard score.

Dick Lyons picked off an Indian pass on the next possession. Then Woolwine found Dooley all alone for a 33-yard touchdown to make it 14-0, just eight minutes into the proceedings. Woolwine's ball handling and passing kept the Indians off balance all day. While the scoring pass was his only completion, Woolwine also rushed for 52 yards and was named the *Richmond Times-Dispatch's* Back of the Week. Servidio had 102 yards on 23 carries, and Foley chipped in 89 more yards.

The Big Red defense had enjoyed a banner day, but VMI nearly gave up a score on the second half kickoff. Johnny Morgan, a local boy from Buena Vista, saved the day, pulling down Jack Yohe at midfield.

Dale Vaughn's four-yard score at the conclusion of a 15-play, 88-yard march meant that VMI was able to snap the four-game losing streak with a 21-0 win before 12,000.

"Fortune smiled instead of scowled on the Keydets last Saturday," wrote McKenna in his newsletter. "The Red (with a 187-pound line, I purposely omit 'Big') capitalized on its good breaks and surmounted the bad ones."

McKenna lauded Foley, who was back at full speed from the broken ankle suffered a year ago. A *Roanoke World News* reporter spotted the talented back limping out of the locker room after the game, but McKenna quipped, "He does that, I think, from force of habit."

Cooper was back at practice the following week as well and gearing up to play in the season finale. The news wasn't so good for Fencel, who had hurt his shoulder in the West Virginia game. He was advised by a Roanoke specialist to sit out the rest of the season. Ray Collins, the *Times* reported, missed a practice to fly to Boston to seek admittance to a dental school the next fall. Such visits were something of a routine for a roster filled with excellent students.

On November 13, the Keydets returned to Washington & Lee's Wilson Field where they met their military rival, The Citadel. VMI dominated this one, 42-0, as the Bulldogs couldn't hang on to the ball against a hard-hitting defense.

First, Byrd separated Citadel quarterback Dickie Miles from the ball, and Jerry Kress scooped it up at the 4-yard line. Foley then scored on a pitchout to open the onslaught.

Woolwine, who had a big day, hit Dooley for a 36-yard score to cap a 75-yard drive, and after another Bulldog fumble, Woolwine hit Vaughn from seven yards for a 21-0 halftime lead.

Freshman guard Jerry Kress of Bristol had a big game, too, including a fumble recovery that led to a score.

McKenna had cleared the bench by the time it was 33-0, Woolwine connected with Vaughn again, and Vaughn scored from two yards on a run. Vaughn had 147 yards rushing, including a 57-yard jaunt in the first quarter, on just 15 carries, and this time he was the *Times-Dispatch's* Back of the Week.

With a chance to again finish at .500, VMI hoped to heal a little in the long week before Thanksgiving and the 50th annual meeting with Virginia Tech. But that wasn't going to happen. On a cold, dreary Thanksgiving Day in Roanoke, the undefeated and 15th-ranked Gobblers rolled to a 46-9 triumph, and the Keydets' record fell to 4-6.

VMI broke on top with a first quarter safety, with Byrd, Vaughn, and Johnny Morgan chasing Howie Wright into the end zone on a punt return. The lead held up into the second quarter until Tech's Dickie Beard threw a 69-yard option pass for a score.

Don Divers, on his way to being named the game's outstanding player, recovered a Keydet fumble to set up another touchdown. VMI closed to 14-9 when Woolwine hit Vaughn from three yards in the second quarter. The Gobblers answered with a Divers' 42-yard interception return for a 21-9 halftime lead. Divers would add a 67-yard interception return after the break.

"From the middle of the second quarter their line controlled the 'briar patch' which is the line of scrimmage," explained McKenna. "Our quarterback was harassed continuously, both on passes and on ground plays."

VMI never found an answer for Tech's speed on the perimeter, and the Gobbler line was dominant up front. Asked if the muddy Victory Stadium track hurt his team, McKenna replied, "No, VPI (Virginia Polytechnic Institute as Virginia Tech was referred to in the 1950s and 60s) did."

Extra bleachers had been installed for the "Military Classic of the South," but the weather limited the crowd to 26,000, including scouts from the Gator Bowl, there to watch Tech.

The storied series, which began in 1894, now stood at 28-17-5 in favor of VPI.

1954 (4-6)

DATE	VMI	LOCATION	OPP
S 18	0	Davidson	19
S 25	16	at George Washington	14
O 2	19	at Richmond	6
O 9	0	at Boston College	44
O 16	0	at Virginia	21
O 23	6	West Virginia (Bluefield)	40
O 30	19	Florida State (Lynchburg)	33
N 6	21	William & Mary (Roanoke)	0
N 13	42	The Citadel	0
N 25	9	Virginia Tech (Roanoke)	46

THE DISASTER

Heading into the 1955 season, McKenna faced perhaps his biggest challenge on Post to this point. The Keydets were readying to field their youngest team since World War II. Among the 40 players the coach hoped to dress out for the season opener at Tulane, VMI had just 10 seniors and six juniors. McKenna would use 17 freshmen that season, easily the biggest sign of immediate trouble ahead.

While the future looked bright with 14 sophomores, depth on the team was more of a problem than ever. Up front, tackles Bill Miller and Lake Westfall, guard Carl LeBourdais, and center Dick Lyons were the only players with any experience.

At end, juniors Billy Elmore and Paul Janshego had a little action under their belts, but there was no experienced depth behind them. Bobby Jordan, Charlie Lavery, Joe Moody and Dale Vaughn could fill the backfield roles, but again, there were no proven alternates in reserve.

Junior end Tom Dooley had moved to quarterback with the graduation of Woolwine, and he was slated to duel senior Jimmy Foster, sophomore walk-on Duke Johnston and freshmen Bill Nebraska, John Engles and Bobby Ross. Fortunately, Johnston came on so strong in summer camp that Dooley, who had injured his shoulder, could move back to end.

Another revelation was sophomore Sam Woolwine, Dave's younger brother and a transfer from Georgia Tech, who had sat out the previous season. He plugged in at fullback as Jordan and Moody won the two halfback jobs.

McKenna called the newcomers his best freshman class ever, and he was particularly pleased with center Jerry Borst, who was about to embark on a Hall of Fame career.

Borst was typical of the kind of player McKenna dispatched his assistants to find. From Pitcairn, Pennsylvania, Borst not only had athletic talent, but he would later win academic honors and go on to a career in civil engineering.

McKenna's youngsters weren't ready, though, which became apparent in a tough opening assignment in New Orleans on September 17. Tulane quarterback Gene Newton came off the bench in the Sugar Bowl to lead the hosts to a 20-7 victory, passing for a score and guiding the Green Wave to two more touchdowns.

Lavery ran four yards for VMI's score midway through the fourth quarter but Tulane controlled the game up front, rushing for 311 yards and making life miserable for Keydet starting quarterback Johnston. Senior Jimmy Foster moved the team in the fourth quarter but was sacked several times to thwart scoring threats.

Worse, Jordan hurt his knee after averaging 42.4 yards a punt and six yards a carry. Lavery took over for him, and McKenna was scratching his head about what to do at quarterback.

He wasn't as confused as the promising freshman, Ross, though. He was sitting on the bench during the game stealthily eating peanuts, which one of his teammates had sneaked in, when he saw Dooley limping off the field.

"(McKenna) called my name, and I thought I was going in the game, but I couldn't find my headgear," Ross recalled many years later. "A guy finally threw me a (helmet), and I was standing up there listening, and my imagination started running away with me. I could see my dad sitting back there (in Richmond) listening over radio station WLEE.

"I heard play-by-play announcer Bob Gilmore, 'Bobby Ross standing next to Coach McKenna, getting ready to go into the game,' and you know I was getting all emotional. He never said a thing to me. He and Dooley were talking, but I wasn't paying a bit of attention, and he turned to me, and said, 'Ross.' I said, 'Yes sir,' and I'm just waiting for a play, formation and all, and all he said was, 'What size shoe you wear, boy?' McKenna had to repeat the query. He again said, 'What size shoe you wear?' I said, 'I wear a size 9 ½.'

He said, 'Take off your right shoe and give it to Tom.'" The next thing Ross knew, Dooley was trotting back into the game with Ross's right shoe.

The following week the Keydets couldn't get off on the right foot either. In a steady rain at Roanoke's Victory Stadium, George Washington poured it on. The Colonials scored on their opening possession and rolled to 235 yards rushing in the mud to drop VMI to 0-2 in a 25-6 rout.

Dooley retrieved a blocked punt at the GW 26 in the fourth quarter to set up VMI's score. Four plays later, Buzz Snyder notched a four-yard scoring run. VMI mustered just 109 total yards. Quarterback Jim Foster was harassed all day by the Colonials, and it didn't help when guard Johnny Johnson went down with a leg injury that ended his season.

Mike Sommers' 84-yard punt return for a score broke the game open and set up a week of hard practice on coverage for the young Keydets.

McKenna called the performance "the worst game since I've been here," and announced an all-out hunt for a consistent quarterback, even including freshman Bill Nebraska in the mix.

"It's an endless search for a quarterback," he said.

The Keydets headed back to Lexington for a rare home game. All-Southern Conference fullback Frank Pajaczkowski ruined the homecoming at Washington & Lee's Wilson Field, scoring all three touchdowns in a 21-0 Richmond win.

Running "like a frightened rabbit," according to *The V.M.I Cadet* report, Pajaczkowski had a 93-yard scamper to open the scoring and added a 65-yarder in the second quarter before 4,000 fans.

"We had them backed against the wall," said McKenna of Pajaczkowski's first long run. "Our boys didn't seem to realize a man can run 93 yards down the middle."

Nebraska, making his first start at quarterback, drove the Keydets inside the Richmond 35 three times in the first half. Points didn't follow, though. VMI looked improved over the first two weeks after McKenna inserted six new starters. Nebraska overcame some early butterflies to rush for 39 yards and give the Keydets a spark. Veteran tackle Lake Westfall went down with a leg bruise and had to be replaced by inexperienced sophomore Bob Rader.

Next, the Keydets met another powerful West Virginia team in Bluefield, but the Big Red held firm early on. Snyder and Nebraska both intercepted passes before a 99-yard punt return by the aptly-named Jack Rabbits opened the scoring late in the first period.

That play opened the door for the 11th ranked Mountaineers, showing off "three balanced elevens" to run up the score with their coal-shaft deep bench for a 47-12 demolition.

The Keydet offense perked up in the second half as Moody and Vaughn rushed for scores, Vaughan's on a 21-yard scamper after Harry Shepherd's 36-yard interception return. Sam Woolwine led the Keydets with 62 yards rushing on 12 attempts.

From there, VMI fell to 0-5 as rival Virginia snapped an eight-game losing streak behind a strong effort from their big Iranian fullback Jim Bakhtiar. The Keydets looked improved in Charlottesville before a homecoming crowd of 16,000 and even bounced back to score after each of the Cavaliers' first two touchdowns.

Lavery zipped 57 yards for a touchdown, unleashed by a Bill Miller block. After a Bakhtiar score for the Wahoos, Foster hit speedy Nick Evanusich for a 32-yard gain to the Virginia 14, and three plays later, Vaughn slashed off left tackle for a six-yard score. Bakhtiar was the catalyst for a 78-yard scoring drive, though Jim McFalls blocked Bakhtiar's extra point kick, putting the Cavaliers ahead 20-13.

The Keydets got the ball back at their own 40 with just two minutes remaining, and Nebraska showed some of the promise McKenna had been touting. First, he hit Lavery for 20 yards to the Virginia 40. He added three straight completions to Woolwine for 10, Vaughn for 12, and then Vaughn for 13 more to the five-yard line, where time ran out.

Nebraska was 5 of 11 for 107 yards passing, and the Keydets rushed for 264 yards.

With injuries and the losses mounting, VMI met Davidson the following week at Alumni Field. Trailing just 7-0 at the half, the Keydets saw the Wildcats tally two more touchdowns to put the game away, 21-7.

After rushing the ball so well against Virginia, VMI could muster just 67 yards on the ground and didn't score until late when freshman quarterback Bobby Ross guided the team. Vaughn rushed four yards to put the final points on the board. Carl Lebourdais and Westfall played well up front, and Woolwine had another good game on both sides of the ball.

The run of losses made it painfully evident that McKenna had to have more players. In his newsletter to boosters, he pointed out that "two years ago, when (VMI) awarded seven grants-in-aid to new cadets, Davidson granted aid to 22."

Harry Shepherd blocked a punt to set up VMI's only score. Ross added the extra point and played a little quarterback. He, fellow freshman Engels, Foster and Nebraska all split time. Ross was the most impressive, hitting four of seven passes for 67 yards. The loss included a little-noticed vignette. Ross angered McKenna when he kept the ball on an impromptu bootleg that wasn't part of the game plan.

"I thought I had played pretty well, but I did one thing on my own," he recalled years later. "I think in the game Coach McKenna thought I had missed the handoff, but basically I just told the guys that I was going to keep the ball. I gained three yards; *it was a magnificent call on my part*. Because of my overall performance, the Richmond paper speculated that I might even be the starter for the upcoming William & Mary game."

William & Mary was also winless, and it seemed like the perfect opportunity for the freshman. "My father was making calls asking for more tickets," Ross remembered, "and I'm thinking this might happen until our meeting in the chemistry lecture room on Monday after lunch. Coach drew the bootleg play up on the board and then matter-of-factly said, "we don't have a play like that." I just wanted to hide. I didn't even make the travel squad for the William & Mary game and was sent instead with the junior varsity team to play Fork Union Military Academy. And I played running back, not quarterback. This is where he was so emphatic about discipline. It was a great lesson learned."

Ross missed a heartbreaker in Williamsburg at Carey Field. VMI went on top early but saw William & Mary rally to hand the Keydets their sixth defeat. Vaughn's 45-yard run on a fourth down had put VMI on top, and Woolwine's 33-yard touchdown made it 13-6 at the half.

Many of the 10,000 fans on hand that day were shocked at halftime as they witnessed a mental patient at Eastern State Hospital climb to the top of the stadium and leap to his death on the ground outside the field.

The Indians struck for two touchdowns in the second half, and despite their 201 yards rushing, the Keydets couldn't find the end zone again, including four chances on four rushes from the one-yard line on one drive. William & Mary used that momentum to score the go ahead touchdown early in the fourth quarter when Charlie Sidwell scored from the one at the conclusion of a 98-yard march to make it 20-13.

"For the first time this year, we got the breaks, but we gave the game away," McKenna observed afterward. "We must cash in on every scoring opportunity."

The road remained unkind the following week, with VMI losing six fumbles and falling to Lehigh 39-0 in Bethlehem, Pennsylvania. Nebraska fumbled on the game's first play to set up the Engineers' initial score, and by halftime, it was 19-0. VMI had driven 60 yards on the final possession of the half, only to come up short of a score inside the one-yard line.

Lehigh opened the second half with an eight-play drive, behind a big, offensive line that put the game away despite, fine efforts by Woolwine and Moody on defense.

Afterward, McKenna painted a bleak picture in his letter to the Sportsmen's Club: "The state of mind of the Keydets before the game was evidently one of indifference. It is that thing which coaches dread most in a losing season. It results in players being injured because they are not mentally keyed and such was the case at Bethlehem where we all but ran out of replacements at several positions. Our biggest problem in our closing games will be psychological rather than technical."

The program did get some good news that week with the "Little Red" freshman team picking up a 19-13 win over George Washington behind Bobby Ross. VMI was trailing 13-0 in the third quarter when Ross sneaked for a score. He then hit Jerry Booth from 15 yards to tie the game. Ray Conkliers' bullish 27-yard run in the fourth quarter provided the victory.

The varsity losing streak – eight games for 1955 and nine games total – seemed a mountain as McKenna prepared his team to take on The Citadel in Charleston, South Carolina. It was so cold on the Thursday before the game that McKenna allowed players to go take warm showers and reconvene for a chalkboard session. The coach was extolling the virtues of line play and how most games were won and lost up front in the trenches when he noticed a tackle dozing off. McKenna shouted his name and said, "Where are most games lost?" The startled player jumped to his feet and replied: "Right here at VMI, I guess, coach."

The team left for Charlottesville the next day to catch a plane to Charleston. It appeared that the Keydets' were headed to another low point in their disaster of season, but when they finally arrived it Charleston, it was 90 degrees. Years later, McKenna recalled that game as a turning point for the program.

The Keydets went 65 yards on the opening drive with Nebraska "bucking over" from the one. To spark the next score, Moody made a big defensive play, knocking the ball loose from a Bulldog ball carrier, and LeBourdais recovered at the 46-yard line. Foster hit Evanusich for a 24-yard gain inside the 10, and Foster scored from the three.

The Citadel drove inside the VMI 20 on the ensuing possession, but the Big Red defense halted the threat on downs. Five more times the Bulldogs would drive inside the VMI 10, and the Keydets would stop them. Citadel's score came after a VMI fumble in the final six minutes, but the Keydets held on, 14-7. It was VMI's only victory since beating the same Citadel team the previous year.

A scuffle broke out after the physical game, perhaps spurred by the Bulldogs' frustration after the VMI line controlled the action most of the contest. The Keydets were happy to avoid the first winless season in school history, and the Corps came out to mob the team in celebration upon their return to Lexington. The moment provided a reaffirmation of the love the school had for its coach, and McKenna would treasure the moment as a highlight of his career, one that came toward the end of his bleakest season.

"It was the first time this year that we have held off repeated drives by the opponent," he wrote that week in his newsletter. "That phase of the game was very pleasing to me as it shows the development of mental maturity. If a boy doesn't learn to surmount bad breaks to really dig in when his back is to the wall, the experience of playing college football is deficient in the most valuable elements the game has to offer."

McKenna could sigh in relief now, his young team was finally in the win column, and would get a little extra rest before the annual showdown with Virginia Tech in Roanoke.

A Thanksgiving Day throng of 24,000 in Roanoke's Victory Stadium saw the underdog Keydets jump out to a 13-0 lead over their arch-rivals in the game's opening seven minutes. Nebraska intercepted a pass by VPI's Bill Cranwell to set up the first score.

Woolwine picked up 32 yards in two rushes to move the ball inside the VPI 10. Three plays later, Nebraska scored, but the point after was blocked. The Gobblers were driving when freshman tackle Jim McFalls recovered a Cranwell fumble at midfield. Vaughn dashed 27 yards, and Paul Janshego made a juggling catch of a Nebraska pass for a 21-yard touchdown.

McFalls recovered another fumble, but the Keydets then coughed up one of their own seven fumbles, losing the ball and momentum. Tech's Don

Divers had a five-yard run to put the Gobblers on the board before the end of the first quarter. Woolwine was then knocked out of the game in the first quarter with a bruised hip, a major blow to VMI on both sides of the ball. The Gobblers ran the ball hard to his side on defense after he was gone.

The speedy Divers and Dickie Beard took control for Virginia Tech, and by half, VPI led 20-13. Divers finished with 74 yards and three scores in what became a 39-13 Tech triumph.

VMI's 1-9 record was the worst since 1944, when the war-time Keydets were 1-8, with youth and injuries a factor for McKenna's third team. Future star Bobby Jordan missed the whole season after undergoing knee surgery. Lavery played with a sore leg, and Miller had a sore back most of the year.

Woolwine led the team with 480 yards rushing on 100 carries. The passing game didn't amount to much. Nebraska was the leading passer with a modest 14 completions in 49 attempts, good for just 216 yards. Vaughn was the team's leading receiver with six grabs for 92 yards on the season. It was becoming apparent passing wasn't the Keydets' forte, at least not yet.

For the first time, the winners of the game were presented with a ceremonial sword, imported from Spain by the VPI Corps of Cadets and VMI's senior class, a trophy to be awarded annually in the series.

McKenna's young team had faced one of VMI's toughest schedules. Game after game, Tom Joynes noted, "it was like a Little League team meeting the Yankees."

1955 (1-9)

DATE	VMI	LOCATION	OPP
S 17	7	at Tulane	20
S 24	6	George Wash. (Roanoke)	25
O 1	0	Richmond	21
O 8	12	West Virginia (Bluefield)	47
O 15	13	at Virginia	20
O 22	7	Davidson	21
O 29	13	at William & Mary	20
N 5	0	at Lehigh	39
N 12	14	at The Citadel	7
N 24	13	Virginia Tech (Roanoke)	39

CHAPTER SIX

NOWHERE BUT UP

When the Keydets reported for duty in August of 1956, the team was still young but now with a little more seasoning. Of the 28 sophomores on the 44-man team, 17 had seen varsity action the year before. Fifteen of them had lettered.

As the season opened, McKenna now had a letterman at each position. In addition, he had brought in a speedy group of freshmen, including a guard from Richmond, Howard Moss, who had been a state junior AAU champion in the 100 and 200 yard dashes. This time, however, there would be no need to throw them into the varsity fray before they were ready. The school's Sportsmen's Club had begun to gather the resources for increased financial support for scholarships. The record hardly reflected it, but a new attitude had taken hold.

"Even the sophomores are veterans," explained the coach, who couldn't help but expand the thought in his typically understated fashion. "(They) have readily improved, but this may not be discernible to the public."

To McKenna's point, the Keydets needed to find suitable replacements for center Dick Lyons, tackle Bill Miller, end Paul Janshego and halfback Dale Vaughn, in particular.

Johnston and Nebraska looked improved at quarterback, and Jordan was back to rejoin Moody and Woolwine in the backfield. Jim McFalls, at 220 pounds, and Bobby Dale, at 205, anchored the line at the tackle positions, and 195-pound Jerry Borst seemed ready at center.

Indeed, the still-young team looked ready in the September 15th opener, pounding Stetson 47-6 in Deland, Florida. Halfback Bobby Jordan, back from the knee injury that sidelined him the previous season, rushed 13 times for 99 yards and four touchdowns.

Fullback Sam Woolwine had 74 more yards, and co-captain Joe Moody and quarterback Duke Johnston also pitched in as VMI rushed for 274 yards, and in a big change from the previous season, didn't lose any fumbles. McKenna also liked the play of Borst and Dale in the line.

Perhaps echoing McKenna's skepticism at this stage, *The V.M.I. Cadet* tempered the early-season enthusiasm, reporting, "Since the opposition by Stetson was inadequate, the score of this contest may not be entirely indicative of what lies ahead."

Those words proved prophetic as VMI entered yet another tough slate of road games, beginning September 22 in Charlottesville. For the second straight year, Virginia's big Jim Bakhtiar led the Cavaliers over the Keydets, this time by an 18-0 count. Bakhtiar rushed for an Atlantic Coast Conference record 210 yards, more than twice VMI's rushing total that day.

Another familiar face, former Keydet Sonny Randle, had a big 46-yard reception early in the game to set up the first score, but it was the Virginia defense that set the tempo. VMI never got inside the Cavaliers' 30-yard line in the first half.

The Keydets' best opportunity came in the third quarter when a Woolwine tackle caused a fumble that Dale recovered. Jordan ran 10 yards for a first down on a fake punt, but penalties stalled the march, and then VMI fumbled.

The game stood at 6-0 until late in the fourth quarter when Bakhtiar scored. VMI's Borst blocked his PAT attempt. After another fumble, Virginia tacked on a 17-yard touchdown run by Randle.

The Keydets, in a bad portent, lost five fumbles at Scott Stadium before the Wahoos' largest crowd (22,000) in three years. McKenna, in his weekly newsletter to boosters, implored help to have alternate year games with Virginia moved out of Charlottesville to neutral sites around the state. He also lamented an official's call which took away a touchdown, offering that "still photographs" of Chuck McLennan's potential scoring grab looked like he had made the catch inbounds. "The movies (game film), not yet back, will tell the story," he wrote.

More bad news came when the Keydets' biggest player, talented tackle Jim McFalls, was declared out of action until his sprained foot healed. Don Basham, a 195-pound sophomore, would replace him in the starting lineup.

In a not-very-surprising announcement, McKenna also said he was considering moving Nebraska to the first unit to replace Duke Johnston, who had been inconsistent so far.

It probably wouldn't have mattered who suited up or who quarterbacked when VMI traveled to West Point, New York on September 29. The trip got off to an ominous start when the plane coming to pick up the team in Charlottesville blew a tire. Sophomore quarterback Bobby Ross picks up the story from there. "Charlottesville was not a big airport, so they had a tire flown down from New York. In the interim, the team was taken to see a movie. It was *Bus Stop with Marilyn Monroe* – not the sort of movie that was on Coach McKenna's top ten list. We get back to the airport and are standing around on the tarmac while the mechanic is changing the tire. All of the delays were not on Coach's schedule and this further time consuming effort was too much. He looked at the mechanic and said, 'Judging by how long it's taking you to fix that tire, you must not to be too good of a damn mechanic.' The mechanic looked back at Coach McKenna and said, 'Judging by your won-lost record last year, you must not be too good of a damn football coach.' [That was the '55 season and we had finished 1-9.] Let me tell you, all of us players scattered. Coach McKenna was like a god to us, and we had never heard anyone say something like that to him. We weren't sure what fireworks might happen. However, he showed his poise and didn't say a word. It was one of the few times that Coach was speechless."

Powerful Army, a six-touchdown favorite in some quarters, ground out 364 yards rushing in a 32-12 win before a crowd of 26,150.

Army drove for two first quarter touchdowns, but VMI bounced back, taking wing on Johnston's aerials. He connected on a 21-yard pass to Jordan that set up Jordan's 19-yard scoring run. Six minutes later, the Radford native scored again. However, the Keydets couldn't trade touchdowns after that.

Johnston had 146 yards passing, and Jordan and Nick Evanusich had good games as VMI played Army closer than most experts had predicted, forcing Coach Red Blaik to stay with his first team until late in the contest.

Despite a slow start in the win-loss column, when the national statistics came out Monday, VMI had a leader. Jordan had 40 points on six touchdowns and four PAT kicks to pace all collegians.

The Keydets got back in the win column the following week, downing Richmond 35-20. VMI's fourth straight road game got off to a great start when Woolwine took the opening kickoff 93 yards for a score in heavy fog at City Stadium.

Over fifty years later, Joynes could still picture that play though few got a very good look at it that night. "It was foggy; the Spiders kicked off, and Sam got the ball. He started up the middle, and you could barely see," Joynes said. "He was knocking people all over the place and went all the way with it. He was pretty fast, and he would catch the ball, tuck it in and just run. He didn't look to see where everybody was; he just ran over people."

VMI coaches had noticed a tendency by Richmond on kickoff coverage and confused the Spiders by crisscrossing their blockers. The heavy fog that limited visibility to about 20 yards may have also aided the tricky play. So did the determined Woolwine's brute strength.

"He killed people," laughed Joynes in a 2006 interview. "He got a reputation. Players were afraid to get in front on him. He was 5-11, 175, but strong as an ox."

Moody took an interception back 55 yards and VMI's front wall on defense limited Richmond as the Keydets improved to 2-2. Ron Swirk, subbing for an injured Carl LeBourdais, was a standout, as were McFalls, Borst and Bob Rader.

Pete Johnson rushed for two scores, and Jordan's punts helped pin Richmond back all day. Howard Moss, the speedy freshman, also added a big interception return in the gloom.

Jordan was kept out of the end zone but kicked his first field goal and continued to lead all state players with 43 points.

McKenna later announced he would continue alternating Johnston and Nebraska under center. "This is a unique situation for us," he said. "In the past, when our first-stringer got hurt, it meant trouble."

The Keydets returned to Lexington but didn't bring their best effort with them on October 13 in a 27-20 loss to Lehigh. Bob Naylor rushed for a school-record 220 yards, as the Engineers spoiled VMI's homecoming, the only home game of the season. The Keydets led early but made too many mistakes, missing too many tackles on a frustrating afternoon.

In his weekly newsletter, McKenna vowed to have "live" tackling the rest of the year in practice if that aspect of the team's effort didn't improve. "The thing that causes us grave concern is the knowledge – and all coaches everywhere agree – that tackling is ninety percent desire," he wrote.

Trailing at the half, the Keydets scored after just two plays in the third quarter with Jordan's 85-yard reception from Johnston setting up the touchdown. VMI closed to 14-13, but Lehigh needed just five plays to answer.

Johnston hit Evanusich for another VMI score after Johnson and Jordan moved the team into position, but that was all the offense could muster. Lehigh tacked on a clinching score, and then recorded a fourth quarter interception to decide matters.

"Johnston, Jordan and Evanusich stood out for us in the good sense," McKenna wrote to The Sportsmen's Club. "Many of the others were conspicuous by their shortcomings."

The game was memorable for another special occasion, though. At halftime, VMI took the opportunity to honor one of its greatest gridiron stars, Jimmy Leech. The certificate of Leech's election into the National Football Hall of Fame was presented to his widow, Mrs. Esther B. Leech of Charlotte, North Carolina.

Teammates of Leech, members of the undefeated 1920 Flying Squadron, were also guests of honor. Leech was elected to the Hall of Fame in January of 1956. His 26 touchdowns had stood as a national collegiate record for more than 20 years.

Scoring was likewise a trademark for McKenna's '56 Keydets. Through five games, they were averaging almost 20 points a contest, but the defense was porous, and that flaw magnified any mistakes, costing the team scoring opportunities.

VMI certainly didn't have enough scoring opportunities the following week, falling 40-14 at George Washington in a Friday night contest. VMI lost five interceptions, a fumble and had problems getting a grip on Colonial ball-carriers all night. GW led 40-0 at one point in old Griffith Stadium in a game McKenna labeled a "tragedy of errors."

GW "pushed the lighter Keydet line all over the field," according to *The V.M.I. Cadet.*

VMI third-stringer Art Brandriff, "a high stepping halfback," came off the bench to score a late touchdown, and Jim Sam Gillespie had a 10-yard reception for a score, but the depth-shy Keydets were again overpowered by a bigger, deeper opponent.

Four Keydet quarterbacks could muster just 6-of-19 passing, all the completions by Johnston, who also had three of VMI's interceptions.

McKenna wasn't pleased with his receivers, who failed "to latch onto the ball in crucial situations," and tackling was still an issue. "Tackling by our players continues to be shoddy, and all our efforts are bent on developing and finding those boys who can and will tackle."

Perhaps partly because VMI was on the receiving end of so many kickoffs, Woolwine now led the nation with 392 return yards.

The ensuing 13-13 tie at Davidson felt more like a win with the way the Keydets fought back in the closing minutes. Sophomore quarterback Bobby Ross hit John Engels for a touchdown with 1:05 to play, and the Keydets salvaged the tie, thanks to that play and Johnston's point after kick.

Engels caught Ross' aerial on the sideline at the goal line and fell into the end zone, as he was tackled. Earlier, VMI marches in the final period, first to the 26-yard line and then to the 14, were thwarted as tension grew on the Keydet sideline.

The big star was Woolwine, who weaved his way for 131 yards on 22 rushes and was also a defensive standout as VMI held Davidson below 200 yards total offense. It marked the first time the Keydets had out-gained an opponent since the season-opener. Woolwine showed that he was a premier two-way player and earned Southern Conference Player of the Week honors.

"He had about half our tackles," said McKenna. "He averaged better than six yards per carry as our workhorse and got the yardage we needed in clutch situations. The only thing he didn't do for us was score, but it was the consensus that he was the best man on the field."

The beleaguered defense held Davidson to 164 yards on the ground and just 53 more passing and turned back first half drives deep in VMI territory. The Keydets did the job, still without captain and steady guard Carl Lebourdais, who had his foot in a cast and missed his fourth game.

McKenna was being extra careful, hoping to get his stalwart back for a closing surge. "A hard lick would put him out for the rest of the season," said the cautious coach.

In his newsletter, McKenna said, "The players felt they should have and could have won."

Even with the injuries, the Keydets got back in the win column at City Stadium in rainy Lynchburg, where they bested winless William & Mary 20-6 before 5,000 fans.

It was their best performance of the season, a result McKenna said came in large part due to assistants Clark King and Vito Ragazzo's scouting of the Indians. Jordan capped a 75-yard, game-opening drive with a five-yard scoring run, but the Indians ran the ensuing kickoff back to tie the score.

In the second quarter, Johnston's 31-yard pass to Chuck McLennan set up the first of Woolwine's two touchdowns. He finished with 87 yards on 20 carries. McFalls was a standout up front, opening holes for the Keydet runners, and on defense, batting down a pass and nearly blocking two punts. VMI held the Indians to just 96 yards rushing, while running up a 252-yard total on their side of the ledger.

Fellow linemen Lou Farmer and Nick Ruffin were also keys up front, but the team took a severe blow when Bobby Dale was lost for the rest of the season with a dislocated forearm late in the contest.

When the "Big Six" standings and statistics came out in papers around Virginia that Monday, Jordan (whom McKenna called "an unobtrusive but highly capable operative" in his newsletter) was still atop all scorers with 55 points, including eight touchdowns. Despite the shuffling at quarterback, the Keydets led all Southern Conference teams, averaging 93.9 yards passing per game.

Not everyone was buying into VMI's improvement, though. The Keydets were a four-touchdown underdog headed to Morgantown but nearly snapped West Virginia's 19-game Southern Conference winning streak in a tough 13-6 setback.

West Virginia ground out 403 total yards, but most of it came between the 20s, as the Big Red defense stiffened whenever the Mountaineers got close. West Virginia never punted, and led 7-0 at the half after recovering a fumble to set up the score.

In the third quarter, the Keydets rolled 87 yards, Johnson slamming in from two yards to make it 7-6. A 10-play, 69-yard drive extended the WVU lead, but VMI wasn't done. Sophomore end Carl Kasko, in for McLennan, who left with a broken nose, recovered a fumble to set up a potential winning drive.

A 31-yard run by Woolwine helped the Keydets move to the WVU 20, but a fourth down screen pass went awry, and the march was stopped. Mountaineers coach Art "Pappy" Lewis thought his defensive front, particularly center/linebacker Chuck Howley (later of Dallas Cowboys fame), was the difference in their victory.

"This was the best VMI team we've played yet," said Lewis. "VMI seems to be getting better as the season rolls along."

Lineman Lou Farmer was named SC Player of the Week for his efforts in helping slow the heavily favored Mountaineers. "I couldn't begin to count the number of key tackles Farmer made or helped with," said McKenna. The 186-pounder from Fries, Virginia, came up particularly big when the Mountaineers moved in close, looking to score. Farmer helped his defensive mates stall Mountaineer marches inside the 20-yard line three times to keep the Keydets in the game.

A week later, West Virginia would beat Furman to claim a fourth straight Southern Conference crown.

The Thanksgiving Day game with Virginia Tech wouldn't have much to do with the Southern Conference title, and VMI fell flat on a miserably cold afternoon in Roanoke. The Gobblers overpowered VMI 45-0 before 24,000 frozen fans in Victory Stadium.

VPI quarterback Jimmy Lugar ran a diverse attack that rolled up 368 yards rushing and controlled the game throughout. The weather hampered VMI's Southern Conference-leading passing attack with Johnston completing just two tosses.

"We simply had a poor day against a good, sharp club," said McKenna. "I think our youth really showed."

Jordan, with a gimpy knee, wasn't able to go, another hindrance to the VMI offense. At a disappointing 3-6-1, the Keydets still finished with two more wins than the previous season, and beating William & Mary and playing West Virginia tough down the stretch gave the team optimism for the future.

Abingdon native Woolwine finished as the team's rushing leader with 107 carries for 507 yards and was named the state collegiate player of the year by the Roanoke Touchdown Club. Johnston completed 41-of-101 passes for 653 yards to lead the aerial attack, a vast improvement over the previous season.

Still, not even the most ardent Keydets' fan or player could envision what was coming. McKenna had an idea, though. He could look down a roster that had what he most admired in his players...experience.

1956 (3-6-1)

DATE	VMI	LOCATION	OPP
S 15	47	at Stetson	6
S 22	0	at Virginia	18
S 29	12	at Army	32
O 6	35	at Richmond	20
O 13	20	Lehigh	27
O 19	14	at George Washington	40
O 27	13	at Davidson	13
N 3	20	William & Mary (Lynchburg)	6
N 10	6	at West Virginia	13
N 22	0	Virginia Tech (Roanoke)	45

CHAPTER SEVEN

UNDEFEATED AND THE VOTE

It's 1957. The tail fins on cars are tall, and the crew cuts on young men are short...a gallon of gas is 24 cents and a new "Hi Fi" portable record player retails for under $80. Most people can own a Hi Fi or a new car, which averages about $2,749, because credit is now readily available. Two-thirds of all new cars on the nation's new interstate system are bought with credit in 1957, a major change in the way daily business is conducted nationwide.

Those expecting business as usual at VMI, where the Keydets hadn't fielded a football winner since 1951, were in for a bit of a surprise.

"We have more depth now than at any time since I've been here," McKenna observed. "We can start a letterman at every position and will have a letterman behind everybody but the ends and right halfback. However, we know we're still no world-beaters. Our reserve guards are small and a football has an odd shape—it takes too many crazy bounces."

McKenna finally had a team with which he could win, assembled largely with players from the Commonwealth. Twenty-two of 48 players were from the Old Dominion. His Keydets had speed and savvy in the backfield. They had decent size and good experience up front, and McKenna had players hungry to turn the tough defeats of the last two seasons into victories.

Sam Woolwine was typical of McKenna's now veteran, hard-edged team: tough, talented and determined. Woolwine had originally enrolled at Georgia Tech but became disenchanted at the school when he was pushed toward industrial engineering. Woolwine, even as a tender-aged freshman, already had his mind set on dentistry.

One of 10 children, all of whom attended college, Woolwine decided to transfer to VMI, where his brother Dave had some success. Sam sat out a year per NCAA rules, but he was allowed to practice with the varsity. He often played on the "scout" team, among the football fodder on a practice squad charged with preparing the top units for the next game.

Woolwine usually took the role of the coming week's top opposing back, mimicking players like Virginia Tech's Don Divers or Richmond's Frank Pajackowski. Woolwine was often tougher on his teammates than those gentlemen would be once the Saturday game actually kicked off.

Howard Dyer, who matriculated to VMI that fall, said Woolwine "was the toughest guy I ever tackled in my life."

Dyer continued that Woolwine was "not that big, but he was just all muscle and gristle, and every part of his body was hard." Even trainer Herb Patchin said Woolwine was so tough it was hard to penetrate his skin and give him a shot with a needle.

"He's a real firebrand," McKenna noted. "Before a game, with other guys eating steak and potatoes, Woolwine has a couple of soft-boiled eggs."

Football was in the 175-pound halfback's blood. In his senior year at William King High School, the school held a special night for his mother, Grace, for contributing "eight football-minded sons" to the program. His father was an engineer for Norfolk & Western Railroad, making the passenger run from Bristol to Roanoke, and back again, for 50 years.

Woolwine was one of 21 lettermen in the fold late that summer, a group that included junior tackle Jim McFalls, the largest man on the roster at 220 pounds. McFalls was also a pre-med honor roll student and the fastest tackle in the state, his desire evident by the way he sped down the field covering punts.

Bobby Dale was back at the opposite tackle spot, and Lou Farmer and Nick Ruffin were the guards. Farmer, now a senior, had joined the Rat team three years earlier, as an unknown, but just kept on impressing coaches.

Junior Jerry Borst returned at center, and Nick Evanusich and Carl Kasko manned the ends. Kasko had been a center in high school, but McKenna switched him to end his first week on Post, noting his size (6'-0", 192) and his experience playing high school basketball.

A three-way battle had played out in the spring at quarterback with Duke Johnston, Bill Nebraska, and Bobby Ross all enjoying moments. Johnston had the job for the most part in 1956, and Nebraska had been good enough to play as a freshman the previous year. Ross, along with junior halfback Johnny Engels, a converted quarterback, had been the talk of spring practices with their sensational play.

Woolwine, a senior, was entrenched at fullback, and Engels and Pete Johnson were atop the depth chart at the tailback slots after the team lost speedy Bobby Jordan temporarily. Jordan was suspended for a military violation – caught in the barracks room next door while under disciplinary room confinement. It was a second offense for Jordan, who had been 19th in the nation in scoring in '56, and 24th in the country in punting with a 38.4-yard average.

McKenna thought Jordan was the most underrated player in the state and was anxious to get him back in practices. The coach thought the problem in the perception of Jordan was that he just made everything look too easy.

"It's like Joe DiMaggio in center field," he explained. "Everybody expects Jordan to kick the ball 50 or 60 yards, and to make sensational runs and catches. We can say without reservation that we haven't seen a better all-round back."

Jordan had uncanny balance and a penchant for the big play, though his biggest challenge was staying healthy. He had hurt his knee as a freshman and again as a sophomore. Somehow it hadn't seemed to affect his speed.

McKenna always liked to joke about recruiting the Radford native. Jordan's father, an army officer, had been transferred to St. Louis while Jordan was in high school. He was All-Missouri at University High School as a junior and senior, scored a St. Louis record 106 points and averaged 42 yards a punt his final season.

But his family roots were back in the Old Dominion, and Jordan hoped to return "home" to play in college. Missouri, Vanderbilt, Illinois and Yale were vying for the high school halfback, but McKenna liked to say he landed Jordan for an investment of $1.09.

That's the cost of three three-cent stamps he used to send letters and the dollar he spent on lunch when Jordan made his visit to Lexington. "We were lucky to get him," McKenna told a reporter.

A pre-med student, Jordan had been winning academic prizes since his freshman year. After he enrolled at VMI, his father retired from the military, and his family moved back to Virginia.

It was one of Jordan's returns – a nifty runback of a punt – that set the stage for the Keydets' season-opening win at Tampa. VMI beat the oppressive humidity and the Spartans in a gutty 7-0 victory on September 21. Using his superior depth, a whole new strategy for the Keydets, McKenna wore down the hosts with a steady ground attack in the Tampa heat.

"At 7:00 p.m. Saturday night, it was 92 degrees in Tampa and the humidity was 95 percent," wrote McKenna in his newsletter. "The figures are from their newspaper. That is no weather for football."

Woolwine had the game's only score with a 5-yard jaunt off right guard, capping a drive in the third quarter set up by Jordan's 16-yard punt return. Behind the hard running of Jordan, Pete Johnson and Woolwine, VMI moved down the field for the decisive score.

Jordan was also a major factor with his punting that pinned Tampa back.

A fourth-quarter goal line stand preserved the lead with Lou Farmer and Woolwine making key plays. "It was a heartening display of defensive determination and the most pleasing effort of the evening to our coaches," wrote McKenna. "It ended the Tampa gesture for the night."

It also hinted at the kind of determination this squad would show all season. *The V.M.I Cadet* took note of the new-look Keydets, saying that "long suffering coach" McKenna and "the Keydets field a team with more speed, finesse, and poise than any of recent years."

Holy Cross was a 20-point favorite the next week on the road at Fitton Field in Worcester, Massachusetts, not far from McKenna's childhood home in Lawrence. VMI opened the scoring, Woolwine going 19 yards to complete a 59-yard, 13-play drive on which the Keydets converted two fourth downs. Holy Cross went ahead 14-7 before the half, but in the third period Duke Johnston made a big play. Seeing the Crusaders guarding the middle on a fourth-and-one, the quarterback switched the play to go outside. Picking up a block from Nick Ruffin, Johnston sprinted 53 yards to make it 14-14.

Holy Cross went up 21-14, but Johnston engineered a drive, and hit Jordan for a 20-yard score. For the third time, Pete Johnson's extra point was true.

To go with all that, there were plenty of big plays defensively. Johnson had an interception, and Woolwine made an interception in the end zone late, on a pass deflected by Bobby Ross. A fumble deep in VMI territory put the game in peril, but Dick Evans got a big sack on fourth down.

Johnston got an interception and ran the ball back to the Crusaders 27, and as time wound down, Johnston hit Johnson – with blockers in front of him – but a jarring hit knocked the ball loose, ending VMI's last threat inside the 10.

The prudent and now standard option of kicking a field goal before that fateful play wasn't available to McKenna because the substitution rules of the day didn't allow him to reinsert his best kicker, Jim True, with no timeouts and the clock running.

The Keydets had twice fought from behind to knot the contest and then kept the Crusaders out of the end zone, stopping them on the eight-yard line with less than five minutes to play before nearly pulling out the win in the closing seconds. They held New England's top team to a 21-21 tie.

The rock-solid Farmer, a team co-captain along with Woolwine, was again brilliant on both sides of the ball, and all in all, this New England homecoming was much more enjoyable for McKenna than the 44-0 loss at Boston College in 1954.

A large rally greeted Farmer and the Keydets upon their return, the Corps carrying the players into the Courtyard. VMI had tied the team favored to win the Lambert Trophy as the top team in the East. The speedy, smart Keydets had also just tied a team that outweighed them 12 pounds a man up front, an indication that McKenna's fundamental, cerebral style of football could truly be successful.

The Keydets opened Southern Conference play on October 5th and got off to a great start with a 99-yard, first quarter drive that keyed a 28-6 victory over Richmond in City Stadium. Johnston scored from the one to put VMI ahead, and a minute-and-a-half later, after a Richmond fumble, Johnson added an 8-yard scoring run.

Penalties kept VMI from taking firmer control, and a Spiders' touchdown closed the game to 14-6 at the half. A key Johnston-to-Sam Horner pass got the Keydets moving in the third quarter, and Jordan rolled five yards for a score to make it 21-6. Ross came on to complete three passes in a late drive that sealed the victory. Art Brandriff capped the win with a 1-yard score.

VMI finished the day as the only major undefeated program in Virginia. Again, "The Boys from the State Capital," as McKenna called them, were bigger and had a speedy backfield but couldn't gain much ground on the VMI defense, which held them to 133 yards rushing and just 16 more passing. VMI had 254 yards on the ground, and McKenna was particularly pleased with his second unit and some new, emerging threats like Brandriff, a former roller skating speed champion, who was also pretty fast without his metal wheels. He had been timed at 9.8 in the 100-yard dash in cleats.

Horner, another newcomer, was a high school swimming star and had hoped to go to Army but couldn't meet the entrance requirement because of his poor vision. He wore glasses off the field and contacts on. His grandfather was a VMI alumnus, and McKenna clearly saw he had a future star.

If a team had depth, the one-platoon system allowed a coach to play multiple quarterbacks if he had a plan to insert an entire unit at once. "Coach had teams he called the gold team, the blue team and the green team," Bobby Ross recalled. "The gold team was the original starters, and the blue team was kind of like a tempo team. They were going to set a fast pace. Then the green would be kind of fillers for the gold and blue. This was his organization. I mean, it was sound and it was solid. Almost everybody who got on that bus knew they were going to play because he would play three teams. Under the rules, he could only substitute at certain points in the game. He had a person who made him aware of when he could substitute and when he could not."

The Keydets next enjoyed their first home game of the year, rolling to a 3-0-1 record with a 26-14 homecoming win over Davidson before about 4,000 at Alumni Field. Home games were a rarity for the Keydets in the 1950s for multiple reasons, chief among them the lack of a quality facility.

McKenna, as he so often did on Post, took a perceived negative and worked it as a positive. "John was unusual because he consciously did not mind playing road games," said Dick Sessoms, who succeeded Joynes as sports publicist. "Why? Because as every cadet knows, you can get demerits on Saturday morning marching down for breakfast if you aren't careful. So John liked to get the team out on the road. I think he thought that getting into a first class hotel would get their minds on playing a football game on Saturday afternoon."

Late in the first quarter against Davidson, Ross moved VMI 80 yards, mostly with short passes. Horner's 10-yard scoring run capped the march.

VMI took command in the third quarter. A 35-yard Johnson run set up Johnston's 6-yard scoring pass to Jordan for a 13-0 lead. Davidson scored, but Jim McFalls pounced on the Wildcats' onside kickoff attempt. Ross then hit Jim Sam Gillespie for a 15-yard touchdown to extend the lead to 20-7.

Davidson came right back with a score, but VMI's Jordan broke tackles on a 49-yard touchdown that settled matters with four minutes left. Woolwine led the ground game with 65 yards on seven carries, and Ross was 7-for-7 passing, for 74 yards, which fueled speculation that he might move up in the quarterback rotation after Duke Johnston struggled.

"Duke had several passes intercepted, and I remember the next day he was on the field practicing," said freshman quarterback Howard Dyer. "He went out there and worked his way back into the lineup and became an excellent quarterback. What I remember most is Duke Johnston had the courage to fight through that adversity and come back and become a better player and a better leader."

Johnston would become a test pilot and fighter pilot in the United States Air Force, retiring as a Colonel after a distinguished 25 year career with leadership learned under the watchful eye of The Eagle.

The Davidson win put VMI atop the Southern Conference standings at 2-0 heading into a meeting in Williamsburg with William & Mary. An estimated 7,500 fans showed up at Carey Field, many of them VMI alums buzzed by the strong start.

Ross started the game but was knocked out in the first quarter with a broken nose. After a scoreless first quarter, the Indians drove inside the VMI 20, only to see Farmer recover a fumble and change the game's momentum. Behind the strong running of Jordan, Woolwine, and Horner, VMI went 81 yards to go ahead when Woolwine crashed over from two yards. Woolwine's point after kick proved large later, when the Indians went 55 yards to score just before the half but missed their PAT attempt.

Mike Chunta scored 30 seconds into the fourth quarter to put William & Mary ahead 13-7, as the Indians used an unbalanced line much of the day. "It was a well calculated move on the part of the Indian coaching staff," explained McKenna. "William and Mary had not shown anything of the sort in its previous four games, and while we warn our boys that any opponent may employ such tactics and while we tell them what to do in such an event, our team hadn't practiced against it. Very limited practice time precludes the opportunity to work against everything that is in the realm of possibility."

Jordan, who did a lot of things opponents thought outside that realm, wasted little time elevating Big Red hopes. He took the ensuing kickoff 46 yards to the Indians 32-yard line – "a thing of beauty," according to his coach

– but VMI was stopped at the 10. Then the Keydets were stymied again at the five when they fumbled on their next possession. On William & Mary's first play after the turnover, Farmer came up with another loose football. Two plays later Johnston hit Johnson for a 10-yard score, and Woolwine put the Keydets back on top with his PAT at 4:16, 14-13.

William and Mary put together a drive that reached the VMI five, but Jordan came up with a fumble at the goal line. With time running out, the Indians forced a VMI punt. However, Horner's interception on the final play sealed a big Southern Conference road victory.

Richmond Times-Dispatch writer Steve Guback reported the scene after that finish: "The grey-clad VMI Corps of Cadets rocked Williamsburg with a volley of cheers and behaved for minutes afterward as if they had just been awarded a five-day furlough."

"McKenna was good at judging opponents," recalled lineman Marty Fisher. "Regarding William & Mary, a powerhouse in the 40s, and still a dangerous team in the 50s, he told me, 'I will never play William & Mary until the fifth or sixth game of the year because by that time they have reduced their good players due to injuries just like we have. Then it's an even game.'"

With excitement building around the undefeated Keydets, the team returned "home" to Roanoke's Victory Stadium to meet George Washington. Advertisements billed the contest as "Southern Conference football at popular prices." Tickets for the game sold for $3, $2, and $1, generally 50 cents to a dollar cheaper than usual.

Four thousand fans turned out to see the Keydets pull out another tight game on a chilly day. "The action was anything but dreary, however," penned McKenna, "and such cash customers as there were surely got their money's worth."

Horner zipped 50 yards on the game's first play, all the way to the GW 15 and four plays later cashed in for the score. A Johnston-to-Jordan touchdown pass made it 13-0, but the Colonials got on the board before the end of the first quarter. Horner had another 1-yard scoring run to make it 19-7 in the second quarter. GW closed to 19-14 before the half.

The Colonials got a go-ahead score and a 20-19 lead late in the third quarter after an interception. However, Jordan's prolific punting late helped change field position, and VMI took advantage with a short drive that ended with Johnston's 5-yard scoring run.

Jerry Borst came up with an interception, and VMI ran out the clock for a 26-20 decision. Horner had 106 yards on 17 carries, and Johnston added 77 on 11 rushes. Jordan's five punts averaged 47.6 yards. McKenna thought it was the best game of the year for his linemen.

Duke Johnston, who had never played on a winning team in high school or prep school, was now 5-0-1. The New Castle, Delaware native would become the star of the November 2 clash with Virginia, a contest that would decide the "Big Six" championship.

The Cavaliers were listed as 6-to-10-point favorites and had beaten VMI three straight. The battle drew 21,000 spectators to Scott Stadium. The Keydets trailed 7-0 at the half, and 7-6 into the fourth quarter but rallied with a balanced attack. Johnston led VMI through the air with nine completions in 17 attempts for 177 yards against a Virginia pass defense ranked fifth in the nation.

McKenna had suspected that the Cavaliers weren't as staunch against the pass as those lofty statistics indicated. Despite Johnston's 33 percent completion rate entering the contest, the game plan was to throw. After the game, Johnston's 393 yards through seven games led the Southern Conference.

Years later, Ross reflected on McKenna's adaptability as a key for the Keydets. "(McKenna) wasn't confined to just one system," said Ross. "He was going to change based on what personnel he had, and that just showed what a remarkably good coach he was."

Confirming that, Johnston engineered three second half scores, the first a 29-yard touchdown throw to Carl Kasko, who made a nice over-the-shoulder catch. After a rushing touchdown by Woolwine, the wily quarterback, having one of his finest days, connected with Jordan for 42 yards to set up a dive for Johnson, who slammed in from three yards with just nine minutes left.

Both rushing scores were behind McFalls, and one of Johnston's favorite plays was rolling out behind the big right tackle. Johnston added an interception on defense to cap his impressive performance. For the third straight week, VMI came from behind to win a game, this one by a 20-7 count.

After the game, cadets swarmed the field to celebrate. The Keydets, undefeated this late in the season for the first time since 1922, were beginning to draw comparisons with the Institute's famed "Flying Squadron."

Woolwine, the bruising fullback, again led the ground game with 63 yards, and it was his one-yard plunge that put the Keydets ahead in the second half.

The Keydet defense did a better job slowing big Jim Bakhtiar, limiting him in the second half, though the Wahoos still managed nearly 200 yards rushing. The bruising Bakhtiar had 102 yards, but just four came in the final 30 minutes.

Coach McKenna had a lot of wry remarks, but Pete Johnson remembers that on the way back from Charlottesville to Lexington, McKenna stopped the team bus at a roadside stand near Staunton and bought the team a bushel of apples. His players were surprised by the gesture. "No roses, but a damn fine game," he told them.

"That," recalls Johnson, "was about the highest praise we ever heard from The Eagle."

Obviously, there was no time to stop and congratulate themselves. Another big test awaited on November 9th, a strong Lehigh team yet again on the road. The Engineers were being called "Little Oklahoma" by Northeastern scribes, thanks to a 10-game win streak.

Oklahoma and Coach Bud Wilkinson, by the way, would run their national-record winning streak to 47 games this same Saturday with a 39-14 win over Missouri in Columbia, Missouri. The following week, Notre Dame's 7-0 upset would end the Sooners' unprecedented run. Although the game's limited substitution rules had their critics, Wilkinson was not among them.

Meanwhile McKenna's biggest fear was within the Keydets' gold helmets. "The (Virginia) victory was satisfying to say the least," he wrote. "It will take a real effort to get them back to earth for the game with undefeated Lehigh next week in Bethlehem. The Keydets deserved to win, and so many were outstanding that the best thing to do is give a blanket stamp of approval."

McKenna's charges encountered 13,500 screaming fans in Bethlehem, Pennsylvania, for the showdown. VMI opened the game with an 80-yard touchdown drive, again highlighted by Johnston's passing.

The quarterback avoided onrushing tacklers to find Horner all alone for a score. But the Keydets failed on the conversion and found themselves behind when Lehigh went 40 yards for a 7-6 lead after an exchange of punts. VMI had two other scoring opportunities in the first half but was stopped on fourth down at the one yard and had a pass intercepted at the Lehigh 15.

Bill Nebraska led a fourth quarter 63-yard march by the "blue team," with John Engels, Verne Keefer and Johnson all picking up chunks of yardage. Engles' one-yard plunge on fourth down put VMI back on top 12-7, though the defense had to thwart a late drive to end Lehigh's winning streak. Horner led the attack for the day with 13 carries for 74 yards, and Johnston was 7-of-14 for 73 yards passing.

The toughest part of the day may have come at halftime when Lehigh students came on the field to welcome their team back and threatened to seize VMI's trademark cannon. The VMI band and many Corps seniors surrounded beloved "Little John" to protect it until two policemen restored order.

McKenna wrote that the "ruckus" wasn't worth mentioning in his news-letter...though he mentioned it. "The Keydets present at the game merely ob-jected to a possible threat of other spectators taking the cannon which plays a supporting role in our rooting section. Their conduct was representative."

End Jim Sam Gillespie was also a big gun, recovering two fumbles which eventually led to both of VMI's touchdowns. The 6'-2", 188-pound junior was a civil engineering major from Pounding Mill and had seen more playing time since Nick Evanusich was injured in the Holy Cross game. Late-bloomer Gillespie had also been effective on offense. While not a virtuoso pass-catcher, he was a thundering blocker and helped trigger the potent Keydet running game.

The hard-fought victory at Lehigh set the stage for a Southern Conference championship game the following week in Lynchburg between 7-0-1 VMI and The Citadel, now 6-1-1.

The Keydets had come from behind for a fifth straight weekend and were rewarded by moving to 13th in the Associated Press national poll. Of the tendency to fall behind and battle back, McKenna opined, "It makes a coach proud and nervous, too."

The *Richmond Times-Dispatch* had offered this assessment of McKenna's persona earlier in the season:

McKenna often sounds more like a banker than a football coach when he talks. He frequently uses words that are heard only in the best literary circles and he has a ready wit that captivates his listeners. Despite his ease as a speaker, it comes hard. He'll often pass up the banquet bill-of-fare or just dabble because of pre-speaking butterflies.

Dick Sessoms, who had dealt with McKenna as a reporter and as his sports publicist, said the coach often charmed the media. "He was very articulate; the sportswriters used to marvel and rush for their dictionaries," Sessoms laughed. "How many football coaches refer to a football as a 'prolate spheroid?' John was well read. He was precise in his use of the English language and didn't mince words, but he chose his words very carefully."

This season, McKenna's team was doing all the talking for him.

The Keydets certainly made a statement in the championship game. They finished off The Citadel in a 33-7 demolition in Lynchburg's Municipal Stadium before 9,000 in the Jaycee Bowl. The Keydets rolled 57 yards with the opening kickoff, as Horner swept the corner from seven yards for a quick lead in the de facto Southern Conference championship game.

One play after the ensuing kickoff, Gillespie recovered a fumble to set up Jordan's 14-yard touchdown scamper. Johnston added a sneak for a score and hit Jordan for a 26 yard touchdown to make it 26-0 at the half in VMI's finest showing of the season.

The Citadel tried to match VMI on the ground after maintaining a strong aerial attack all season. The strategy backfired. Though the Bulldogs ground out 184 yards, VMI was better with 244 yards by land.

Now only Virginia Tech stood between the VMI and an undefeated season. Despite the big win, the Keydets would actually fall to 16th in the national poll, and move to 17th with the Saturday off just before the Thanksgiving showdown.

VMI remained an eight-point favorite over the Gobblers in Dunkel's rating system, which was so prominent in the 1950s that its predictions often ran in daily newspapers. Dick Dunkel created the "Dunkel Index" in 1929 as a way to "settle a debate over which teams were the best." The index used statistics to establish "power ratings" for each team based upon strength of schedule and the team's most recent results. Newspapers and "enthusiasts," who enjoyed paying close attention to point spreads, often used the index to forecast outcomes.

A crowd of 25,000 rain-soaked fans and several bowl scouts filled Victory Stadium on Thanksgiving Day and saw Jordan score twice for the Southern Conference champs, the field lights on the entire afternoon because of the gloomy skies overhead. The heavy, slow track was another advantage for the larger Techmen, but VMI was not to be denied, not this season.

Jordan's first score came on a four-yard rush early in the second quarter for a 7-0 advantage VMI would carry into the half. The Gobblers took to the air early in the fourth quarter and got a touchdown but missed the extra point attempt. The two teams exchanged punts and turnovers, but Farmer came up with a big play, scooping up a fumble at the VPI 14. Four plays later, Jordan crashed in from three yards to make it 14-6, the play punctuated by the now familiar blast of the team's celebratory cannon, "Little John."

The Gobblers had one more drive in them, moving to the Keydet 25, but they stalled there, and Johnston was able to run out the clock. With his two scores and 43 yards rushing, Jordan was named the game's outstanding player as the Keydets beat VPI for the first time since 1953. He had two clutch late punts, one from the end zone and one a booming 59-yarder on third down to help keep the Gobblers at bay in the final minutes.

"Bobby Jordan won that game for us," said Ross years later.

McKenna employed the "quick kick" often that season because of Jordan's punting prowess. VMI would often punt before fourth down, particularly when penalties set them back or when inclement weather dictated a strategic advantage. On this day, Jordan punted the wet, heavy ball for an average of 40.5 yards.

With mud all over their grinning faces, the Keydets cheerfully collected the saber that went with the win in the series between the two teams. Sam Woolwine hoisted it high in the locker room as his happy teammates gathered round. McKenna was there too, still wrapped in his overcoat. He tilted his gaze up to the saber and allowed the slightest trace of a smile. The happy faces would soon disappear, however, as the coach moments later addressed the team behind closed doors in the National Guard Armory adjacent to Victory Stadium. They discussed postseason options, and then he and the coaches left to allow the team to vote on the bowl opportunities now available to the team.

Those options included either a trip to the Sun Bowl in El Paso, Texas, or to the Tangerine Bowl in Orlando, Florida. Earlier, it has been thought that the Keydets were more interested in the Sun Bowl because the December 27 date of the Tangerine Bowl would mean missing Christmas at home.

HOW DID THEY VOTE

By a 2-to-1 margin, the team voted to stay home and not go to either bowl.

Co-Captain Woolwine addressed the team and afterward said, "I thought we owed it to the school and the coaches to make the trip. I voted to go, but I'm happy with whatever the team wants. I think the biggest factor was that we have so many boys from the Pittsburgh area, and they would have had to leave home Christmas Day in order to get to school in time to leave. It's hard for a boy to miss that vacation when you don't get any more time off than we do."

In his newsletter that week, McKenna disputed that notion. "The squad's vote to decline all bowl bids surprised me. Contrary to what appeared in print more Virginia boys voted against the post-season game than did Pennsylvanians. The proposition was carefully explained to them with practice restarting on Dec. 16 with five days off starting the 21st and including all Christmas Day at home. No player would have had to start back before the morning of the December 26. A refusal was their prerogative, of course. They exercised it by a 2 to 1 majority."

McKenna hid his disappointment to the media after the game. "They sure fooled me," he said. "But the kids have had a great season, and I guess they feel that beating VPI caps anything they could do from now on. I'm satisfied if they are."

Ross, who would later understand more about McKenna's emotions when he became a highly successful coach himself, couldn't remember how close the vote was. He just remembered McKenna.

"I remember seeing Coach McKenna's face, and I probably didn't fully understand the disappointment until I became a coach," he recalled. "That would have been a crushing blow to me, too. Clark King was the same way, kind of shocked about the whole thing. Tell you why it happened, I think the guys wanted the Christmas vacation. We were probably good enough to have won the thing too. We were a pretty good football team, had depth, had speed, the whole thing. I think it was a tremendous set back to the program financially."

Jordan was overheard saying, "I'm sorry about that bowl vote," to McKenna as he was leaving the building. To the media, the senior said, "I think this victory was a good way to end the season."

For many Keydets, it wasn't until years later that they truly realized what they had given up. Eileen McKenna heard them talk at reunions, heard the things they later said to her husband. "After they voted they were all sorry, but not right away. John said it was a mistake later on, that he should have handled the voting differently. Years later, they all admitted they would have voted differently."

For players who had begun practice under the late summer sun, had the long season with no weekend breaks, in addition to the demanding life on Post, the allure of getting away was too much, particularly for players not playing a big role other than in practice.

"They didn't want to miss their vacation," said Eileen McKenna. "These were kids who had been under the gun since they came into school, and they couldn't wait to get out from underneath. I think from underneath John, too."

Crusty end coach Vito Ragazzo was more direct. "I think they ought to have their heads examined. These kids just don't know what a bowl trip means."

"The thing that people don't understand is that in '57, there was a Rose Bowl, Sugar Bowl, Orange Bowl, Gator Bowl and Sun Bowl, and that might have been it," said Tom Joynes years later. "There weren't many bowls like there are now."

Joynes had a good memory. The Bowl line-up that season had Tennessee nipping Texas A&M in the Gator Bowl, the only game played before New Year's Day. Oklahoma beat Duke in the Orange; Ohio State over Oregon in the Rose; Navy defeated Rice in the Cotton; Mississippi bested Texas in the Sugar; Southern Mississippi got past Texas A&M Commerce in the Tangerine Bowl, and Louisville beat Drake in the Sun Bowl, the bowl that most wanted VMI.

"The guy from the Sun Bowl told the press that he invited us, but we turned them down," said Joynes. "As I recall, the original report of that sounded like VMI turned it down, not the players. Eventually somebody had a story in the paper that explained it was the team."

Joynes also recalled the shock on McKenna's face at the outcome. "He told me that night that he should have let the starters do the voting," Joynes remembered. "The coaches wanted to go, and it hurt them that the players didn't want to go."

McKenna later hid his feelings well, but Joynes was of the opinion that the vote troubled the coach for years afterward.

"I am sure that it did," Joynes said in 2006. "Because you seldom have a team like that, a season like that, an opportunity like that. There were so few bowl games. That would have been their first time ever on television. At that time, they had never been on television. In fact, no school in the state had probably other than Virginia once or twice playing an ACC team. It was the Sun Bowl. The guy said we would love to have VMI, so John held a meeting. John said later, 'We should have done it over.' However, he let everyone vote."

The vote proved devastating for VMI's emerging fan base of alums, Dick Sessoms recalled, adding that boosters were angry for a long time afterward. It wasn't easy to explain just how the little school in Lexington had even put themselves in a position to turn down a bowl game.

Perhaps *The V.M.I. Cadet* said it best in a congratulatory editorial:

"We felt proud (a word used often this year) of the whole big picture, and we could see that pride and admiration on the faces of alumni and friends as well. They seemed to have proven a point for VMI, something about taking available material, scholarships, a lot of experience, effort, and spirit and turning it into a team...a fine one. We have no Physical Education majors at the Institute, no padding of athlete's grades, no separation of sports from the military life. There are Honor List Students, members of the Honor Court, men with rank in the Corps of Cadets, men soon to become dentists, engineers, doctors, lawyers, businessmen, the like, all members of an undefeated football team, from a school of less than a thousand students...no wonder people are proud, both of the team and VMI."

The undefeated season brought the team and the school more attention than perhaps any time since the Civil War when the Cadets were thrown into the fray in a brave showing at the Battle of New Market.

Mary Garber, the pioneering female sportswriter at the *Winston-Salem Journal*, addressed the situation and explained what made VMI's season so special across the college football landscape:

VMI is one school where the players are students first and then players. All-conference fullback Sam Woolwine and halfback Bobby Jordan are pre-med students. Halfback Pete Johnson is a cadet officer and a major in electrical engineering; halfback John Engels is going into law; quarterback Duke Johnston (one of the conference's top passers) is a qualified jet pilot and an air cadet; tackle Jim McFalls is a pre-med student, made the Southern All-Scholastic team for top grades; tackle Bobby Dale is studying to be a research chemist; another tackle, George O'Neill is majoring in chemistry (and) plans to be a professor; guard Dave Martin has trouble with some subjects. He even got a B in one (his worst grade).

Maybe this shows that a school which wants to can preserve its educational integrity, stick to its school traditions and requirements, but still put out a fine football team manned by students.

But VMI was vastly different than many of the "football factories" they joined in the national rankings. The Keydets were ranked 20th in the final AP poll after going 9-0-1, their only national ranking in the 20th century.

And McKenna did it at the smallest school playing major college football, with only two fulltime varsity assistants, a freshman coach and another a basketball coach available only until November 1. Scholarships are a precious commodity at VMI, where only seven players were awarded "full rides" this season, and two more newcomers received partial aid.

Larger schools were offering as many as 30 football scholarships a year, and could afford to "hit" on perhaps 50 percent of those recruits becoming successful and still maintain a successful program. The Keydets had no such margin for error.

There were other obstacles most powerful football programs don't face either. Besides the military lifestyle, VMI cadets must have had two years of high school algebra, a year of geometry, a principal's recommendation and a C-plus average to be admitted to the Institute.

Practices don't begin until 4:30 in the afternoon because 8:00-4:00 is academic time at the Institute, and everyone – even football players – must engage in military drills either Monday or Friday, so there are only four football practices a week. The team also practices on the parade ground or sometimes in the school's antiquated 4,000-seat stadium. This year, the Keydets played nine games off campus.

The 1957 team more than passed muster.

There were other rewards, besides the bowl invitation. McFalls, Farmer, Johnston, Jordan and Woolwine all earned First Team All-Southern Conference honors, and Gillespie and Borst were second team, while Kasko and Horner garnered honorable mention. Jordan was selected Conference Player of the Year.

For the third straight year, Woolwine led the team in rushing, racking up 531 yards, his best showing ever, on 105 carries (an average of over five yards per rush). Johnston completed 37-of-90 passes for 520 yards, and Jordan was the top receiver with 19 catches for 317 yards,

McKenna was named Southern Conference Coach of the Year and given a three-year contract extension. "I didn't do as much coaching this year as in some of the losing seasons we had," he responded.

He summed up the program's progress thusly: "They say you learn something in defeat and for two years we must have been learning."

1957 (9-0-1)

Southern Conference Champions

DATE	VMI	LOCATION	OPP
S 21	7	at Tampa	0
S 28	21	at Holy Cross	21
O 5	28	at Richmond	6
O 12	26	Davidson	14
O 19	14	at William & Mary	13
O 29	26	George Wash. (Roanoke)	20
N 2	20	at Virginia	7
N 9	12	at Lehigh	7
N 16	33	The Citadel	7
N 28	14	Virginia Tech (Roanoke)	6

CHAPTER EIGHT

HUNGRY STILL

With the fallout from the bowl vote still being processed among alums, McKenna welcomed 24 lettermen back to Lexington in 1958. But there was more talk about who wasn't back in summer camp. Graduation hit the undefeated and defending Southern Conference champs hard. In the backfield alone, Johnston, Woolwine and Jordan were all gone, and up front the indispensable Lou Farmer had graduated, as well.

As always, these problems would play out as concerns in VMI's depth. McKenna and coaches Ragazzo, King, Chuck McGinnis and the newest addition, basketball/baseball/assistant football coach Louis "Weenie" Miller, had answers in the starting slots. Finding able alternates was the challenge.

Co-captain and fiery linchpin Bobby Ross, all 5-9, 172 pounds of him, would start at quarterback if he could beat out Bill Nebraska. Pete Johnson would slide into Woolwine's fullback slot, and speedster Art Brandriff would take over for Jordan at left halfback. Horner, at right halfback, could handle the punting chores.

Gillespie and Kasko would man the ends, and McFalls and Dale were a sturdy tandem at the tackles. Nick Ruffin was back at one guard slot and Jerry Borst had – as predicted – developed into a fine center. *The Roanoke Times* wrote that Borst had been so good for so long "that he's taken for granted like a good breakfast."

Colleges had taken a long look at Borst as he came out of Pitcairn High

School in Pennsylvania, but at 180 pounds, he didn't fit the mold of most major college linemen. His two brothers played at West Virginia but Pappy Lewis deemed Jerry too small. What the sheer numbers of height and weight didn't account for was Borst's leadership skills. There were times he ran the huddle for the Keydets, and he always commanded the line. It was a very good, veteran line ready to open holes for a "lightning-fast" backfield.

Lightning struck in the season-opener at home against Morehead State. The new class of 385 rats, pushing VMI's enrollment over 1,000, was on hand, part of an Alumni Field crowd of nearly 4,000 as the Keydets looked to continue their winning streak from the previous season.

Horner, the only non-senior starter, had a 61-yard touchdown run early, and Kasko recovered a fumble on the ensuing kickoff. Two plays later, Brandriff raced 28 yards for a score on McKenna's "belly play" off right tackle, and VMI was up 16-0 as intermittent rains came and went.

The Eagles were further ruffled when Borst deflected a pass that Ross picked off. McKenna inserted his second team and though they didn't score, their drive pushed Morehead State back deep and set up end Tom Kurkoski tackling Bert Dixon for a safety.

Nebraska hit Dick Evans for an 11-yard touchdown to make it 24-0. Ross returned the second half kickoff 74 yards for another score. Big Pete Johnson, just two years after surviving a bout with polio, recovered another MSU fumble to set up a Horner 7-yard run and a 39-6 Keydet lead to get the 1958 season off to a rousing start. VMI had comfortably won its ninth straight game, rolling over the Eagles, 46-20.

McFalls "was all over the field making tackles," according to McKenna.

The crusty coach found enough faults with his team's performance to drive them harder in practice the next week. "The green team, which is our third, looked better than the blue team, which is actually our alternate rather than a second team," he wrote in his weekly newsletter. "There'll be some changes made."

Ever the competitor, McKenna opined, "It was TOO easy, and we hope it doesn't prove harmful. Future opposition will be much, much sterner."

Around the state, some were calling Horner and Brandriff "The World's Fastest Backfield." Both halfbacks were capable of running the hundred-yard dash in 9.7 seconds.

"Yes, our first unit played very well, but I was far from satisfied with the showing of the reserves," said McKenna to the media, trying to calm some of the expectations for his retooling team. "We have a lot of work to do."

The coach would have trouble quelling the excitement the following week in a contest at Villanova, his alma mater. McKenna had played there in the mid-30s on teams coached by Harry Stuhldreher, an infamous member of Notre Dame's "Four Horsemen" in the 1920s. Another member of that Notre Dame backfield was James Crowley who, later, became head coach at Fordham where he mentored another legend, one Vincent Thomas Lombardi. Lombardi and his fellow defensive linemen also garnered a nickname at Fordham, "The Seven Blocks of Granite."

The Keydets apparently still had their horses in the barn as the Wildcats drove 78 yards to score on their opening possession before 7,000 fans in Philadelphia. But the hosts only had 13 seconds to enjoy that lead because that's the amount of time it took Pete Johnson to haul the kickoff back 97 yards. Horner's conversion run put VMI ahead 8-6.

McKenna described the play in his letter to the Sportsmen's Club that week. "We hit them with a bomb on the kickoff to us. Pete Johnson took the ball on his three-yard stripe, barreled straight up the middle to about our 35 staying in the apex of our wedge, then broke right through a pair of tacklers and out legged everyone into the end zone – truly a picture play."

Nebraska, subbing for an injured Ross at quarterback, blew the game open. He hit Kasko for 33 yards into Villanova territory and two plays later found Kasko for a 30-yard touchdown. The next time VMI had the ball, he needed one play to hit Brandriff for 45 yards and another score.

McKenna said Villanova was stacking the line to stop "our wide running game," and "we had good execution to begin with."

Leading 20-6, McFalls keyed a defensive stand in the third quarter that decided matters. Horner and Johnson added touchdown runs in the fourth quarter. McKenna cleared the bench, and youngsters like Rats Stinson Jones from Texas and Waynesboro native John Traynham played well in the 33-6 win.

The news wasn't all good. Ross who left the game in the first quarter, had a broken bone in his foot and would be lost for some time. The young quarterback had already begun showing the leadership traits that would serve him so well in the future. Ironically, he was hurt in punt coverage. Ross would often line up over center, and the ball was snapped between his legs. The center and the guard would block opposite directions, clearing a hole for the speedy Ross to get down quickly in coverage.

"They had a guy sit right there waiting for me to release off the line and when he hit me, I caught my leg in the ground," Ross recalled.

The V.M.I Cadet, reflecting Ross' popularity on Post, took his loss hard. "Bobby wasn't only a good player, he was a team man, and kept the spark glowing that often is the difference between a group of boys and a team of athletes," the newspaper reported.

McKenna was equally disappointed in the loss of his field general. "Bobby Ross, our co-captain and a quarterback, had his ankle broken in the first quarter mishap," he wrote. "We will miss him for more reasons than just his playing ability. You folks don't have a finer representative."

Minus Ross, the Keydets faced a big challenge with Southern Conference foe Richmond coming to town. Nebraska still had his hot hand at quarterback, connecting with Horner for a 69-yard touchdown to put the Keydets ahead 6-0. But the Spiders blocked a quick kick just before the half and tied the game.

Johnson dashed 40 yards for the decisive score early in the third quarter, taking a page from his faster backfield mates. As the interior of the Spider defense crashed into the backfield on a trap play, he cut to the right and turned on the speed.

The VMI defense again came up big to preserve the victory. Richmond had a first down on the VMI 10 late but was unable to score. The Keydets overcame three fumbles and 99 yards in penalties to keep their winning streak alive with a 12-6 win over the Spiders.

After the game, McKenna appraised: "Only our speed saved us. Thank the good Lord for it. We made more mistakes than we usually make in three or four games. Richmond was a lot tougher than we thought – more durable, more determined. We figured we could wear them down but we couldn't."

McKenna wrote that "penalties and fumbles kept us in hot water all afternoon making it hard to mount a sustained offense." This, despite the Keydets averaging a whopping eight yards per play, said the coach, who was searching for an answer for the lackluster overall effort.

"There were many anxious moments endured by the faithful, and I admit to a little apprehension myself," he wrote. "The coaching staff is at a loss to explain the reversal of form from the scintillating performance at Villanova the previous week and that which marked Homecoming Day – Trying too hard? – A natural let down after a superlative effort? – Preoccupation with the dance weekend? – Selling the determined and spirited Richmond team short?...You guess."

To the trained eye, the Keydets weren't playing their best football, and it would catch up with them in Bluefield's "Coal Bowl" in a 6-6 tie with William & Mary that included a controversial penalty at the end of the game that may have prevented a VMI victory.

Nebraska drove the team 67 yards to the two-yard line with 11 seconds remaining and the score tied. After a delay penalty moved the ball back five yards, Joe Morabit missed a field goal to the left, but the Indians were offside. Brandriff ran into the VMI huddle with Morabit's kicking tee, which had been tossed off the field after the miss. He drew a 15-yard illegal substitution penalty, which moved the ball all the way back to the 17.

Morabit missed wide left again, this time with one second remaining, ending VMI's 11-game winning streak but leaving the Keydets still undefeated in their last 14 outings.

McKenna later said that "the movies" (game film) showed Brandriff's reentry was actually legal. He had started the fourth quarter with the second unit, and then he returned in the last minute, legal under the rules of the day.

"It's a shame that our fine winning streak should be terminated on a note of confusion and error," the coach complained.

But he also acknowledged that a lot of mental and physical errors had led to the Keydets' undoing. They had three fumbles against the Indians, including one grabbed out of the air and returned 65 yards for a touchdown. VMI had lost 10 fumbles already in 1958, after recording just 10 all of the previous season.

Fumbles were the Keydets' friend in a 13-12 squeaker the following Saturday night in Tampa. Early in the game, a low snap to the Tampa fullback trying to quick-kick went awry, and he was tackled at the two-yard line. Horner crashed in from the one six minutes into the game.

Three minutes later, the Spartans tied the game when 248-pound Fred Cason scored. However, punting was a problem for the home team. After a bad snap on a Tampa punt, the Keydets smothered the punter at the seven-yard line. Three plays later, Nebraska banged in from the three 40 seconds into the second quarter, and Johnson's PAT kick was good.

VMI led 13-6 at the half, but Buddy Williams dashed 68 yards for a score in the fourth quarter. Tampa elected to go for two points, but the quarterback dropped the ball trying to run to his right on an option play.

"Nick Ruffin, our left linebacker, broke through, forced their quarterback to fumble, and then recovered the ball on a very fine defensive effort,"

McKenna described in the weekly newsletter.

The Roanoke Times and other newspapers took a dim view, often literally with the illumination technology of the day, of night contests. "These night games are strictly for the birds," the newspaper complained. "Players and coaches alike have too much time to think about the upcoming contest. Pressure of football leaves the boys keyed up and that tension makes for a sleepless night following the game. If the play is in the afternoon enough time elapses before bedtime and the kids can go to bed relaxed."

Not too relaxed, though. The Keydets lost three fumbles, but Tampa left the ball on the ground eight times, losing the pigskin on five occasions. McKenna noted that the Spartans were "sky high" for the game, "which is one of the few ventures they make against nationally known competition."

After three tight games, VMI blew out Davidson 42-7 on October 25th, spoiling the Wildcats' homecoming. The Keydets rolled 63 yards on their opening drive, and Nebraska scored from six yards out. He had another three-yard score behind great blocking from Borst and company.

A highlight of the day was Verne Keefer's 86-yard interception return for a score, aided by several fine blocks along the way. It was 20-7 at the half, but the Keydets were even more dominant after the break. Johnson had a 43-yard scoring run. Substitute quarterback Howard Dyer added a 59-yard touchdown pass to Evans in the fourth quarter when McKenna was utilizing a much-improved bench. Rats Stinson Jones and John Traynham also had big runs.

"We were able to alternate three teams giving the green team some valuable game experience which they had failed to acquire in the three previous contests," McKenna wrote. "The Richmond, William and Mary, and Tampa games had been so close right down to the wire that we had been playing only 22 to 24 men."

McKenna even let tackle Bobby Dale punt – VMI's only punt of the afternoon – and that was a tricky proposition under the substitution rules of the day. The coach explained, "When a lineman is brought back to kick it means that he must be replaced by a back. The assignments are strange to the back in replacing a tackle; he might well be giving away forty or fifty pounds in weight."

VMI's improved depth would play a big role in the 33-0 victory over Virginia the following week at Foreman Field in Norfolk. Fifteen thousand turned out for the first Civitan Bowl and saw VMI blast the Cavaliers for the second straight season. In fact, this was the Keydets' most lopsided win in the series since a 35-0 win in 1935.

It was a bittersweet victory for the Institute and the Corps of Cadets, all of whom travelled to the game by train for the annual Corps trip. However, on the ride down, senior Samuel P. Adams fell off the train and was killed. Adams, a leader within the Corps, was a civil engineering major from Newport News, Virginia and a cadet captain and commander of Delta Company in the regimental system.

Pete Johnson led a powerful ground assault and broke loose for several long runs, including a 39-yard sprint early. Jimmy O'Dell's one-yard run started the scoring, and Horner's four-yard run in the second period made it 14-0, on the way to a 27-0 halftime lead. Johnson ground out 94 yards on 12 carries and was voted the player of the game and would earn Southern Conference Player of the Week honors.

Another key against Virginia was the defensive secondary shutting down Sonny Randle, who came in as the nation's leading pass catcher. He latched on to just three balls for 32 yards thanks to some sticky coverage from John Engels and Johnson. Randle did break loose for a long punt return to the three-yard line in the third quarter, but the Big Red defense slammed the door to preserve the shutout. If fact, three times in the second half, Virginia drove deep into Keydet territory, but McKenna sent the first unit back in each time to thwart the Cavaliers.

McKenna poured all 38 members of his traveling squad into the fray, while first-year Virginia coach Dick Voris stuck with his starters most of the afternoon. Where depth had been a VMI weakness early in the year, it was now a weapon to wear opponents down.

Despite always having someone on the sideline to help keep track of substitutions, McKenna had a remarkably thin staff on game days, Dick Sessoms recalled. "It always amazed me to look down at that VMI bench and (McKenna) was standing by himself. There was Herb Patchin on one end, and Dr. Martin Delaney (VMI Class of 1928), the team physician, was on the other end. In those days one assistant coach was always scouting next week's opponent, and the other assistant was up in the box on the phones to the bench. The Rat coach was coaching the Rats somewhere else. It wasn't until Thanksgiving Day that the full coaching staff assembled on the sidelines."

Now 6-0-1, VMI was being called a Gator Bowl hopeful by the Associated

Two photographs of John McKenna during his senior year at Villanova University... That fall, 1937, the Wildcats were undefeated and he was Honorable Mention All America at center. On defense he was the team's leader for a unit that allowed only one touchdown the entire season. He graduated in the spring of 1938 with a BA in philosophy.

John McKenna was an assistant coach at Loyola Los Angeles for three season (1949-51). With his former teammate at Villanova Jordan Oliver as head coach, they revived the Loyola program, losing only one game and barely missing out on a trip to the Orange Bowl in 1950. Among those he coached at Loyola were Don Klosterman, the NCAA's leading passer in 1950 and renowned professional football executive and Gene Brito, a five-time pro bowler, who was named one of the 70 greatest players for the Washington Redskins.

The 1952 VMI football staff, Coach McKenna's first year at the Institute... (L to R) Colonel Sam Heflin, John McKenna, head coach Tom Nugent, Vince Ragunas, Clark King, and Chuck Noe. Nugent is the "Father" of the I-formation. He introduced this backfield set in 1950 season opener, in which VMI upset William & Mary. Nugent took the head coaching position at Florida State following the '52 season.

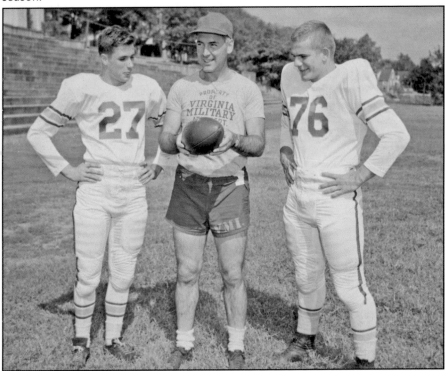

Coach McKenna in his first year as head coach is pictured with co-captains Johnny Mapp (L) and George Ramer. Both of these players are members of VMI's Sports Hall of Fame, Ramer as a rugged offensive and defensive lineman and Mapp as an All Southern Conference performer in both football and track and one the best running backs in Keydet history.

Coach McKenna (L) with assistant coaches, Vito Ragazzo and Clark King (R)... Ragazzo was an assistant coach for five seasons (1956-60). He returned to VMI in 1966 replacing Coach McKenna as VMI head coach, a position he held from 1966-70. King came to VMI with Coach McKenna in 1952, serving one year under Tom Nugent and ten years with Coach McKenna. In 1963 he became head of VMI's physical education department, a position he would hold for 28 years until his retirement in 1991. King Hall, one of the Institute's physical education buildings, was dedicated in his honor in 2007.

Nick Servidio bulls his way for yardage in VMI's 42-0 win over The Citadel in 1954. The big, strong fullback led the Keydets in rushing that season with 524 yards on 124 carries, a 4.2 yards per carry average. Note that the use of facemasks had not yet come of age.

Ⅴ MI's 1955 starting unit...(linemen L to R) Paul Janshego, Bill Miller, Lou Farmer, Dick Lyons, Carl LeBourdais, Lake Westfall, Nick Evanusich. (backfield L to R) Dale Vaughn, Sam Woolwine, Bill Nebraska, Charlie Lavery. Though this team finished 1-9, Coach McKenna felt that the late season win over The Citadel was the turning point for his future teams.

Ⅽ huck McLennan gathers in a pass from quarterback Duke Johnston for a 35 yard gain in a VMI's 20-6 win over William & Mary in 1956. The game was played in Lynchburg, Virginia, one of two neutral site games that season. The Keydets had only one home game in '56, a trend throughout Coach McKenna's tenure.

A classic photo of the 1957 undefeated team, which reached a ranking of 13th and finished 20th in the Associated Press poll of major colleges...Fullback Sam Woolwine (31) and quarterback Duke Johnston (15) lead halfback Pete Johnson (44) with a power sweep against the University of Richmond.

Coach McKenna (L) with assistant coach Chuck McGinnis on the sidelines... Though not identified, it is likely one of the season finales against VPI, one of the few times McKenna had the "luxury" of a sideline assistant. McGinnis joined McKenna's staff in 1957 and served with him through the 1963 season.

All Southern Conference fullback Sam Woolwine takes advantage of a hole in the William & Mary line in the Keydets' 14-13 win over the Indians in 1957. Blocking for Woolwine is #60, co-captain and All Southern Conference guard Lou Farmer.

Halfback Bobby Jordan is about to take on a defensive lineman of the University of Virginia in VMI's 20-7 win over the Cavaliers in 1957, the year he was selected Southern Conference Player of the Year. Blocking for Jordan is #88 Carl Kasko.

VIRGINIA MILITARY INSTITUTE

SOUTHERN CONFERENCE CHAMPIONS   1957   VIRGINIA BIG SIX CHAMPIONS

Record: Won 9, Lost 0, Tied 1

VMI	7—Tampa	0	VMI	26—George Washington	20
VMI	21—Holy Cross	21	VMI	20—Virginia	7
VMI	28—Richmond	6	VMI	12—Lehigh	7
VMI	26—Davidson	14	VMI	33—The Citadel	7
VMI	14—William and Mary	13	VMI	14—Virginia Tech	6

FIRST ROW, LEFT TO RIGHT: Jim McFalls, Pete Johnson, Nick Evanusich, Bobby Dale, Duke Johnston, Bobby Jordan, Co-Captains Lou Farmer and Sam Woolwine, Nick Ruffin, Carl Kasko, Jerry Borst.

SECOND ROW, LEFT TO RIGHT: Herb Richardson, Bobby Ross, Chris Koumparakis, Ron Swirk, Tom Daniel, Jimmy O'Dell, Sam Horner, Benny Day, Howard Moss, Bill Kirkland, Bob Rader, Verne Keefer, Dave Martin.

THIRD ROW, LEFT TO RIGHT: Ken Scott, Marty Fisher, Mike Ondos, Joey Sisler, Jon Quinn, Phil Hamric, Truman Baxter, Dick Evans, Tom Kurkoski, Bill Nebraska, Lloyd Thacker, Harry Shepherd, George O'Neill, Joe Morabit.

TOP ROW, LEFT TO RIGHT: Jon Parnell, Jim True, John Engels, Managers Jim Wood and Roland Tharp, Assistant Coach Clark King, Head Coach John McKenna, Assistant Coaches Vito Ragazzo and Jack Null, Trainer Bobby King, Assistant Manager Doug MacArthur, Jim Sam Gillespie, Art Brandriff.

C oach McKenna (left) with fullback Sam Woolwine (#31) and quarterback Duke Johnston and other players celebrate the season ending 14-6 win over VPI on Thanksgiving Day 1957. The victory, which secured VMI's undefeated season, was bittersweet for its coach, as the team voted not to accept a bid to the Sun Bowl in El Paso, Texas.

C oach McKenna at the proverbial chalkboard diagramming a Keydet play for a touchdown...With him are coaching staff members from 1958-59-60 (L to R) Lewis "Weenie" Miller, Chuck McGinnis, Clark King, and Vito Ragazzo. This must have been a "formal" session with the shirts and ties. NOTE – Miller was also VMI's head basketball coach from 1958-64 and led VMI to its first Southern Conference Championship in 1963-64.

Quarterback Bill Nebraska runs for a big gain in VMI's 33-0 rout of Virginia in a 1958 game played in Norfolk, Virginia. The VMI Corps of Cadets attended the game traveling by train from Lexington. The victory was overshadowed by the death of First Classman (senior) Samuel P. Adams, who fell from the train on the trip to Norfolk.

Quarterback Bobby Ross, co-captain of the 1958 VMI team...Ross' collegiate coaching career included head positions at The Citadel, Maryland, Georgia Tech, and West Point. He won three consecutive Atlantic Coast Conference championships at Maryland, and his 1990 Georgia Tech team finished 11-0-1 and shared the National Championship. In the professional ranks, he was head coach at San Diego and Detroit leading the Chargers to their only Super Bowl appearance in 1995 and the Lions to the NFL playoffs in 1999.

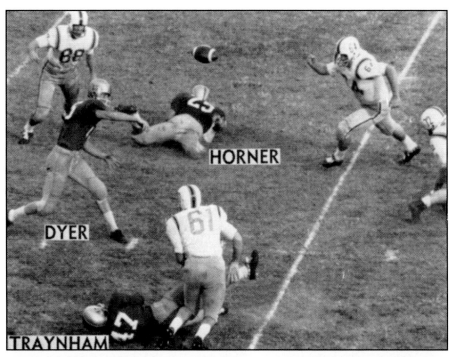

HORNER

DYER

TRAYNHAM

The Howard Dyer to Dick Evans combination during the 1959 season was one of the key reasons for VMI's 8-1-1 record. In this series of photos, the duo connects for a long gainer in the Keydets 32-8 win over The Citadel. Evans caught 35 passes for 698 yards that season, an average of almost 20 yards per reception. Dyer completed 55 of 105 passes for 1,072 yards with 13 touchdowns and only two interceptions.

End Tom Daniel recovers a fumble in VMI's 19-12 win over Virginia in 1959, one of Coach McKenna's four Southern Conference Championship seasons. A Bristol, Virginia native, Daniel served 20 years as an officer in the United States Air Force.

Howard Dyer, known as the "Mississippi Gambler" for his daring play calling is set to release a pass in the 1960 opener against William & Mary. Dyer led VMI to a 7-2-1 record and a second straight Southern Conference Championship.

Quarterback Howard Dyer, in cadet uniform, with the trophies he garnered following his First Class (senior) season, 1960. He is holding the Southern Conference Player of the Year plaque. Dyer remains the only VMI quarterback to have received this honor. The other trophies (L to R) are Outstanding Football Player in Virginia, Roanoke Touchdown Club Outstanding Virginia Back, and Sportsmanship Award for the Southern Conference. His career passing efficiency remains #1 in the VMI record books, and the Keydets lost only three games in which he was the starting quarterback.

This photo of the McKenna family was taken at their home on Edmondson Avenue in Lexington, circa 1960. Coach McKenna is holding Steve and his wife Eileen is holding the youngest son Peter. Their three daughters are (L to R) Margaret, Kathleen, and Mary. Coach McKenna would say that he and Eileen had the "makings" of a football team, a center and starting backfield.

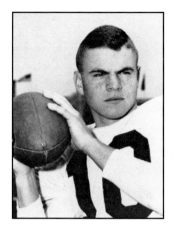

VMI's fourteenth Superintendent J.H. Binford Peay III, better known as "Binnie" Peay, in his playing days at quarterback for Coach McKenna from 1958-61...As a cadet, he was a battalion commander in the Corps of Cadets and received the Cincinnati Medal, presented for efficiency of service and excellence of character, at graduation in 1962.

1960 Co-captains quarterback Howard Dyer (15) and center/linebacker Lee Badgett. This duo led VMI to combined 15-3-2 record over their last two seasons. Dyer, though drafted by the New York Titans, chose law school after serving in the United States Army and returned to his hometown of Greenville, Mississippi to practice law. Badgett, a Rhodes Scholar and Regimental Commander (highest ranking cadet in the Corps), served with distinction in the United States Air Force for 24 years and returned to his alma mater as Provost and Dean of the Faculty in 1990.

1961 Tri-captains Quarterback Bobby Mitchell (11), Stinson Jones (45), and John Traynham (47)...Mitchell's five touchdown passes vs Buffalo that year still stand as VMI's single-game record. Jones and Traynham, both members of the VMI Sports Hall of Fame, are considered one of the fastest halfback combinations in Keydet history. Mitchell became an attorney, Jones a pediatrician, and Trayhnam an orthopaedic surgeon.

Absolutely the two best photos from the VMI-VPI game on Thanksgiving Day, 1961...The annual game at Roanoke's Victory Stadium, played entirely in a driving rain storm, was won by VMI 6-0 on an option pass from wide receiver Kenny Reeder, who lined up in the backfield, to halfback Stinson Jones. The photo at right shows quarterback Bobby Mitchell throwing a jump pass with fullback "Dee" Worrell blocking. In spite of the conditions, Mitchell completed 9 of 21 passes for 73 yards. Mitchell said that on each snap from center, the ball would slide from his hands to his stomach where he could finally grip it. In the photo above, the central figure is fullback Worrell, who has received one of Mitchell's "belly handoffs," on a dive play. Blocking for Worrell appears to be #47, halfback John Traynham.

Running Back John Traynham sets sail on a 61 yard punt return in VMI's 33-21 win over William & Mary in 1960. Blocking for Traynham is #79 Bob Polk. Either Traynham or his backfield partner Stinson Jones led the Keydets in rushing for three consecutive years.

Coach McKenna and his staff for the 1962 season...(L to R) Lewis "Weenie" Miller, Chuck McGinnis, Clark King, Bo Sherman, and Richard Bell.

Hall of Fame wide receiver Kenny Reeder breaks into the open after catching a pass from Butch Nunnally in the 1962 win in Lexington over William & Mary 6-0. Reeder led the Keydets in receptions in both 1961 and 1962.

1963 Co-captains quarterback Butch Nunnally (15) and center/linebacker Bill Tornabene...Nunnally was also an outstanding punter, whose 67 yarder vs Iowa State in 1963 stilll ranks 4th in the VMI record books. Tornabene returned to VMI in 1976 as an assistant coach under Bob Thalman for four seasons.

Halfback Donny White (#45), at 155 pounds. soaking wet, gains yardage in a 14-6 win over George Washington in 1963. White was also a standout defensive back, as well as an All Southern Conference baseball player. Blocking for White is quarterback Mark Mulrooney...something that was part of a quarterback's responsibility in that era.

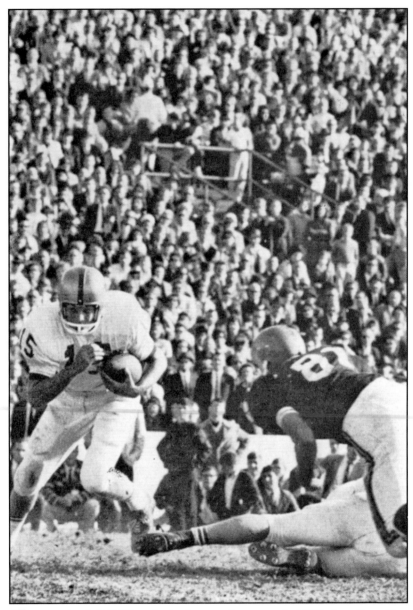

Quarterback Hill Ellett looks for running room in VMI's heartbreaking 20-19 loss vs Virginia in the 1964 Tobacco Bowl in Richmond. A 23-yard two point conversion by the Cavaliers, following two consecutive penalties during extra point attempts, provided the winning margin. Ellett was the Keydets passing leader in 1965 and 1966.

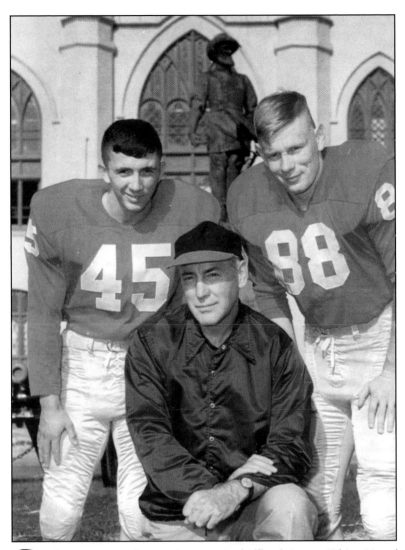

Coach McKenna with 1964 Co-captains halfback Donny White (L) and end Joe Bush, both members of the VMI Sports Hall of Fame. These two longtime friends were assistant football coaches together at VMI from 1971 to 1980, when White, an All Southern Conference baseball player, took the head baseball coaching position at VMI which he held for seven years. White returned to VMI in 1998; serving as Athletic Director until his retirement in 2013. Bush left VMI in 1984 and became head football coach at Hampden Sydney College in 1986. He was named Athletic Director in 1992, serving in both positions for five more years. He retired from the AD position in 2010.

Halfback Ted Mervosh (#44) with lead blocker Granville Amos picks up yard-age during a rare home game vs William & Mary in the 1964 season. In that game, Amos set the VMI record, which still stands, for longest run from scrimmage, a 98 yard touchdown. Amos would later become a Brigadier General in the United States Marine Corps.

IN HONOR OF

COACH JOHN McKENNA

"A TRUE COACH AND GENTLEMAN"

PRESENTED BY THE
1953 – 1965 VMI FOOTBALL TEAMS AND FRIENDS

This plaque is featured at the entrance to the John McKenna Campus Champions room at the Virginia Sports Hall of Fame in Portsmouth, Virginia. Every college and university in Virginia with an athletic program is celebrated in this room. Coach McKenna was inducted into the Virginia Sports Hall of Fame in 2007 and is also a member of the Sports Hall of Fame at Villanova University, Loyola, Los Angeles (now Loyola Marymount), and of course VMI. He is an honorary alumnus of VMI and Georgia Tech.

Coach McKenna on the sidelines with his "top assistant coach" the legendary Herb Patchin, who served as VMI's athletic trainer for 34 years...Patchin was McKenna's lone sideline companion for the majority of the games each season. Herb - never at a loss for words – was, no doubt, ready to give Coach McKenna some sage advice.

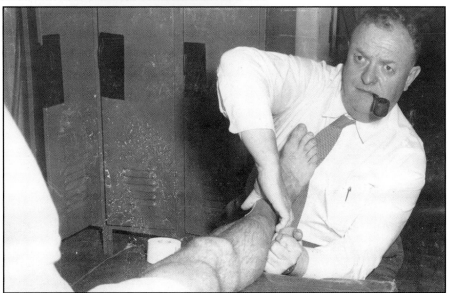

A vintage picture of iconic athletic trainer Herb Patchin, with pipe – sometimes cigar – taping a player's ankle...Patchin is a member of the Helms Athletic Foundation Hall of Fame and VMI's Sports Hall of Fame.

Halfback Paul Hebert picks up yardage during the 1965 season. Hebert went on to earn his PhD in Environmental Engineering and worked to promote and support humanitarian causes in under-developed countries throughout the world for more than 30 years. In 2011, he was the first VMI alumnus to receive the Institute's Jonathan Daniels Humanitarian Award. The first two recipients were President Jimmy Carter and Ambassador Andrew Young. Daniels, a 1961 VMI graduate, was an Episcopal Seminarian, who was murdered in Hayneville, Alabama in 1965 during the Civil Rights struggle. He saved the life of a black teenage girl, Ruby Sales, pushing her aside and taking the full force of a shotgun blast.

Coach McKenna's captains for his final season (1965) at VMI, fullback Tom Slater (left) and defensive tackle John Turner... Slater, who led the team in rushing that year, is a partner with the law firm of Hunton-Williams in Richmond, Virginia and served as president of the VMI Board of Visitors from 2008-2011. Turner was a First Team All-Southern Conference selection as both a junior and senior and is a member of the VMI Sports Hall of Fame.

Bob Thalman (kneeling), VMI head football coach from 1971-1984, was much like Coach McKenna in his disciplinary approach to the game and his great respect for the value of a VMI education. Coach McKenna (13 years) and Coach Thalman (14 years) have the longest coaching tenures in VMI football history. This photo was taken at West Point during the 1981 season. The game marked VMI's only win over Army, 14-7, and it was the last winning campaign (6-3-1) for a VMI team going into the 2014 season.

Plaques at the VMI Football Complex
Foster Stadium, Alumni Memorial Field, Clarkson-McKenna Hall

CLARKSON-McKENNA HALL

Honoring two Keydet coaches who led
their teams to undefeated seasons

BLANDY B. CLARKSON, '14
1920 season, 9-0-0

JOHN McKENNA
1957 season, 9-0-1

Dedicated during the one hundredth season
of VMI football
October 27, 1990

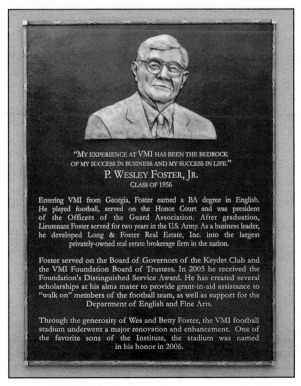

"MY EXPERIENCE AT VMI HAS BEEN THE BEDROCK
OF MY SUCCESS IN BUSINESS AND MY SUCCESS IN LIFE."
P. WESLEY FOSTER, JR.
CLASS OF 1956

Entering VMI from Georgia, Foster earned a BA degree in English.
He played football, served on the Honor Court and was president
of the Officers of the Guard Association. After graduation,
Lieutenant Foster served for two years in the U.S. Army. As a business leader,
he developed Long & Foster Real Estate, Inc. into the largest
privately-owned real estate brokerage firm in the nation.

Foster served on the Board of Governors of the Keydet Club and
the VMI Foundation Board of Trustees. In 2005 he received the
Foundation's Distinguished Service Award. He has created several
scholarships at his alma mater to provide grant-in-aid assistance to
"walk on" members of the football team, as well as support for the
Department of English and Fine Arts.

Through the generosity of Wes and Betty Foster, the VMI football
stadium underwent a major renovation and enhancement. One of
the favorite sons of the Institute, the stadium was named
in his honor in 2006.

Wes Foster was a lineman and letterman on McKenna's 1957 team. Through the generosity of Wes and Betty Foster the VMI football stadium underwent a major renovation and enhancement, which was completed in 2006.

THE McKENNA ERA

Four Southern Conference Championships
Five State Championships
Six Consecutive Winning Seasons
Eighteen Straight Games Without a Loss
Undefeated 1957 Team Ranked 13th in the Nation

John McKenna

Head Football Coach, 1953 – 1965

Coach McKenna's impact on his players and coaches set
the standard for excellence in VMI football.
A disciplinarian, fundamentalist, mentor, and coaching legend,
his teams were successful in every phase of the game.

Coach and Mrs. McKenna are held in highest respect by
the Institute and the citizens of the community.
We were blessed by his leadership.

Placed in honor of Coach McKenna,
by his players and staff on the occasion of their reunion
21-22 October 2005

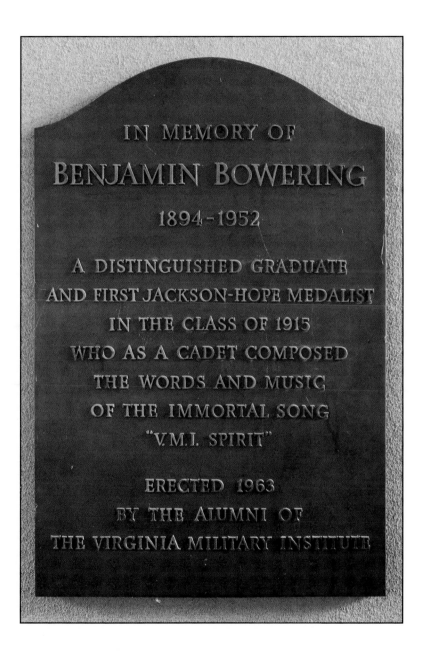

IN MEMORY OF

BENJAMIN BOWERING

1894–1952

A DISTINGUISHED GRADUATE
AND FIRST JACKSON-HOPE MEDALIST
IN THE CLASS OF 1915
WHO AS A CADET COMPOSED
THE WORDS AND MUSIC
OF THE IMMORTAL SONG
"V.M.I. SPIRIT"

ERECTED 1963
BY THE ALUMNI OF
THE VIRGINIA MILITARY INSTITUTE

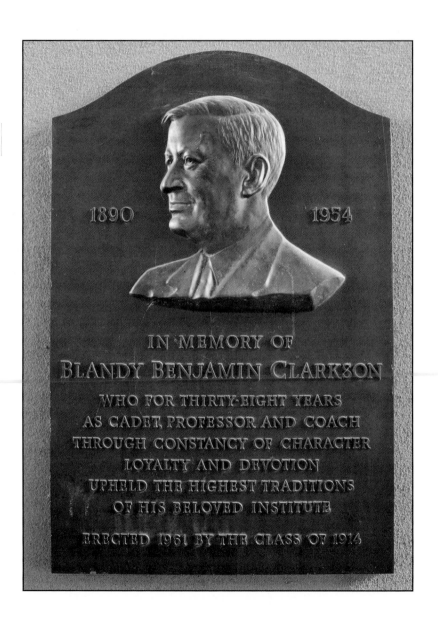

1890 1954

IN MEMORY OF
BLANDY BENJAMIN CLARKSON
WHO FOR THIRTY-EIGHT YEARS
AS CADET, PROFESSOR AND COACH
THROUGH CONSTANCY OF CHARACTER
LOYALTY AND DEVOTION
UPHELD THE HIGHEST TRADITIONS
OF HIS BELOVED INSTITUTE

ERECTED 1961 BY THE CLASS OF 1914

Press. Horner led the Southern Conference in scoring with 44 points. The staunch, veteran defense was giving up just eight points a game and the first unit had only allowed one touchdown via a sustained drive in the first seven contests. McKenna thought the team's speed, perhaps even more so on defense, was the key to success.

"We consider the performance of our defense one of our greatest achievements," he said. "If the defense had not been able to rise to the occasion, I don't know where we'd be."

More good news came that week when Ross rejoined the team in practices.

None of those factors prevented a disappointing showing against Lehigh in Lynchburg in the Jaycee Bowl. In a 7-7 tie that felt more like a loss, VMI moved deep inside Engineer territory three times only to come away scoreless on each occasion. Nebraska did cash in from the one on another opportunity in the third quarter, and Johnson's extra point tied the contest.

The Engineers were effective at shutting down the ends and limiting Horner and Brandriff, with a steady diet of stunts out of their 6-3 and 5-4 defensive alignments. Nebraska fell victim, too, tackled for 41 yards in losses while attempting to pass. He was sacked for a big loss on the game's final play, falling into the end zone under a host of Engineers, but the officials spotted the ball at the two-yard line – much to the Engineers' dismay – preserving the tie.

The Keydets' paltry 129 yards represented their worst offensive showing in three years.

Lehigh, which had scored in the second quarter on a tricky halfback option pass that went 77 yards, missed a 21-yard field goal with 19 seconds to play.

VMI's Jim True missed a 16-yard field goal in the second quarter, one of the Keydets' squandered chances. When someone mentioned that True's toe was generally true from in close, McKenna snapped "except on Saturdays."

The coach wasn't happy. "We didn't give our passer any protection at all. We made some dumb plays, and we couldn't come up with the key play when we needed it."

McKenna had reason for concern. Lehigh had created a template for bottling up VMI's "Lightning" offense, and now the Keydets faced what the coach called their toughest game of the season, the long trip to Charleston, South Carolina, to meet military rival The Citadel. McKenna said VMI was a bigger rival for The Citadel than vice versa, because VMI had the annual in-state game with Virginia Tech.

Still, under McKenna, VMI had never lost to the Bulldogs.

The Citadel turned a couple of Keydet fumbles into touchdowns, and in front of a raucous crowd of 12,000, as VMI's 18-game undefeated streak came to a bitter end. The Keydets hadn't lost since Thanksgiving of 1956, but on this day, they just couldn't get the offense going against the fired-up Bulldogs.

The Citadel prevailed 14-6, a win so joyous for VMI's southern rivals that Citadel cadets were granted extra liberty to celebrate. The Keydets could manage just eight first downs and didn't score until late in the third period on a 30-yard gallop by Horner. By then, The Citadel had built a lead, scoring after a Johnson fumble on a punt in the first quarter and then after another punt fumble in the second.

"The law of averages is an inexorable thing," said McKenna. "It finally caught up with us. You can theorize and conjecture. There was the emotional and physical attrition of a tough season, a long winning habit. We had been 'up' for a long time. It was a game we had to play, sooner or later. We just came to the end of the trail as everyone must."

Nagging injuries caught up with the Keydets, too. Ross was still out of the lineup, and Brandriff and Don Rishell had both missed multiple games now, as well. McFalls was heavily taped during games to hold together. Even McKenna wasn't exempt, battling a flu bug that was partly the reason for his scuttling a trip to Hattiesburg, Mississippi, to scout the Gobblers. There was more to his decision, though.

"I can't leave the boys now," he said.

The VMI footballers weren't the only Keydets that had a bad day. Charlotte police stopped the school's cheerleaders en route to the game after police got a report that the cab they had rented was stolen. Even with that confusion cleared up, the police confiscated the ammunition for the Keydets' cannon, Little John II.

Little John wouldn't have been used much anyway in Charleston. Still, reports surfaced the following week that the Tangerine Bowl was considering VMI, along with Mississippi Southern, East Texas State, Tulsa and Miami of Ohio. Florida State was considered the front-runner, though, to meet Buffalo, which had already been invited. It probably didn't help the Keydets' chances when The Citadel lost 76-0 to Georgia the following Saturday.

"Now we have Virginia Tech coming up, and we'll know soon whether we have real football players or just spoiled kids," said McKenna, obviously planting some messages to his team in the media. "You've got to be able to get up off the deck."

Subsequently, though, the coach knew his team needed a break. McKenna gave the "down in the dumps" team three days off.

In a contest that would decide the state championship, the big Thanksgiving showcase in Roanoke had a lot of fireworks before 27,500 fans in Victory Stadium.

Horner had a 34-yard run on a fake punt play that set up the game's first score, Johnson's two-yard burst. VPI came right back, consistently out-flanking the Keydet defense.

Ross, returning from his injury, completed two of three passes to move the ball down to the 20-yard line and set up a field goal by Johnson that made it 10-7 in the second quarter.

VPI's All-Southern Conference connection of quarterback Billy Holsclaw and end Carroll Dale moved the ball in for a score, and then Holsclaw hit Dale for the two-point conversion and a 15-10 lead. VMI drove inside the 30 on the ensuing drive but fumbled before the half.

The Gobblers dominated the third period, out-gaining VMI 126-19. The key play came early in the fourth quarter when VMI moved to the Tech 24, and on a fourth-and-one, Horner was stopped for no gain on a play where it looked like the Keydets got a terrible spot from the officials. VPI drove 76 yards for a clinching score.

Asked after the game if he questioned the official about that key fourth down ball mark, McKenna said he "didn't ask about it," he "told (the official) about it."

He wrote to the Sportsmen's Club: "The rules state clearly that the ball is placed at the point of the farthest advance. The head linesman, whose responsibility is the placing of the ball on plays to his side, did not, in my opinion, place the ball properly. It was my firm conviction immediately following the game, is now, and will always be that that was the turning point of the game."

Sophomore quarterback Howard Dyer came on to lead the Keydets on a final drive and scored from four yards for the final margin, 21-16. VMI finished 6-2-2, a disappointment after the great start and because the Keydets failed to defend their Southern Conference and Big Six titles. This time, a long, grueling season had simply worn them down, even more so than the previous year. West Virginia, which had seen VMI snap the Mountaineers' four-year reign, regained the championship.

McFalls, Borst and Horner all earned First Team All-Southern Conference honors, and Ruffin and Johnson were second team. Kasko nabbed honorable mention. Horner led the team with 612 rushing yards, the most for a Keydet since Johnny Mapp's 656 in 1953.

McKenna singled out First Classman (senior) Johnny Engels for praise, citing Engels' comeback from an Achilles tendon injury the previous spring and then trying to fight through a pulled muscle suffered at The Citadel. "This youngster deserves more credit than verbal approbation from me," the coach wrote.

He lamented the loss of his 18 First Classmen not just for the football team but for the Institute. "All of the departing players have been a real credit to themselves, their families, the Institute and you folks," he offered the Sportsmen's Club. "Their record of achievement in every phase of cadet life is something of which we can all be justifiably proud."

Three of the seniors became NFL Draft Picks. Pete Johnson was drafted in the third round by the Chicago Bears. He played in Chicago for a year before being selected for the new Dallas Cowboys team from which he was later released. Art Brandriff was a fourth round selection of the Detroit Lions but was released at the end of the exhibition season. Jim McFalls was drafted in the sixth round by the Washington Redskins but declined in order to begin medical school.

McKenna's achievements were also gaining attention. In January of 1959, rumors surfaced that he might be interested in the Colgate head job. In the end, McKenna stayed on Post.

That year the editorial staff of the VMI *Bomb,* the school's yearbook, dedicated its 75th edition to their coach. When given, the dedication was usually reserved for iconic faculty, staff, or Superintendents of the Institute. Some excerpts from the dedicatory page provide insight into the respect held for McKenna and the uniqueness of this football coach:

He (McKenna) has done very well with VMI athletics, coming at a time when subsidized football had reached a very low ebb with scandals in a number of schools. McKenna succeeded in raising the standards of football and the prestige of collegiate athletics in the state…he follows a simple – if not easy – rule of trying to instill in the players' minds the feeling that each game is an entity in itself, and that what has gone on before or may be coming in the next week/weeks has nothing to do with the game at hand.

Coach McKenna deals in two commodities – fundamentals and facts. On the football field at practice, it is the former. At the banquet table, it is the latter. McKenna's attributes as a speaker and as a VMI ambassador make him an excellent advertisement for VMI and athletics in general. His modesty, sincerity, and flow of words at the speaker's rostrum would do credit to a college president.

Newspaper columnists have called Coach McKenna "an articulate and entertaining speaker, spirited competitor, a deep thinker who doesn't speak unless he has something to say."

The Corps is extremely proud to have been associated with this extraordinary gentleman and coach. The dedication of the seventy-fifth edition of the 'Bomb' is but a small measure of the esteem with which he and all the coaching staff are held....

1958 (6-2-2)

DATE	VMI	LOCATION	OPP
S 20	46	Morehead State	20
S 27	33	at Villanova	6
O 4	12	Richmond	6
O 11	6	William & Mary (Bluefield)	6
O 18	13	at Tampa	12
O 25	42	at Davidson	7
N 1	33	Virginia (Norfolk)	0
N 8	7	Lehigh (Lynchburg)	7
N 15	6	at The Citadel	14
N 27	16	Virginia Tech	21

Chapter Nine

THE MCKENNA MIRACLE

It would come to commonly be referred to as the year of the "McKenna Miracle." And 1959 was no doubt the year that McKenna cemented his reputation as one of college football's top coaches.

Coming off the 6-2-2 campaign of '58, the Keydets returned just one starter – Sam Horner, who had led the team in rushing and led the Southern Conference in punting with a 42.6-yard average. While not devoid of talent, VMI's players were as green as spring grass and certainly not highly regarded as a threat to contend in the conference or in the Commonwealth.

However, by season's end, a lot of experts would be eating crow along with newly invented "french fries" that were becoming all the rage. Also making news, President Dwight D. Eisenhower signed an executive order making Hawaii the 50th state that August, and Bobby Darin's new hit "Mack the Knife" began rapidly moving up the charts.

Sam Horner was also trying to move up the charts. He was a proven commodity in the backfield but nagging injuries would limit him early in the year, allowing speedy sophomore John Traynham, defensive standout Stinson Jones and promising Don Kern, back after a year's absence from school, to get more work.

The ends were solid with Tom Daniel back, and fellow senior Dick Evans poised for a great season. Big (6-3, 218) Tom Kurkoski could help, as well. Up front, pre-med major Bill Haeberlein was back from injuries, and Howard

Moss was one of the game's fastest guards. Not too many teams of that era - and certainly none from the present era - had an offensive and defensive lineman who ran a 9.8/ 100 yard dash and was a sprint standout in track. Moss garnered numerous top three finishes in the indoor and outdoor sprints for the Keydets' State and Southern Conference Championship teams, and once, in an outdoor tri-meet vs William & Mary and Virginia Tech, he won the 100, 200, and the broad jump. Moss went on to a distinguished career in the United States Air Force and was a decorated fighter pilot in Vietnam.

Senior Jimmy O'Dell would get a long look at quarterback, but McKenna thought he had a couple of youngsters who might open up the offense and the airways like never before.

As two-a-day practices opened in late August, McKenna was again stressing fundamentals, defense, and eying that potentially potent passing attack. The coach was quietly confident that the Keydets could do well, but the fate of the season rested on instilling that same feeling in his young team.

Bobby Mitchell, a promising quarterback from Alexandria, who joined the team that fall, was already getting a sense of what it meant to play for the great coach. "The thing about Coach McKenna was the way he conducted the program," recalled Mitchell years later. "You always felt that he had done everything that he could do to put you in position to win. If you look back at his teams, they were all strong fundamentally, good blockers, good tacklers, very few penalties, very disciplined.

"It's kind of like a soldier with a general. You knew he had put you in the position to win the battle. You may not win, but you knew he had put you in position."

Mitchell recalled McKenna's practices as crisp and efficient. In season, practices usually ran about an hour and a half and were meticulously organized. "There was a schedule and you were going here and there for periods of time. The whistle would blow, and you would go."

McKenna, and really VMI itself, built confidence in young men through conditioning and physical fitness. "Conditioning was a big factor," added Mitchell. "We prided ourselves that we never played another team in better condition than we were."

In addition to running, push-ups and chin-ups, the "duck walk" – players on bended knee awkwardly "walking" on the field – was a popular conditioning tool, now all but disappeared from the scene. Weight training hadn't become as vital to football as it is today, and that was for a common sense purpose, particularly at VMI. Playing both ways required quicker, lighter players.

"(McKenna) was here at the right time," said Dick Willard, whose younger brother, Ken, who played ten years in the NFL, mostly with the 49ers. "That's when you could take good, general athletes and mold a good team. We didn't do the weight training then. We didn't do a lot of the things they do today. But we played both ways, and that's why we didn't weigh as much."

Likewise, a norm of the day was also to deny players water during practices, the thinking that dehydration toughened them. It wasn't uncommon for players in morning August workouts to suck the dew off the practice field grass.

In addition to the fundamentals and the conditioning, McKenna poured a steely focus into the team regarding the season opener, particularly of importance for the confidence of his rebuilding squad. "If you can't win that one, everything is uphill for a young squad," he said of the crucial opener September 19 in Huntington, West Virginia.

Fortunately, Marshall University (then Marshall College), which had lost the last five games of 1958, and now under new management in Coach Charley Snyder, was the perfect fit for what McKenna wanted to impart. The Keydets rolled to a 46-0 win at Fairfield Stadium in the first meeting of the two schools.

Traynham scored twice, and Kern, Jones, Horner and the Keydets rolled. Traynham ran 49 yards for one score and also hauled in a touchdown toss from quarterback Bobby Mitchell.

Promising junior quarterback Howard Dyer completed three out of five passes, including two touchdowns, as VMI rang up 341 yards of offense and 22 first downs. Daniel, the pre-med senior end, and scrappy Dick Weede had touchdown receptions.

The VMI defense held the inexperienced "Big Green" of Marshall to just 101 yards of total offense. McKenna was apologetic that his third-stringers tacked on two late scores, mostly of Marshall's making with mistakes, and he was worried that expectations for his rebuilding team would be ratcheted up quickly.

Some of McKenna's fears for his team were realized the following Saturday in State College, Pennsylvania. Powerful Penn State ground down the Keydets, though the final 21-0 score was misleading.

Before 20,000 at Beaver Stadium, the Nittany Lions couldn't get a first down on their first three possessions. VMI hung tough with the nationally-ranked team, even without Horner, who was limited to just punting with a leg injury suffered in the opener.

Penn State eventually struck just before halftime to go up 7-0, but the Keydets missed a golden opportunity to tie the game in the third quarter. Jones intercepted a pass in Penn State territory, and Dyer marched the Keydets to the 11-yard line. He hit Evans for an apparent touchdown, but a leaping Evans couldn't get a foot down, and the Lions ultimately intercepted a pass to squelch the threat.

"One official signaled touchdown, and the other said it was out of the end zone," recalled Dyer. "We thought we had a touchdown in the third quarter."

Kern made an over-the-shoulder catch for a 45-yard gain from Mitchell to put VMI inside the 10 later, but again the Keydets came up empty. Penn State added two fourth quarter scores, including a 16-yard run by Dick Hoak out of the Nittany Lions' vaunted Wing-T formation, guided by All-American Richie Lucas, who would be the top pick in both the NFL and the new AFL draft in 1960.

McKenna eschewed field goal attempts when the Keydets got close, hoping to cash in for touchdowns and stay in the game. He lamented that strategy, which caused his team to be shutout for the first time since Thanksgiving of 1956. But he showed no remorse for playing to win and was pleased with the effort his team gave.

"There were deficiencies in the play of some individuals, but overall the effort was highly commendable," he wrote that week. "Any objective observer must concede that the better team won, but the lesser team certainly made them work for everything they got."

Dyer, the 6'-1", 190 pounder out of Mississippi, had made an impression against top-flight competition. Going against essentially the same secondary that led the nation in pass defense in 1958, Dyer completed eight of 12 passes for 81 yards. McKenna named him as starter, taking over for O'Dell, heading into the Southern Conference opener against Richmond.

Dyer earned *Richmond Times-Dispatch* Back of the Week honors for his late-game heroics in a night game inPortsmouth against the Spiders, a contest in which the Keydets were probably still recovering from playing a titan like Penn State. Trailing 14-7, and taking over at their own 44, the Keydets mounted the determining drive on the strength of Dyer's arm. He hit Evans and Kurkoski for key gains, and then scored himself on a sneak with less than a minute to play. Nelson Elliot's kick tied the game 14-14 and left the Keydets 1-1-1 on the season.

McKenna, responding to criticism for kicking the extra point, instead of going for a victory, pointed out how little success the Keydets had against the Spiders' over-shifting 6-3 defense most of the evening. He added in his newsletter:

"It occurs to me that some of the second guessers might be likened to the folks who go to Indianapolis on May 30th looking for a car or cars to overturn and set on fire. I have quoted to you before the football pundit who said that 'a tie is like kissing your sister.' Granted, that comparison is an accurate one. Even that is a whole lot better than a kick in the pants from a non-member of the family."

"We played (Penn State) well, we really did, and then the next week we played Richmond, and we were so beaten up from that Penn State game we had to come from behind in the fourth quarter," explained Dyer years later.

Dyer's rise to the top of the depth chart at the most visible position must have come as a surprise to recruiters who thought him invisible during his modest career at Greenville High School in Mississippi.

"I remember that the college coaches used to come over and invite some of our boys to the college games," Dyer told the Associated Press in 1960. "I was never invited."

Like most Mississippi boys, the skinny Dyer grew up wanting to play at Ole Miss, but their staff wasn't interested, even after Dyer stood out in a losing effort in a high school state championship game. Davidson College turned Dyer down when he scored low on a math test. His situation became so desperate that his father turned to the unorthodox-for-the-time course of mailing reels of high school game film to college coaches.

A VMI alumnus, local Greenville banker and one of McKenna's "bird-doggers," Wade W. Hollowell '31, insisted they send a tape to McKenna in Lexington. They sent film of that championship game. "I looked at two films," said McKenna, "and wired back: 'Send boy next.'"

McKenna had invited Dyer to early practices, and in spite of his initial intimidating remark – "Dyer, I thought you were a bigger boy than this" – he liked what he saw but didn't put him on scholarship until his sophomore season. By then, Dyer's math scores and his passing statistics were both on the rise.

A hip injury kept Dyer out of all but the first five minutes of the Jaycee Bowl in Richmond's City Stadium, and VMI struggled with the now perennially struggling Cavaliers, who were off to an 0-3 start. Sophomore Butch Armistead intercepted a Virginia pass and ran it back 20 yards for a fourth quarter touchdown to preserve a third-straight win over "Our brethren over the Blue Ridge," as McKenna called the Cavaliers.

Even without Dyer, the Keydets jumped out to a 13-0 lead before 7,000 rain-soaked fans. Mitchell, in at quarterback, hit Stinson Jones for a 5-yard score. Ox-strong Mike Ondos recovered a Cavalier fumble to set up the next touchdown, a Mitchell one-yard sneak.

Virginia opened the second half with an 85-yard drive for a touchdown, and then trimmed the VMI lead to 13-12, when Fred Shepard scored on a two-yard run.

"Whereas in the first half Virginia had seemed bent on proving they were a worse football team than we, our players did an about face and seemed equally determined to prove that we were worse," McKenna wrote to the Sportsmen's Club.

Besides Armistead's big defensive play for the clinching score, the glue-fingered Evans had a big day on offense with four receptions for 54 yards. VMI prevailed 19-12, in a performance that McKenna said "left something to be desired."

Kurkoski added another interception "to quell Virginia's final uprising and give me two or three easy breaths before the game's end," wrote McKenna. "Our lack of depth in quality has been much in evidence this season. Some individuals on the blue team handle themselves well under fire, but our inexperience and lack of speed in spots poses a real problem. An outstanding job of recruiting must be done by all of us, coaches and sportsmen, for the 1960 Fourth Class or there are hard times ahead."

The hard times weren't here yet, even without Dyer. Mitchell was still under center the following week as the Keydets blew out William & Mary 26-7 in what was expected to be a tight game in Norfolk. Mitchell earned *Richmond Times-Dispatch* Player of the Week honors after guiding both VMI's first and second units to scores. He was also the game's outstanding player, as voted by the media.

McKenna later wrote to the boosters: "Bobby Mitchell, Third Class Cadet and, until three weeks ago third string quarterback, guided his Keydet teammates to a fine 26-7 win over William and Mary. For his performance,

Mitchell was selected the game's outstanding player and awarded a beautiful trophy. Few people in the park would have disputed the decision of the judges."

The sophomore from Alexandria was pressed into his first start with Dyer and O'Dell both shelved by injuries. O'Dell had separated his shoulder against Penn State and wouldn't return until the last game of the year. Mitchell completed 4-of-7 passes for a whopping 123 yards and added 22 more yards on the ground, including a 7-yard touchdown run.

Mitchell had been recruited by Virginia but wanted to major in engineering. The Cavaliers' coaching staff basically said that engineering and football were not compatible. McKenna had no such qualms about tough majors and football. He just needed players, and he preferred smart ones.

"Coach McKenna assured me that there were a lot of engineering majors at VMI, and you could tell he had a full grasp of what someone would be thinking about when they are going to college," recalled Mitchell years later. "With Coach McKenna, you knew there were other things important in his life, and he knew there were other things important in your life. Yet when you're on the practice field or in a ball game, you were focused, and that's what his attention was on, too. I think his character and integrity set the tone for the whole program."

Besides Mitchell's heroics that day, it was Traynham's 10-yard scamper that put VMI on top of William & Mary early at the end of a 60-yard drive. The VMI defense set up Mitchell's score when Kurkoski recovered a fumble on the Indians' nine-yard line.

William & Mary cut the lead in half with a touchdown early in the third quarter, but the Keydets bounced right back with another 60-yard drive. Jones scored from seven yards. "This boy bids fair to become one of the better backs in the area," McKenna wrote that week. Later that period, Mitchell scrambled away from pressure and found Evans for 45 yards. A couple of plays later, he hit Kurkoski for an 8-yard score.

VMI twice ended Indian uprisings in Keydet territory with interceptions in what was becoming somewhat of a theme for the team. On the season VMI would lose the ball just 13 times through fumbles or interceptions and on defense, the Keydets would swarm to recover 40 takeaways, including a nation's best 28 interceptions.

"Our team was opportunistic and played heads-up determined football all afternoon," wrote McKenna of traits that always marked his best teams. "We are no means out of the woods, but our season's record of 3-1-1 at the moment is highly pleasing to the coaching staff and surprising to just about everyone else."

Dyer was back October 24 for a big 34-7 homecoming win over Davidson, one of many teams that had shunned him in recruiting. He passed for three scores and ran for another as VMI slipped and sloshed to a win on a muddy Wilson Field on the Washington & Lee campus. Damage to Alumni Field had forced that game and the upcoming tilt with The Citadel to be moved to W&L's field.

Only the nomadic Keydets could host homecoming on someone else's field. While Alumni Field hadn't handled the seemingly weekly Saturday rainfall well that fall, McKenna wasn't overly pleased with the track at Wilson. "An amphibious tank would have had heavy going," he wrote that week. "We bagged our lowest ground yardage this current season."

Traynham wasn't deterred, though. He fielded a quick kick and zipped 58 yards in the muck to put the Keydets on top. Dyer was deadly efficient despite a wet ball. He completed 7-of-9 passes for 185 yards and three touchdown passes to Evans, all in the first half, as VMI went up 27-0. The Wildcats had hoped to play an eight-man front and gang up on the running game, but Dyer did them in when he came in with the second unit early on.

Horner, also coming back from nagging injuries, was another key. The senior captain averaged 42 yards on his high punts and continued to impress his teammates.

"He was a great guy, very quiet," said Dyer, "but just unbelievable ability. He was fast, probably ran a 9.7–100. He could play for anybody. Today, he would play at Southern Cal, or he could play at Notre Dame. He was a great, great football player."

"Sam is a reliable performer, and his teammates know it," said McKenna after the game. "And who'd have thought we would be 4-1-1 at this stage, particularly with Horner out for three games."

McKenna got to play all his reserves in the closing minutes, and that really pleased him. "There is something about game experience which simply cannot be matched by any amount of practice," he wrote to the Sportsmen's Club.

The following week, Dyer threw for three more scores, and VMI ground up George Washington 28-6 on a Friday night in Griffith Stadium in Washington, D.C. Led by the blocking of guards Lou Shuba and Bill Haeberlein, the Keydets rolled to 229 yards rushing.

VMI scored on the initial possession, going 68 yards with Horner crashing in from the six. After an Armistead interception, the Keydets moved in for another score, Dyer hitting Evans for the first of three touchdowns the skillful end would notch during a torrid stretch. Evans hauled in five passes for 99 yards on the night.

Evans, the 6-2, 185-pound history major, would make some history of his own on this season, setting VMI season records with 35 receptions and 698 receiving yards. The Wilmerding, Pa., native would go on to sign with the Buffalo Bills of the fledgling American Football League.

"There is no way to tell you how great a receiver he was," said Dyer of the senior end. "He had big hands. He was about 6'-2", and he could catch anything. He was absolutely the best receiver during my four years at VMI, by far, and I dare say, he's as good a receiver as we ever had at VMI. I don't recall one ball that I threw him that year that was catchable that was dropped."

Shuba earned Lineman of the Week honors from the *Richmond Times-Dispatch*, and Horner looked back to full-speed. He had punts of 64 and 63 yards and ground out 67 yards in nine rushes, while, "being his own formidable self on defense," McKenna said.

McKenna reflected on the improbability of VMI's 5-1-1 record. "The team lost fifteen of the first twenty two men of last year's squad, including ten of the starting eleven. During the absence of Sam Horner in the early part of this year, we were not playing a single man who had started a varsity game before the current season. Needless to say, we are very pleased and feel that you should be too."

The pleasing tenor of the season continued, though narrowly the next week at Lehigh. VMI took the Engineers' best shot, and cheerleaders and members of the band fought off another halftime raid trying to take the Corps' cannon. VMI made a point, staving off some 300 charging, would-be cannon-snatching students, and won by a point when sophomore kicker Nelson Elliott's extra point was the difference. The Keydets escaped with a 7-6 road win in Bethlehem, Pa.

On the rainy, chilly afternoon, VMI scored early and then held on to the victory and their cannon before 4,500 spectators. Evans continued his sterling offensive play, taking a short pass from Dyer and turning it into a 40-yard touchdown in the second quarter. He eluded seven tacklers on a muddy meander.

"Howard Dyer hit Dick Evans, his favorite target, against the right sideline for what appeared to be a 16-yard completion," described McKenna. "But Evans shook off the tackler covering him, side-stepped a couple more, and aided by three good downfield blocks, went into the end zone for six points. It was an outstanding display of effort on the part of Evans and alert action on the part of several of his teammates."

Eight minutes later, Lehigh scored on a 19-yard pass play, Bob Scheu to Boyd Taylor. On the conversion attempt, though, VMI's Randy Campbell appeared out of nowhere to bat down a pass.

Dyer led a late drive that ran out much of the clock in the fourth quarter as VMI won its fifth straight game. The Engineers never got past their own 45-yard line in the second half. Dyer was 9 of 18 for 172 yards passing, and VMI had 327 yards to Lehigh's 152, in a commanding performance that didn't translate to the scoreboard.

The stage was set for a huge game with The Citadel at Wilson Field. The Keydets exacted revenge against their military rivals for the 14-6 loss the previous season that broke the Institute's 18-game unbeaten streak.

VMI recorded a convincing 32-8 win before a Parents Day crowd of 8,500, including 800 cadet visitors from The Citadel. The loss eliminated previously once-beaten Citadel from the Southern Conference race.

"Desire and determination to excel are sufficient motives to win any football game, but our demonstration against The Citadel smacked of a revenge incentive," McKenna wrote that week. "It looked as though we were bent on getting even."

To the media, McKenna praised Horner and Traynham and the two-way efforts of Shuba, whom he called "a behind-the-scenes player" who didn't get enough credit for the team's success.

It was again the passing combination of Dyer and Evans that ignited the offense. Evans caught three passes on a 74-yard drive that set up a 34-yard Elliot field goal. The Keydets then drove 63 yards, Kern scoring from the two, and Kern adding a two-point conversion run for an 11-0 lead in the second quarter.

After a short punt by Citadel star Paul Maguire, Dyer orchestrated a 58-yard drive to open the third quarter, with the quarterback plunging in from a yard out for a 19-0 lead.

VMI shackled receiver Maguire all day, and he was eventually ejected from the game for fighting with Keydet end Tom Daniel late in the fourth period.

Randy Campbell's interception, another part of a solid day for the Big Red defense, set up a touchdown. It also set up a Southern Conference championship showdown with Virginia Tech.

"The win was highly gratifying, but I must admit to a special pleasure in getting this one," McKenna wrote. "It keeps us alive as possible winners of the Southern Conference and adds special luster to the Thanksgiving game against VPI in Roanoke. If you have tickets and the time, don't miss it. It should be a good one."

McKenna was correct, particularly from a Keydet perspective. A record-breaking Roanoke crowd of 27,500 saw VMI win its second Southern Conference title in three years, routing rival Virginia Tech 37-12. In the process, VMI also claimed the Big Five (Washington & Lee had de-emphasized football in the 1950s) crown in convincing fashion.

Dyer was again superb, accounting for four touchdowns. He intercepted a pass to thwart a Gobbler drive in the first period, then he drove the Keydets 81 yards, hitting Evans, who had missed the two previous Thanksgiving games with injuries, on fourth down for a 29-yard, go-ahead touchdown.

It was a fourth-and-12 play, and part of the reason Dyer was becoming known as the "Mississippi Gambler."

"I knew he would be open, Dyer told The *Roanoke World-News.* "On third down I told him to go down and out. They knocked the pass down, but I saw the way their halfbacks were playing. So this time I told him to go down and in. Sure enough he was in the open."

Horner, who had infuriated McKenna earlier in the week by telling a reporter that VMI could win the rivalry game by three touchdowns, got an interception to set up the second score. Another fourth-down Dyer-Evans hook-up gained 18 yards and set up Horner's two-yard touchdown plunge. On this day Evans easily bested the Hokies All-American wide-receiver Carroll Dale, who would go on to a 13 year professional career. He was a three time Pro-bowler with the legendary Green Bay Packers' teams under Coach Vince Lombardi and is a member of the Packers Hall of Fame.

Virginia Tech came back with a 15-play drive, Pat Henry diving in from one yard. The Keydets had time to score again before the half, though. The big play was a Dyer pass deflected to Traynham for a 32-yard touchdown that put VMI up 18-6. "Traynham fell flat on his back while embracing the ball in making one of the great catches I have seen this fall," McKenna said later.

Dyer directed a 63-yard march in the third quarter, and again, got some luck when Tech's Alger Pugh batted his pass right into the hands of Evans for a 29-yard score. It was a tough day for Pugh, who got smashed by center Lee Badgett on the opening kickoff, cracking his helmet. Keydet players still talked about the hit 50 years later.

McKenna wrote about it in the opening of his missive to the Sportsmen's Club that week. "Lee Badgett's tackle on the opening kickoff set the tone for the Turkey Day game against VPI. Sam Horner's boot traveled to the VPI five where it was fielded by Alger Pugh, Tech's All-Conference back. As the latter started across the field diagonally, Badgett hurled himself through the air on a diving tackle. The impact was so great that it knocked the ball loose from Pugh's grasp and broke the face guard on Badgett's helmet. A fast whistle, properly so, saved the ball for Tech, and they retained possession."

Pete Candler, VMI Class of 1971, whose brother "Big" John Candler was already making himself known as a standout tackle for the Keydets, tells it this way: "I was ten years old and in the stands watching the game with a number of family members. John was the first in our family to attend VMI; all the others had gone to Tech. After the opening kickoff and the hit by Badgett, one of my uncles stood up and said, 'This game is over; I'm going home.' He left Victory Stadium and did not return."…his prognosis could not have been more succinct – and correct.

VMI's defense intercepted six passes as a Keydet team predicted to finish no better than fourth in the tough Southern Conference claimed the crown and finished the season with seven straight victories and an 8-1-1 overall record.

McKenna was named Conference Coach of the Year and could look back over a three-year run that saw VMI post a 23-3-4 record. He said this team came closer to achieving its potential than any other team he had ever coached.

Dyer was named the Thanksgiving game's outstanding player. Playing in front of his parents for the first time in his college career, he hit on six of 15 passes for 152 yards and the three scores. He also rushed for another 46 yards.

"That was what you would call a perfect weekend," Dyer remembered in a 2006 interview. "It was a beautiful day. It was Ring Figure weekend; I got my class ring. My parents saw me play for the first time in college, and I was selected the outstanding player. We beat the hell out of them."

Despite injuries that forced him out of two games and the fact that he wasn't the team's starter until three games in, Dyer racked up a school record

1,072 yards passing, almost double what anyone else had ever achieved at the Institute since the formation of the Southern Conference in 1953. He completed 55 of 105 passes, had 13 touchdown tosses and ran for four more scores.

He and Horner were named First Team All-Southern Conference, and Evans, Haeberlein and Traynham, who led the Keydets with 491 yards rushing in 92 carries and totaled nearly a thousand yards in a variety of methods, landed on the second team. Shuba was an honorable mention choice. Dyer, Evans, Horner and Shuba were selected to the All Big Five Team named by the Associated Press, and Dyer and Horner were honorable mention AP All-America.

Horner was a second round draft pick by the Washington Redskins, and played a lot as a rookie the following season. He would play two seasons there and one more with the New York Giants.

McKenna was a popular choice as Southern Conference Coach of the Year, the second time he had won the honor. With 15 of his top 22 players lost to graduation, he cobbled together a big winner, taking to the air with Dyer and relying on that spectacular, ball-hawking defense. His team was true to his base fundamentals, too, losing a nationwide low six fumbles.

McKenna confided *to Richmond Times-Dispatch* columnist Chauncey Durden that VMI had just 27 scholarship players on the team, and some of those were partial grants…small numbers, big achievements for the unlikely champions.

Veteran trainer Herb Patchin, Durden reported, was the calmest man on the VMI sideline during the big win over Tech. "I knew the second game of the season that we'd have a real good team," Patchin was quoted. "Penn State has a powerful squad, but our inexperienced boys were hitting just as hard as they were."

Durden added, "Patchin's standard, succinct summation of VMI's whopping victory over Virginia Tech: 'The Christians ate the lions.'"

McKenna had the final word in his season-ending newsletter to boosters:

"The fine season with eight wins, one loss and one tie has been concluded. Over the past three years, only three teams have beaten the Institute's Big Red, two of those defeats have already been avenged. With a winning tradition established and outstanding cadets representing the Institute on the gridiron, let's maintain to the best of our ability the established standard of excellence. It requires your efforts, your material and moral support, as well as the strivings of the players and the coaches, to get the job done.

"The poet John Milton said, 'they also serve who only stand and wait'. We will all get on better if everyone keeps busy while we are waiting."

1959 (8-1-1)

Southern Conference Champions

DATE	VMI	LOCATION	OPP
S 19	46	at Marshall	0
S 26	0	at Penn State	21
O 3	14	Richmond (Portsmouth)	14
O 10	19	Virginia (Lynchburg)	12
O 17	26	William & Mary (Norfolk)	7
O 24	34	Davidson	7
O 30	28	at George Washington	6
N 7	7	at Lehigh	6
N 14	32	The Citadel	8
N 26	37	Virginia Tech (Roanoke)	12

CHAPTER TEN

SO CLOSE

Dyer and fellow senior, center Lee Badgett, were named co-captains for 1960. Preseason pigskin prognostication magazines – the colorful covers usually featuring helmetless quarterbacks jumping toward a camera, one arm spread wide and the ball cocked back, behind a well-coiffed, albeit short mane, in the other hand – touted Norm Snead of Wake Forest, Roman Gabriel of NC State, and VMI's Dyer as legitimate All-America quarterback candidates in the Mid-Atlantic region.

True ("The Man's Magazine") gushed about VMI in its *1960 Football Yearbook*, available on newsstands that summer for 35 cents:

The point has been reached in the Southern Conference at which it has been deemed unsafe not to give Virginia Military Institute the benefit of every doubt...John McKenna is unquestionably one of the country's most underrated coaches. He has built quite a dynasty at VMI in his seven years.

Dyer, who was good enough to set records and win conference honors the previous season, had come back to summer camp an even better quarterback. He explained it was "because of a little trick he learned this summer" while in ROTC training at Fort Knox.

"I worked out with Jim Ninowski (of the pro Detroit Lions) quite a bit, and I was really impressed with the way he got back from under center. I learned a lot from him, and I think I'm at least a step faster getting back with the ball ready to pass."

The Sporting News had details, too, further explaining that Dyer was a tank driver. "Just like Elvis Presley," Dyer laughed of his stint at Fort Knox.

One day, minus the tank, Dyer ran into the Detroit Lions quarterback on the base, which, as it turned out, was even better than meeting "The King."

Elvis, for the record, had just left active duty that March. By the end of the 1960 football campaign, he would be, football diehards in Lexington argued, only slightly more famous than Dyer.

Dyer was big in another way, too. He also added 10 pounds of muscle, now weighing 195. The passing concern in Lexington that summer, though, was who would replace Dick Evans, one of the top VMI ends in program history. Dick Weede was back from knee surgery, and Ken Legum and Dick Willard were "top drawer" defenders. It was enough of a concern that McKenna moved track speedster Wyatt Durette from halfback to end and started accelerating the end education of promising sophomore Kenny Reeder of Wilmington, Delaware.

Weede, who liked to catch balls with his wrong hand on top, was sometimes called "Wrong Way," and McKenna confessed to trying to correct that technique the previous year. "We tried making him catch the ball the conventional way," said the coach. "He dropped almost every one."

Another concern was replacing Horner, particularly as a punter. The leading candidate, John Traynham, hit line drives, which were all too returnable. Less of a concern was that strong defense. Up front, VMI had some size in 6'-2", 224-pound veteran Martin Caples and promising 6'-5", 242-pound John Candler. All told, 20 lettermen returned for the defending champs, and the team was deeper than ever. There were no sophomores on the first or second units and only four on the third team.

McKenna had those 20 returning lettermen and some unproven talent coming up, too. Most of all, though, he and the Keydets had Dyer, who was making a national name for himself. *The Sporting News* loved the senior quarterback:

Because Dyer is a ruggedly-built 6'-1", 191-pounder, he frequently turns a quarterback sneak into a power play. He's not reluctant to run with the ball either when his receivers are covered.

While Dyer was becoming nationally known for what he did on offense, his defense also attracted some attention. Tom Joynes, the team publicist, remembers Dyers' penchant for big hits at linebacker.

"Dyer was a big guy," he said. "The truth of the matter is Dyer just liked to hit the other quarterback. He was an outside linebacker, and he loved it when the other quarterback would come around on his side with the option."

Truth be told, players had a lot of fun in "one-platoon" football. They had more ownership in the game, and it took fewer of them to be successful, something VMI certainly exploited. "I think it's a complete game that way and it enables a school like VMI to be more competitive," said backup quarterback Mitchell.

Mitchell had a unique perspective. He had only played on offense in high school. "Now I had to play defense," he said. "Basically, and this happens with quarterbacks, they had to find a place to hide you. So I was weakside linebacker all the time."

Dyer, apparently, wasn't hiding unless you count lying in wait for opposing quarterbacks to come his way.

McKenna didn't downplay the Dyer publicity, but he did often wryly temper it. For instance, he would compare the quarterback with a less polished though nonetheless accomplished athlete, like, say Yogi Berra, the star catcher of the New York Yankees dynasty in full bloom during this era. "Neither of them looks particularly impressive, but look what they've done," he would say, breaking into a smile.

The Sporting News continued: *Dyer is anything but a satin-smooth quarterback. His moves often are herky-jerky, and he throws the ball with a snap from off his ear and with the long, sweeping motion the pros cherish. Some people claim Dyer could complete passes while on his back. Unlike some quarterbacks who have their places filled under the new wild-card substitution rule, Dyer operates both ways and serves as a corner linebacker.* "He's one of the best defensive men we have," said McKenna.

McKenna's assessment of Dyer's throwing motion was different from *The Sporting News.* "He's not the full-arm thrower like that in the pros. He throws with a three-quarters motion like a baseball catcher. The results speak for themselves. We don't fool around with a passer's style unless he throws sidearm."

Of course, a big reason McKenna was smiling was that Dyer would operate behind a veteran offensive line, the largest in the coach's tenure, averaging 210 pounds tackle to tackle and anchored by all-conference pick Shuba.

"Lou Shuba at guard was pound for pound, John (McKenna) always said, the best player he had in those days," said Joynes' successor as Keydets' publicist, Dick Sessoms. "And he had a lot of good ones. (Shuba) was a heck of a football player. He was better at his position, John always said, than even Dyer was at quarterback."

Another big factor was Badgett, a man of few words but a lot of influence, teammate Binnie Peay remembered years later. "He was a quiet leader in his own way, and we respected him. I think some of their (Dyer's and Badgett's) personality had a lot to do with the whole concept of winning."

Badgett's accolades off the field were equally impressive. He was the Regimental Commander (highest ranking cadet) in the Corps and was vice-president of his class. A brilliant student, he graduated with distinction as a mathematics major, a Rhodes Scholar. He later earned a Ph.D. from Yale. He had a distinguished 24-year career in the United States Air Force and returned to his alma mater in 1990 to serve as Provost and Dean of the Faculty.

Meanwhile, the schedule, while still plenty challenging, was minus the one team – Penn State – that beat VMI in '59. A tough road stretch of Virginia, Boston College and Memphis State would test the team plenty, though.

The season opened on a sunny September 17 in Williamsburg before 7,500 fans at William & Mary's Carey Field. A lead was elusive in Williamsburg. The Keydets nearly doubled up the Indians statistically, but the game was tied 21-21 at the half, with the Southern Conference and Big Five favorites seemingly stumbling out of the gates.

The Indians scored first, but Mitchell hit Don Kern for 25 yards to set up Stinson Jones' seven-yard scoring run. Dyer capped a 70-yard drive with his one-yard plunge for a score, but the extra point failed.

After William & Mary went ahead 14-13 on a 77-yard fumble return, Kern had a big 37-yard run and then scored from five yards. William & Mary tied the score and had a chance to regain the lead in the third quarter but fumbled at the 24-yard line.

VMI scored twice in the fourth quarter to pull away in a 33-21 victory over the surprisingly pesky Indians, who had somehow sneaked on the schedule early that season, against the McKenna strategy of playing them deeper into the season.

Dyer scored on a one-yard keeper for the go-ahead score midway through the fourth quarter, and Badgett's interception set up a Dyer-to-Dick Willard touchdown pass from 12 yards to seal the win.

"The game," wrote McKenna in his newsletter, "was very hard fought and there was a considerable collection of bruises on both teams. The resistance from William and Mary was stiffer than anticipated and will doubtlessly prove a confirming lesson to our ball club. Each game is truly a brand new season, and nobody can be sold short. To use an old cliché, 'Uneasy rests the head that wears the crown,' and it is harder to knock off one's head if the latter is kept level."

The following week at Buffalo, Dyer ran for a touchdown and passed for another as VMI beat Buffalo 28-14 in War Memorial Stadium before a crowd of 18,675.

"Howard Dyer was the principal contributor to the offensive derring-do as he chipped in with 124 yards passing and 34 yards on the ground," wrote McKenna. "He was aided and abetted principally by Stinson Jones who once again turned in one of the sterling efforts of the evening."

Early in the second quarter, Dyer hit Kern for 42 yards to set up the first score, a Dyer sneak from less than a yard. Four minutes later, VMI went up 14-0 as Traynham bulled in from seven yards, set up by Jones' 29-yard catch and run from Dyer.

Reserve Buffalo quarterback Joe Oliverio got hot and moved the Bulls 67 yards for a touchdown and a two-point conversion. Caples recovered a Buffalo fumble early in the fourth quarter, and Pat Morrison scored on a 17-yard sweep. Dyer added a 7-yard touchdown pass to Jones to make it 28-8, ensuring the Keydets' ninth consecutive victory.

"Dyer is big league," opined Buffalo coach Dick Offenhammer. "We couldn't contain him. We had him trapped several times but could not hold him. He rolls out, runs the option, does everything."

After two games, Dyer's 239 total yards was ahead of his Southern Conference-leading pace of a year ago.

The Mississippi native, who was living up to his "Mississippi Gambler" moniker with his penchant for big plays, was at it again in VMI's 21-6 Homecoming win over Richmond. Dyer completed 15 of 22 passes for 177 yards and scored two touchdowns to stave off Richmond before 6,500 fans.

"The team's performance during the first two quarters was unfortunately typical of many Homecoming occasions," McKenna wrote to the Sportsmen's Club. "This is not peculiar to Virginia Military Institute since almost every coach I know has a feeling of dire expectancy born of sad experience on Homecoming Day. It is our great good luck that the dire in this case is spelled Dyer."

The Keydets, with the jitters to which the coach referred, fumbled on their first play, though their defense would hold. Traynham recovered a fumble late in the first quarter, and Dyer took the Keydets 42 yards for the first score, with Dyer carrying three yards for the touchdown. His conversion pass to Willard made it 8-0.

Dyer then added a one-yard scoring run in the third period as VMI went up 15-6. He had a fourth quarter touchdown pass to Willard nullified by a holding penalty but came back later to hit Willard again on a fourth down play for the game's final points.

The Southern Conference Player of the Week, Dyer ranked fourth in the nation in total offense and led the Southern Conference in passing.

McKenna was distressed about his team's depth, as he shared in his newsletter:

"Our gold team or starting unit played the bulk of the afternoon and did not get the rest which is needed to maintain top efficiency. The performance of our blue team or alternate unit in the last two games has not warranted playing them for any considerable length of time since their defensive play has been sub-standard to say the least. Unless there is definite progress in the quality of play by our reserves, our days – or weeks – as an undefeated team might well be numbered. Monday scrimmages are indicated as a therapeutic measure until we can trust them to hold the fort for at least a half period at a time."

McKenna would look prophetic the following week. On October 7, with their 10-game winning streak in jeopardy against George Washington, the Keydets turned to enigmatic backup halfback Don Kern in Washington, D.C. He dashed 38 yards for a score, the first of his four touchdowns to tie a Southern Conference record and lead a 34-10 victory.

Kern's first score cut into a 10-0 George Washington lead and started a 20-point VMI second quarter outburst. McKenna credited assistant Clark King, "our man upstairs," for spotting how aggressively the Colonial linebackers were coming up "to stem our wide game. It set the stage for a quick inside shot." Kern did the rest, then Mitchell hit Willard for two points.

Kern hauled in a 15-yard pass from Dyer for another touchdown on a piece of flim-flam, Dyer rolled right and threw all the way back to the left for an easy score. The "ubiquitous Mr. Kern" had a four-yard touchdown run that made it 20-10 at the half.

Kern was known among teammates as a "free spirit," a cadet many thought cocky, and who had ups and downs even with teammates. While McKenna never started Kern, he did love to bring him off the bench and for a couple of years the speedster played a key role, especially on offense.

One story that made the rounds in the barracks had Kern getting in trouble for calling a professor "stupid." When McKenna got word of the incident, he sent Kern to apologize, and Kern supposedly said, "I'm sorry you're stupid." True or not, teammates thought Kern capable of such shenanigans.

Dyer found Kern for a 32-yard touchdown pass in the third quarter, and the quarterback had another big day. He had 223 total yards, moving into the national lead in total offense with 772 yards in three games. His four-game total was the second most in history behind only Notre Dame's Paul Hornung in 1956.

The strong-armed quarterback wasn't quite as effective statistically at Virginia the following week, but he impressed his teammates, playing with a sore shoulder and after being bedridden for three days with the flu. He hit 11-of-22 passes for 205 yards and handed the Cavaliers their 22nd consecutive loss, this one 30-16, part of the longest losing streak in the nation at the time.

Virginia had even scored first, to the delight of 21,000 in Scott Stadium, marching 66 yards and culminating with a 10-yard run by quarterback Carl Kuhn. VMI then drove down and scored on a Kern plunge from the one, and Dyer hit Willard for a two-point conversion to tie the game.

Virginia muscled the ball down the field, and Kuhn scored on a keeper play from 15 yards, adding two points to go up 16-8. On the day, Virginia out-gained the Keydets 297-85 on the ground, attempting to keep the ball away from Dyer & Co.

"The ease with which our line was handled in the game's early stages was disconcerting," said McKenna.

Dyer hit Jones for 40 yards to bring VMI back quickly. He connected with Willard for a touchdown and then Kern for a tying two-pointer. Jones then recovered a Virginia fumble to give VMI the chance to go on top. Dyer hit Traynham, Kern and Jones to move the team into scoring position, Jones making a great catch while on his back after slipping. McKenna thought that play was the game's turning point.

Dyer scored from two yards, and then passed to his roommate Weede for a 24-16 advantage before the half.

A long Traynham kick return set up a late, clinching score, Dyer's two-yard run, and the Big Red defense rose up to stop Virginia on the ground. Armistead intercepted Cavalier quarterback Gary Cuozzo on the game's final play after Virginia had driven deep into VMI territory against the "prevent defense."

"This is designated to keep the opponent from scoring while placing little emphasis on the ground gained short of the goal line," McKenna wrote the boosters. "The prevent defense may have looked ineffective, but it did what it's intended to do."

McKenna exulted in a fourth straight victory over Virginia, but offered that the Wahoos were building "...and are coming fast. If we are going to play on even terms with them in future years, a steady flow of Alumni Educational Fund help is required. Football victories do not come about by chance."

Dyer's shoulder, hurt while making a tackle, kept him from playing defense against the Cavaliers, and the Keydets were also without Bill Haeberlein, out with a knee injury. Haeberlein still found a way to contribute. He spotted – helping identify players from the press box – for the public address announcer.

Banged up but still rolling, VMI headed north on October 22 to meet Boston College. Twenty miles from McKenna's hometown of Lawrence, Massachusetts, the Keydets needed two quick scores in the third quarter to salvage a tie and keep their 13-game unbeaten streak alive.

McKenna credited Boston College with outflanking the Keydets, with two wide receivers and a back in motion creating overloads to one side. The Eagles were able to complete passes to their ends or the back in motion and sustain a running game behind a typically hulking offensive line.

The Big Red defense made adjustments at halftime and held BC to just 21 yards rushing the final 30 minutes. "After intermission, it appeared, although identically clad as earlier, that there were two different football teams on the field," McKenna explained. "The Keydets dominated play in every respect, and, before the third period was over, they had tied the score."

The Eagles took advantage of Keydet miscues to take a 14-0 first half lead. VMI turned the tables on their hosts in the third quarter, driving 72 yards in 12 plays to get on the board, running the ball well, often behind the fine blocking of Haeberlein, who was still spotting players, only now knocking them down as well. Dyer scored on a play-fake, dashing five yards for the score.

A two-point attempt failed, but the next time the Keydets got the ball, Dyer drove them down the field again, hitting three consecutive passes. Kern's five-yard run and then his conversion run, tied the contest.

"From this point on, we threatened almost continuously, but miscues on the part of some of our players and excellent defensive play on the part of our opponents blunted our several sallies short of the promised land," wrote McKenna. "The movies showed conclusively that the Keydets played their best football game of the season. It sometimes happens that a team plays extremely well and cannot win. Conversely, it also happens that a team can play poorly and emerge a winner."

Dyer had the Keydets on the march again on their next possession but the drive stalled inside the five, with Kern stopped on fourth down. Late in the game, Dyer was driving his team again, but an interception ended VMI's last threat, and the game ended in a 14-14 deadlock.

"We coaches are pleased with what the boys did in a fine team effort even though we had to settle for a tie," added the coach.

The good folk of Lawrence had declared the afternoon "John McKenna Day" in their fair town, but the coach's only speech came during a halftime admonishment to the Keydets that helped save the day for VMI.

Dyer was still on a blistering pace with 1,076 yards and still the national leader in total offense.

VMI's 14-game undefeated streak was finally stopped on October 29, in Memphis on a rainy night and a muddy field. Dyer's return near his Mississippi Delta home was spoiled by the 21-8 setback.

Memphis State controlled the game, driving 86-yards for an early touchdown. Fullback Charles Killett, on his way to 111 yards rushing, plunged in from the one on the last play of the first quarter. The Tigers tacked on another score early in the third quarter, driving 59 yards with Killett crashing in from the five. The "bulldozer" fullback "rambled off our tackles, gathering large chunks of real estate much of the night," according to McKenna.

The Keydets just missed a big play when Durrette got behind Tiger defenders but couldn't get a handle on Mitchell's pass after a full team substitution by McKenna. The Tigers also intercepted a Mitchell pass early in the fourth quarter to set up another score and a 21-0 lead.

The Keydets finally got on the scoreboard after a 91-yard drive, Dyer smashing over the goal line from two yards out with just 18 seconds remaining. Dyer then hit Kern for two points on the conversion.

VMI had just 19 yards rushing, and the Tigers kept the heat on Dyer all day, regularly blitzing linebackers from varying angles. Dyer totaled 161 yards, below his 179-yard average, and he got most of the stripes against the Tigers in the final period, while playing catch-up.

"Their superiority on that particular evening was not open to question as they dominated play," wrote McKenna, who later in his newsletter explained the odd scheduling of a Midwest opponent, a concession to the economic realities of the day for the Keydets.

"The game with Memphis was a one-shot deal, and we are not scheduled to play them in the future," McKenna wrote. "Actually, we have nothing whatever in common with this opponent academically, traditionally, geographically or in any other way. It seemed to provide an opportunity to make some money, but the rain took care of that."

Now 5-1-1, the Keydets got back in the win column with a hard-fought 18-14 win over Lehigh the following Saturday on Parents Weekend in Lexington. The Big Red defense indeed came up big with four fumble recoveries, including two scooped up by Weede.

Again, though, Dyer got the big headlines, breaking Southern Conference records for passing and total offense, pushing his season totals to 1,093 yards passing and 1,300 total yards.

The VMI offense was in high gear early on. Traynham had a long return of a quick kick to set up a short Dyer touchdown pass to Jones, the speedy back evading six or seven tacklers to score on a screen pass. Two minutes later, Badgett recovered a fumble at the four-yard line, and Dyer powered in for a 12-0 lead.

Traynham had a 41-yard punt return to the Lehigh 29, and a 24-yard run by Kern put the Keydets up 18-0. McKenna went with his second unit for much of the second half, and they held on for the victory. Mitchell, halfback Pat Morrison and little-used senior Don Rishell, who picked up 19 yards in three carries, acquitted themselves well, but the second unit couldn't score.

Dyer dropped to third in the national total yardage race behind Oregon State's Terry Baker and Washington State's Mel Melin. Others in the top 10 included NC State's Roman Gabriel, UCLA's Billy Kilmer, Georgia's Fran Tarkenton and Ohio State's Tom Matte.

Dyer and the Keydets nailed down their second straight Southern Conference title and the third in four years with a convincing 20-6 win over The Citadel in Charleston, South Carolina, in front of a raucous

Homecoming Day crowd of 13,970.

Kern scored two touchdowns, and Dyer did yeoman work on defense, helping a secondary that intercepted two passes. VMI dominated the game, rolling up 366 total yards to The Citadel's 149, denying The Citadel a chance to win the school's first conference football crown in 55 years.

McKenna was particularly pleased with the line-play in Charleston, singling out Bill Hoehl, Shuba, Haeberlein and Badgett in his newsletter.

The Keydets jumped on top with a 13-play, 60-yard drive in the first quarter, Kern tallying from 14 yards. Dyer then hit two of three passes to help the team move 76 yards in the second quarter. Once inside the 10-yard line, Kern was able to bull into the end zone from three yards. Dyer hit Jones for the conversion and a 14-0 lead.

The Bulldogs took advantage of a short punt to score just before the half, Bob Crouch running it in from two yards.

The VMI second unit earned their stripes with an impressive 66-yard drive for a clinching score in the fourth quarter. Morrison and Ken Reeder did most of the damage on the ground, but Dyer got the score from one yard on the 14th play of the march. McKenna surprised The Citadel, putting his potent passing attack on the shelf most of the game, concentrating on a suddenly powerful running game.

Kern, who had just been moved to fullback this week, finished with 88 yards on 13 carries. VMI improved to 7-1-1, while the Bulldogs dropped to 6-2-1.

The Keydets also came away with a souvenir, specifically for right tackle Marty Caples, who had broken his hand and didn't make the trip. A faux cemetery had been set up near the stadium entrance and fake tombstones with the names of nearly all the Keydets were spread there to inspire the Bulldogs.

VMI players, on the bus pulling away from the stadium, implored McKenna to stop and let them collect the tombstones. McKenna relented, allowing only Caples' marker to be taken. "It might cause a riot," McKenna told the team.

The tombstone, as reported in the *Roanoke World-News*, turned out to be a small bookshelf covered in cloth. "The boys proudly displayed it on the chartered plane back to Roanoke. They had it ready for a cheering Caples when the bus arrived at the VMI barracks on Saturday night."

The Keydets also took home the Cadet Memorial Trophy, emblematic of the winner of The Citadel-VMI football game, returning it to Lexington where it had resided nine of the 10 years since its inception. In 1976 a new symbol of what is now called the Military Classic of the South was unveiled – The Silver Shako. A shako is a hat worn at military dress parades at both schools. The Silver Shako still resides at the school of the winner of the The Citadel-VMI game, and the scores of all games are engraved on the base of the trophy.

The Citadel's coach, Eddie Teague, told media after the game that he believed Dyer was actually a "ringer" down from the NFL. "Dyer and (John) Unitas are almost exactly the same size, and Dyer fakes and throws with the Unitas moves," he said. "That's why it's scary to watch him. He looks for all the world like a Colt in VMI uniform."

Teague said he had watched film and seen Dyer completing passes standing up, falling down, and almost lying on the ground and with tacklers "clinging to him like a grapevine."

Despite all the accolades, trophies and souvenirs, the season ended on a disappointing note November 24 in Roanoke with a 13-12 loss to the Gobblers on Thanksgiving. Playing an inspired game, though the conference title had already been decided, Virginia Tech dominated up front and upset VMI before a Thanksgiving Day crowd of 28,000 in Roanoke's Victory Stadium.

The Gobblers ran the ball 56 times to net 155 yards, while holding VMI to just 45 yards on the ground, numbers reflective of the Gobblers' effort, but also the absence of Caples and then Hoehl, who injured his knee in the game. Traynham, playing with a cast on his right hand, thanks to a broken finger, was also limited.

VPI went ahead in the second quarter on Warren Price's 14-yard touchdown pass to Terry Strock, then built a 13-0 halftime lead.

The Keydet offense didn't shift into gear until the fourth quarter. After a fourth-down sack of Price, VMI took over at the Tech 32 and drove in with Morrison scoring over right guard from eight yards with 12:45 remaining. However, the extra point attempt failed, and Tech still had a seven point lead.

Dyer took VMI 80 yards in 20 plays for another score, his eight-yard bullet finding Willard in the end zone with just 63 seconds left. Dyer put both arms in the air – McKenna's signal for going for two points – and he turned to see McKenna signaling the same way.

"I went back to throw a pass, and I didn't see anybody open," recalled Dyer years later of the conversion play. "I tried to run around the right side to get in, and I was tackled on the one-yard line by Charlie Speck from

Virginia Tech. I never forgot how disappointed I felt. We had already won the (Southern) championship, but I certainly didn't want to lose there, and I have always felt guilty because I didn't find a way to get that ball in the end zone."

Speck tossed Dyer to the green-dyed dirt in Victory Stadium, and the Keydet rally came up short. The *Roanoke World News* highlighted those two combatants in an interesting anecdote immediately following that fateful play:

Charlie Speck, Tech's big junior end, had just bear-hugged Howard Dyer to earth as the great VMI quarterback attempted to run to his right for the vital extra points after finding his receivers covered.

Speck and Dyer walked back up the field together and shook hands along the way. What were they talking about? Was Speck gloating over the fact his play had ensured a Tech triumph? Was Dyer losing his temper at the heartbreaking defeat?

Not with these two warriors, who in the heat of battle showed their true colors.

'I just told him that he might have missed the extra points,' Speck explained later in the Tech dressing room, 'but he was still a great ball player.'

Speck said Dyer simply replied, 'Thank you, sir.'

Into his late 60s, Dyer said he still thought of that play, even dreamt of it. "I'm still not over it," he said.

McKenna had no qualms about going for the win instead of a tie. "We had to go for the two-point play at the end," he said. "Nothing was to be gained by not trying for it."

The veteran coach admitted that the fact that his Keydets had already wrapped up the Southern Conference title made it easier to "go for broke" in pursuit of the Big Five crown.

Dyer called the play, which McKenna endorsed after the game, on the field. Quarterbacks worked from a game plan drawn up by the coaches, but they often called the plays on the field themselves.

Players from that era observed that one-platoon football was more a player's game than a coach's game.

With a couple of smart, quick-on-their feet (and at VMI, just plain quick) players with a cerebral coach, who could prepare them for all contingencies... well, then you had something special. It was the McKenna Era at VMI.

"He trusted me and my judgment," said Dyer. "Coach King and I would talk, and he would often script the first two or three plays (of the game). After that we were on our own."

Dyer admitted that, true to his "Mississippi Gambler" nickname, he was "prone to gamble more than Coach McKenna," but he didn't change the plays McKenna and King told him to run. Deep on his own end of the field, Dyer was even more careful in his calls, especially avoiding throws down the middle that could be tipped and intercepted.

"You didn't cross Coach McKenna," he said. "If I pulled anything like that, I wouldn't have gone back on the field."

Peay recalled Dyer's cool under fire and the great faith McKenna had in him to call the proper plays. "I remember Howard having a career day against Boston College, and there was just a little time remaining in the first half. Howard said, 'Coach, I've got it.' Lord knows none of the rest of us could have ever said that to Coach McKenna."

Mitchell, the backup quarterback, remembered that Clark King, McKenna's longtime backfield coach, actually diagrammed the plays and set the strategy, especially with the quarterbacks. "Coach McKenna was behind the scenes setting the game plan with his assistant coaches but we dealt more directly with them. He let them do their job, and as a quarterback, most of my direct coaching was done by Coach King. But you knew that (McKenna's) hands were on the game plan."

The bond between coaches and players, a trust forged on the football field and within the structure of day-to-day life at VMI, was a factor in the team's success. "I felt like Coach McKenna and I were on the same page," said Dyer. Dyer and the other backs also had a great rapport with King. "Clark King was a fantastic offensive coach," said Dyer. "He knew defenses. He knew who to attack. He knew the strategy of helping quarterbacks succeed. He would point out certain tendencies, and he was invaluable. He worked with me for hours."

King and Dyer watched endless film, and King worked with Dyer daily, honing his mechanics.

That work paid off, and the honors rolled in for VMI following the season, Dyer, Kern and Shuba all named First Team All-Southern Conference. Dyer was tabbed SC Player of the Year for the 7-2-1 Keydets, and Shuba won the Conference's coveted Jacobs Blocking Trophy. Dyer led the Conference in scoring with 72 points, and Kern was second with 68. Willard, Jones, Haeberlein and Badgett all earned second team All-Conference honors, and McKenna lauded Dyer and Badgett for their leadership.

Jones led the Keydets in rushing (82 carries for 289 yards) and receiving

(26 receptions for 394 yards). Dyer set school and Southern Conference records with 87 completions in 168 passing attempts for 1,222 yards. Although his 1,478 yards of total offense was bested by Billy Holsclaw's Southern Conference record, Dyer's passing yardage broke his own record.

Dyer, who played in the North-South game in Miami, and the Senior Bowl in Mobile, Alabama, was named the Outstanding Football Player in Virginia and won the Sportsman of the Year Award in the Southern Conference.

During his career, VMI only lost three games with Dyer at the helm, and one of those was to powerful Penn State. In 1999, Dyer was named to the *Richmond Times-Dispatch*'s All-Century team for the state of Virginia.

The United Press International All-America team featured Heisman Trophy winner Joe Bellino of Navy as the leading vote-getter, but Dyer was Honorable Mention. The first team included future football household names like Ernie Davis of Syracuse, Bob Lilly of TCU and Mike Ditka of Pitt.

Eighteen professional teams contacted Dyer, and he was drafted by the New York Titans, but wound up playing more military football. In 1964, he was selected the outstanding quarterback of U.S. Army field teams throughout the world. However, he decided on law school after the Army and became a highly successful trial lawyer in his hometown of Greenville, Mississippi.

1960 (7-2-1)

Southern Conference Champions

DATE	VMI	LOCATION	OPP
S 17	33	at William & Mary	21
S 24	28	at Buffalo	14
O 1	21	Richmond	6
O 7	34	at George Washington	10
O 15	30	at Virginia	16
O 22	14	at Boston College	14
O 29	8	at Memphis State	21
N 5	18	Lehigh	14
N 12	20	at The Citadel	6
N 24	12	Virginia Tech (Roanoke)	13

CHAPTER ELEVEN

THANKSGIVING FEASTS AND A FOURTH SOUTHERN CONFERENCE CHAMPIONSHIP

The college football landscape, particularly in the Commonwealth, was changing by 1961. First, neighboring Washington & Lee had officially dropped out of the scholarship football arms race, leaving the state five major college teams. Second, the biggest schools, Virginia Tech and Virginia, both introduced new coaches in 1961. At Tech, it was Jerry Claiborne, a master of fundamentals and defense who would usher in a new era in Blacksburg. In Charlottesville, it was Bill Elias, who would last four seasons and win 16 games.

In the Southern Conference, defending champion VMI had 18 letter winners back but none up front in what certainly was McKenna's most pressing concern as practice opened that August.

Meanwhile it was another wall making international headlines. East Germany erected the Berlin Wall that month, to halt the flood of refugees to the West.

McKenna wanted to find the pieces to rebuild his front wall. "We sustained heavy losses up front through the graduation of five starters," he said. "Our line is particularly thin at guard and tackle, and we will be forced to rely on untried sophomores to provide second unit depth."

Experts were saying the league was as wide open as it had been since the Atlantic Coast Conference split off in 1953. VMI and Virginia Tech looked a little weaker, and The Citadel and Furman looked a little stronger. Young *Roanoke Times* assistant sports editor Bill Brill wrote: "The Keydets still lay claim to the SC's most versatile back in towhead Stinson Jones, demon on defense and an accomplished runner. The backfield, even without Dyer and Kern is solid, but like a certain cigarette (Winston), it's what's up front that counts. What's up front in Lexington is a big, big question mark."

And if you were going to compare the Keydets with cigarettes, you'd have to say they were lights. With the rest of college football bulking up, VMI had just 12 players, out of 58, at preseason drills that weighed 200 pounds or more. While substitution rules were becoming a little more liberal each year, McKenna was looking at a depth chart minus six 1960 starters who played both ways.

Most significantly, senior Bobby Mitchell, who had been understudying for Dyer the past two seasons, would move in as starting quarterback. Dyer had left huge cleats to fill. He had been fifth in the country in total offense, led VMI to 10th nationally in passing, and had won more accolades than any Keydet football player ever.

Joe Bush, who would join the varsity the following year, recalled Mitchell's toughness. "Bobby Mitchell didn't look like a quarterback. He was sort of heavyset, but he was a real competitor, and he could get it done."

McKenna was hoping that observation was true of his entire team in 1961.

Rising sophomores Mark Mulrooney and Butch Nunnally would back Mitchell. First Classman Binnie Peay was also trying to get into the mix. Nunnally had been a scholastic All-American at Richmond's Manchester High School and was a dual threat runner and passer. Delaware native Mulrooney was showing promise as a poised and accurate thrower. Peay, who could move the team, would go on to demonstrate significant leadership skills in the United States Army, retiring as a four-star General and head of the U.S. Central Command in 1997. After becoming a Director and Chairman & CEO of Allied Defense Group, he returned to his alma mater in 2003, becoming the school's 14th Superintendent, a position he still holds as this book is published.

Mitchell said practices were more democratic, particularly among the signal-callers, than most fans knew. "Now you hear about teams where the first team quarterback is getting all the reps (practice repetitions), but you couldn't do that back then. Because you knew it wasn't just going to be that first team quarterback or first team end or whatever that would be in there the whole game. If you substituted you would be out for a period of time."

Along with Mitchell, the rest of the backfield was star-studded. Jones had 36 catches in 1960 and might have been an All-American at a larger school, with that kind of production and more of a spotlight. Traynham, slowed by injuries the previous fall, after a spectacular sophomore season, was healthy and again the kind of broken-field runner who inspired pretty prose from the sportswriters with his daring moves. He had been second in the nation, with a 24.6-yard average, on punt returns the previous season.

They were, as *The Roanoke Times* said, a couple of "three-year regulars… that may be the best under McKenna. From the standpoint of speed, experience, depth, they may be the finest array of offensive and defensive operatives in the Mid-Atlantic area."

Kenny Reeder, the 175-pound "pass-catching sensation" of the previous season, was back, as were DeWitt Worrell and Randy Campbell. Spring game standout Andy Tucker, from Cocoa, Florida, was up from a quick-striking freshman team, as were Chuck Beale, Tracy Hunter, and Pete Mazik.

At fullback, the hope was that 185-pound Pat Morrison could stay healthy, while sophomores Bill Davis and Doug Walker held promise. Walker was likely to line up primarily on defense, like veteran Butch Armistead. Dick Willard, J.R. Dunkley, Ken Legum, and Bob Modarelli manned the ends.

New line coach Bo Sherman, formerly the head coach at George Washington, had the biggest challenge, piecing together respectable units from some leftover parts and an array of newcomers. At tackle, 238-pound John Candler was back, and he and 205-pound Bill Hoehl were the only returning lettermen on the line. Center Fred Shirley was moving to guard to lend some experience there, and 212-pound Gil Minor looked encouraging, as well. The center spot was up for grabs, a battle from the spring between senior Dennis Merklinger and sophomore Bill Tornabene spilling over into the summer camp.

Another candidate, Richmond senior Cliff Miller, was out for the season with a dislocated vertebra suffered in a recent swimming accident.

McKenna looked out over a team that lost 15 letter winners, who had lost only five games in four years and pronounced that the Keydets would play a wide-open style, stressing passing and speed. "If the center position generally and a couple of sophomores come through, we'll have a pretty good football team," said the coach. "And we're still the champs until they beat us."

Sherman, so long on the outside looking in at VMI, and now on the inside, was starting to understand more of what made these Keydets special. One thing that stood out to him was simply all that speed in the backfield. "I remember his talking about it after one of the practices," recalled Sessoms. "He said, 'I knew VMI had speed, but I didn't know we had this kind of speed.' Just watching Jones and Traynham in the early practices was like watching lightning."

Meanwhile, another blistering hot summer was causing the already light team to shed more weight each day. McKenna went to more night practices and began tapering back in advance of the September 16 opener at Marshall, a team that outweighed the Keydets at nearly every spot.

"It should be a most interesting season," said McKenna. "Last year we felt like we could beat everyone we played. This year we just don't know."

The Keydets got some answers in the opener in Huntington, West Virginia. A hard-fought defensive struggle turned into a 33-6 rout in the second half thanks to that stellar Big Red defense. Morrison's three-yard run put the Keydets ahead early, but Marshall closed to 8-6 in the third period.

Following Marshall's score, some of that lightning struck. The speedy Traynham took the kickoff back 90 yards for a score, and, soon after, Stinson Jones ran an interception back 42 yards for a 20-6 lead. Dick Thompson wrote in the *Richmond Times-Dispatch* that VMI responded "with all the indignant fury of a Southern gentleman who had just been slapped in the face."

Reeder turned a fourth quarter interception into a touchdown, and then his 62-yard punt return set up Nunnally's three-yard scoring run as the defending Southern Conference champs opened with a convincing win.

McKenna, though, was not convinced about what he had yet. "Although we came up with the big play repeatedly on defense, we did not move the ball with the same alacrity and consistency which have been the VMI hallmarks in recent years. It might be attributable to first game crudeness, the preponderance of sophomores who played, or the improvement of the Marshall team over two years ago. It's too early to tell at this point, but after the Villanova game, we will have a clearer picture."

The next week, returning to McKenna's alma mater, the VMI offense struggled, and a big, strong Villanova squad blanked the Keydets 22-0 in Philadelphia. In 90-degree heat, the Wildcats took advantage of two VMI fumbles in rapid succession in the second quarter to go on top 16-0. Villanova's size and depth wore down the young Keydets.

Villanova added a second half score on an interception. Jones had three interceptions for the Keydets and ran well on offense, but that unit never got going, as VMI fell to 1-1. In front of several pro scouts – and McKenna was convinced Jones was a pro prospect – Jones had 31 of VMI's 58 rushing yards and 63 of the Keydets' 75 passing yards on four catches. He also stood out on defense.

This was the first time VMI had been shutout since the second game of 1959, when the Keydets fell at Penn State.

Mitchell and the passing game had yet to take wing, with the senior hitting just 6 of 21 tosses and throwing four interceptions. McKenna's homecoming, which included a matchup with second-year Villanova coach Alex Bell, a teammate of his when both played for the Wildcats, was a disaster.

Years later, Sessoms recalled that day as a prime example of how patched in Herb Patchin was to the Keydets. "Herb had a feeling about trips," said Sessoms. "You know, he always had a feeling about our football team before a game. He said, 'This is going to be a bad day because we're just not ready and I feel it.' And sure enough, we didn't play well, and they beat the living daylights out of us."

That loss was particularly galling for McKenna, who had lots of friends in attendance. "John hated to lose to Villanova," recalled Sessoms.

And McKenna didn't let it stand. Displeased with the "gold team" or the starters, McKenna made some changes in practice that week, promoting some sophomores and a non-lettered senior. Up front, center Bill Tornabene and guard Del Black earned their first starts, and halfback Chuck Beale also moved up. The veteran guard J.W. Price moved in, and DeWitt Worrell replaced Morrison at fullback.

Worrell had walked on as a Rat (freshman). Peay recalled he and Worrell tried out in boots and fatigues. McKenna kept two or three freshmen that first fall. Worrell wasn't one of them, but he would make the team the next year and become a starter by his First Class year.

Nunnally moved up to the blue team or second unit, taking some of the heat off Mitchell, who had been quarterbacking the first two teams. Mitchell's passing had been a little off so far, and Nunnally was a better runner and punter.

McKenna had been effusive in his praise of Mitchell before the season, calling him a "clever runner and field general" and praising his play-calling.

"We don't expect any step-down in our quarterbacks. Mitchell is very intelligent and a good play-caller. He'll give us a better called game than any quarterback we've had."

While not all Mitchell's fault, the offense wasn't producing at the pace the coaching staff had expected, and changes were being made as the team prepared for Richmond, a squad they hadn't lost to since 1955.

"We have been disappointed in the play of our seniors, while the sophomores, about whom we had some reservations before the season started have been performing well," said McKenna, making the changes to send a message to the team that no more such efforts like that at Villanova would be tolerated.

It was again VMI's defense at the forefront of another victory, this one in the Southern Conference opener at Richmond by a harrowing 8-6 count. Andy Tucker intercepted a Spider pass in the end zone and carried the pigskin all the way back 102 yards for a score, on the game's biggest play.

"Andy Tucker, a fine prospect from Florida, plucked the ball from the air and returned it the entire length of the field," wrote McKenna. "It was a brilliant run displaying the fleetness of foot and alertness of this youngster, who is also president of his class as well as a fine athlete."

Mitchell hit Bob Modarelli for the two-point conversion, and the Keydets would make that score stand up, even after Richmond recovered a fumble at the VMI 17 when Nunnally dropped a punt snap. Four plays later, the Spiders scored on a bootleg pass, but Morrison broke up the conversion pass attempt.

Morrison, Jones, and hard-hitting Ken Legum led the sterling VMI defensive effort, while the Keydet backs, particularly Jones, were noted for their physical play. Traynham helped keep the ball away from the Spiders with his efforts on the ground ,but penalties nagged VMI all game. Richmond ran 85 plays to VMI's 52, and outgained the Keydets 299-152.

McKenna pointed to the "hidden yardage" which helped VMI win – the long interception return and punt and kickoff yards, which fans often overlook in combing through the box scores.

Mitchell was 1 for 7 passing, and VMI again failed to sustain drives. So far this season, only one VMI touchdown had come on a long march. Still, the Keydets were alive in the Southern Conference title chase, tied with Virginia Tech at 1-0 in conference and chasing 2-0 Furman in the standings.

There was some excitement the following week, October 7, at George Washington. VMI helped open the new $20-million, 50,000-seat District of Columbia Stadium (later to become RFK Stadium) on a sun-swept afternoon, but host George Washington was rough on the visitors from the south, pounding out a 30-6 victory.

The Colonials scored after a VMI fumble on the Keydets' first possession, and the entire second quarter was played in Keydet territory. GW notched another touchdown pass by Bill Hardy for a 12-0 halftime lead before the crowd of 25,000.

GW continued to control the contest in the second half, consistently able to move the chains on third down with a frustratingly efficient passing attack that accounted for four scores. VMI's Mitchell finally passed the Keydets down the field for a late touchdown, pitching to Jones on a fourth-and-one play at the goal line. Peay had his best day in relief of Mitchell.

"Although the performance of the team was disappointing, we are not discouraged and feel that from this group a good football team will emerge," wrote McKenna to the boosters. "How soon is the big question mark?"

It was the Colonials' first win over VMI since 1956, and it was now becoming apparent that 2-2 VMI wasn't the team they were a year ago. That notion, took root in newspaper stories around the state and picked up momentum when Virginia beat VMI 14-7, in Norfolk, also the Cavaliers' first win over the Keydets since 1956.

VMI started out like gangbusters, blocking and running like never before, at least this season. They scored the first time they got the ball. Mitchell put together the team's best drive of the year, leading VMI 73 yards in seven plays. Beale crashed in for a six-yard score, and Mitchell's extra point kick made it 7-0.

Virginia came right back, though, marching 67 yards in 14 plays to tie the game on quarterback Stan Fischer's two-yard run. They then added a 10-play, 75-yard scoring drive to take the lead in the second quarter. That drive began after a controversial fourth-down spot left the Keydets short of a first down deep in Cavalier territory. Fischer then hit Doug Thomson for a 13-yard score just 1:01 before the half.

Twice in the fourth quarter VMI was denied. Mitchell drove the Keydets into Virginia territory, but was intercepted at the 28. In the closing minutes, he guided the team 69 yards, only to have his pass intercepted in the end zone, when it glanced off Reeder's fingertips with 57 seconds left. Mitchell hit 10-of-26 passes for 136 yards in the 14-7 setback, but VMI had now dropped to 2-3, halfway through the season.

"Our young Keydets played their best football of the season, and we hope that we have started to move along the comeback trail," McKenna wrote. "Our overall play was much improved, and we displayed our best offense of the year. Virginia overpowered us at the tackles which was the big difference. They also came up with the big play on third down which enabled them to retain possession. This as much as any other single factor displays the inexperience of the third classmen who are seeing so much time."

McKenna went to work on the team's bruised psyche that week in practices, and the Keydets snapped their two-game losing streak with another great defensive effort at Davidson, in a 13-0 win on a grey afternoon.

"He made it so we never felt pressure to perform," recalled Willard. "We wanted to please Coach McKenna and the coaches because they invested their time with us. But, as a player, I didn't feel pressure. I think we all had camaraderie. I think we all had mutual respect. We were all good students. Of that team, I think five went to graduate school, and four became physicians."

One of those future physicians, Willard, came up with the right prescription in the third quarter. After a scoreless first half, he recovered a fumble at the Davidson 7-yard line. Three plays later, "Dee" Worrell powered his way in for a touchdown. Nunnally's precision punt out of bounds at the four-yard line had set up the scoring sequence.

With Nunnally's punting keeping the Wildcats pinned deep, the Keydets ran out the clock late, as Morrison capped a 60-yard drive with a one-yard run on the final play of the game. Nunnally averaged 39 yards on a whopping 10 punts, and the Keydets had won in their old, opportunistic style, improving to 2-1 in the conference and evening their record overall.

"We are not overjoyed by the team's performance, although we are the first of Davidson's opponents to shut them out and hold them to less than 200 yards offense," McKenna wrote. "Our third classmen (sophomores) are continuing to improve in most departments, and one of these fall afternoons they could come of age."

The offense still wasn't firing on all cylinders, but McKenna attributed that problem to Davidson's tricky, stunting defense that often confused his young line. Injuries were taking a toll, too. The big tackle Candler was out with torn knee ligaments, Traynham and Worrell had banged-up ankles, and Jones left the game with a neck injury. "Tiger," as his teammates called Jones, had played with sore ribs all season and regularly took a beating down near the goal line, where he was a ferocious blocker on offense. He led the team in scoring, rushing, receiving, and in interceptions.

The Keydets next picked up a crucial conference road win with a solid 14-7 victory at William & Mary. Nunnally came off the bench to complete 6-of-14 passes for 67 yards and a touchdown to help VMI improve to 3-1 in the Southern Conference. Trailing 7-0 in the second quarter, the Keydets got a break when Gil Minor recovered a fumble. Nunnally came on and tossed a nine-yard touchdown pass to Tucker, but the Keydets missed the extra point.

After the second half kickoff, Nunnally guided the team 59 yards and went over from the one himself to put the Keydets ahead. He then passed to Traynham, who made a one-handed, circus catch for the two-point conversion. Reeder's one-handed catch for an 18-yard gain had already kept the drive alive on a 4th-and-12 play.

The Indians drove 64 yards in the closing minutes of the game, quarterback Dan Henning hitting four passes for 39 yards. A pass interference penalty and one for unnecessary roughness, both against VMI, aided the march. The roughness penalty was particularly unpleasant for McKenna, who offered after the game, "I am not enamored of the job done by the referees."

Doug Walker saved the day with an interception of Henning with 25 seconds remaining, corralling the ball that at one point was behind his back as he tried to catch it. "How he caught the ball I don't know," said a chagrined Milt Drewer, the William & Mary coach.

"Once again the Soldiers beat the Indians just as they do in the TV Westerns," McKenna joked in his newsletter.

The win, improving VMI to 4-3 overall and 3-1 in the Southern Conference, set up a huge showdown with The Citadel (5-2, 4-1) the following week. McKenna announced that Nunnally, who had played so well at William & Mary, would start at quarterback.

For the third straight season, The Citadel needed a win over VMI, this time in Lexington, to win the Southern Conference crown. The Keydets had won the last two meetings and Bulldogs coach Eddie Teague was wary even though he had his best team.

"This is a typical VMI team," he said. "When we use that term down here, we mean fast, rangy and well-coached. They may not run from as many offensive formations as some other teams we play, but everything they do, they do well. If you don't play your best game, you don't beat VMI."

Experts were still scratching their heads as to how these two teams had met at the apex of the Southern. In the conference statistics, VMI was seventh in total defense, and The Citadel ranked last. VMI was last in rushing offense, and The Citadel was eighth. In fact, VMI was last in total offense but had shown a stubborn ability to win close games, an ability their fellow military school combatants to the south shared.

This big game was so anticipated – the one and only home game for the nomadic Keydets this season – that Washington & Lee's Wilson Field was augmented with 2,500 bleacher seats and a special 45-seat platform was built for Citadel superintendent General Mark Clark, pushing capacity to 6,800. Five hundred and fifty Citadel cadets arrived by train that Saturday, and somehow, attendance came to be listed at 9,000.

The lack of a "real" home football stadium, until 1962, and thus its proliferation of road games, cannot be overemphasized. In what would now be considered football suicide, during McKenna's 13 seasons at VMI, his teams had 24 home games (that's less than two per season), 32 games at neutral sites, and 74 away games…and there were only 10 games on the schedule in those days.

The Citadel had a lot to cheer at the end when quarterback Bill Whaley led the Bulldogs 79 yards. He hit Henry Mura for a 22-yard score with just 2:30 left for a 14-8 lead.

The gutty Keydets weren't done, though. Mitchell completed three long passes, hitting Reeder for 19, then Jones for 19, and finally, Willard for 13. With 1:39 left and the ball at the 14, it looked like Mitchell had found Reeder for the winning score, but Reeder had to leap and came down just out of bounds beyond the end zone. Mitchell's fourth-down pass to Traynham picked up just a yard and left VMI short of the first down and their third straight conference crown.

Mitchell was 8-of-15 for 78 yards and had a touchdown off the bench. VMI had no offensive punch in the first half and trailed 7-0 but looked like a new team in second half. Mitchell took the Keydets 75 yards in 16 plays after the kickoff, hitting Reeder for an eight-yard score midway through the third quarter.

The Roanoke Times described VMI taking the lead:

Despite the VMI cannon misfiring while the extra point play was in progress, and despite a heavy haze cast on the field from VMI-colored smoke bombs, VMI's Pat Morrison slipped over for the two extra points and an 8-7 lead.

But with the late score, The Citadel got a measure of revenge, claiming the Southern Conference championship from VMI with a win in Lexington, much the way the Keydets had taken the title in Charleston the year before.

"It was a tough one to lose but the Keydets went down gallantly. Returning alumni could feel nothing but pride for the outstanding job the Big Red did," wrote McKenna.

There was more bad news, though, with the loss of sophomore guard Bill Black, who broke his ankle in the first quarter. "This youngster has been one of the bulwarks of our team's play throughout the season, and we foresee for him a place among VMI's best linemen," wrote McKenna.

A tough week continued with the VMI freshman team falling to Virginia Tech's junior varsity in the 11th annual Shrine Bowl in Roanoke's Victory Stadium. The "Kiddets'" high-powered offense, averaging 348 yards per game, was stymied by a Tech team that out-weighed them 20-pounds per man up front.

The "Gobblets" kept quarterback Charlie Snead, younger brother of Norm, then the Washington Redskins' quarterback, under wraps, also limiting the speedy backfield of Donny White, Granville Amos and Dale Boyd in a 14-6 Tech triumph.

On a brighter note, the VMI varsity found its offense the next Saturday at Buffalo in a 39-6 victory over the Bulls. Mitchell set three school records. The civil engineering major from Alexandria had five touchdown passes, 349 yards passing, and 344 yards of total offense, all Southern Conference records as well.

Mitchell broke Dave Woolwine's 1954 record of four touchdown tosses against The Citadel, and it all came to pass as part of McKenna's plan. "We knew we could throw on them," said the coach. "With their line massed in tight to stop our inside running, they had to give us room in other areas."

Assistant coach Weenie Miller had scouted Buffalo twice that season, and McKenna gave him much of the credit for coming up with the plan. Often, Reeder lined up at split end, and Jones went in motion to the opposite side. Buffalo had trouble matching up, out-flanked by the shifty and shifting Keydets.

"We had Stinson Jones and Johnny Trayhnam as running backs, and we played the system, but sometimes we would have two in the backfield, and one of the two would be spilt as wide receiver," Mitchell recalled years later. "They both had such speed. Dee Worrell was a small guy and played fullback, but he was really tough. Kenny Reeder was a year behind us and was very fast and a good receiver. We were always known for our speed back then."

Minor blocked an attempted quick kick to set up the first score, and two plays later Mitchell hit Reeder from nine yards out for a touchdown. Mitchell then marched the team 86 yards, capping the drive with a 13-yard pass to Jones. Later, Mitchell's 50-yard scoring pass to Reeder made it 26-0 at halftime.

Jones had three touchdown catches, Reeder two, and the long-awaited offensive explosion finally arrived, the Keydets hoping in time to salvage a winning season. Mitchell was 20 of 38, and VMI rolled to 472 total yards and 22 first downs. McKenna had third and fourth-stringers in the entire fourth quarter and exalted in Mitchell "buffaloing" the University of Buffalo with "the peak performance" in his career.

Bill Hoehl, Jack Boyda, and Conrad Davis excelled up front on the offensive line, and fullbacks Doug Walker and Bill Davis also played well.

The Keydets now looked ahead to Thanksgiving in Roanoke, and a game that, while not for any championships, would decide if VMI finished with a winning record or not. They received a little incentive in the week leading up to the game, a plane flying over the Institute dropped "pamphlets" on the campus predicting a score of "VPI 65, VMI 0."

"I can only say that I believe we can do a little better than that," McKenna told the Roanoke Touchdown Club at the Hotel Roanoke the Monday before the Thursday game.

McKenna was more concerned about how many Keydets had missed the second half of the season. He was still without Candler, the biggest player on either team, and Bill Black, who broke his ankle against The Citadel. Sophomore fullback Bill Davis of Rocky Mount, a solid linebacker, was moving to guard to replace Black for the Tech game.

When November 23 came, it was another rainy Thanksgiving but the Keydets were all smiles at the end of the day. That stingy defense recorded a 6-0 shutout over the rival Gobblers on a muddy Victory Stadium field as 20,000 braved the elements to observe the spectacle and the pregame pageantry.

The two teams combined for just 254 yards of offense. VMI moved the ball early but came up empty. In the second quarter, though, McKenna resorted to a little trickery. With wide receiver Reeder lined up at halfback, Reeder took a pitch from Mitchell and then threw to Jones for the game's lone score, a 15-yard touchdown pass. It was Reeder's first career passing attempt.

"We saw in the scouting reports that their backs came up fast," said Reeder. "I was worried to death that I couldn't grip the ball. I saw Stinson out there, and I just tried to loft it over the head of the defensive back."

VMI had six legitimate scoring chances and controlled the action all day, but as the field became such a quagmire, offensive success was defined in the smallest of terms. "Players became mud-splattered non-entities within minutes," wrote Bill Brill in *The Roanoke Times*.

VMI's defense held Tech to minus-one yard, no first downs and no pass completions in the first half, and things didn't get a lot better in the second half. The Gobblers finished with 74 yards and four first downs. Neither team could score as the field became more and more unmanageable. VMI drove inside the Tech 10 after recovering a fumble, but couldn't add an insurance score.

Mitchell was 9 for 21 for 73 yards with the wet ball, and said he could feel the ball slide across teammate's jerseys every time he handed off. "Mitchell's performance was phenomenal under the conditions," said McKenna. "It was a wonderful job."

"It was a downpour the whole game," said Mitchell years later. "It's the wettest I have been my whole life. By the end of the game when I would take a snap from center, it would slip up and I'd catch it with my belly."

McKenna thought it was the defense's best effort of the year, and the season-ending victory caused smiles all around, even after the muddy Keydets found out they didn't have any clean towels for showers. "We used all of them to keep the ball clean," laughed McKenna.

VMI finished 6-4, in what had to be considered another remarkable effort. While the Keydet offense scored 72 points against Marshall and Buffalo, they hammered out just 62 against the rest of the schedule and still managed to win four of the last five games to post a winning slate. No VMI players earned first or second team All-Southern honors, though Gil Minor and Stinson Jones were honorable mention picks.

Jones's 60 carries for 256 yards led the Keydets in rushing on the season, and Mitchell was 69 of 162, for 949 yards to pace the passing attack. Reeder had 26 catches for 323 yards as the top receiver, a fine accomplishment under any circumstance but more impressive because Reeder was a diabetic. There weren't any famous football players, who were diabetic at the time, and in athletics, only tennis stars Bill Talbert and Hamilton Richardson had really enjoyed any athletic success while battling the disease.

Overall though, the Keydets as a team were coming off their worst season in five years, a season made acceptable only by the Thanksgiving victory over Virginia Tech. VMI claimed the Big Five crown for the fourth time in nine years and posted a fifth consecutive winning season, something the Keydets hadn't done since 1891-1895.

In the moment, just the win over Virginia Tech, a team that was starting to come into its own under Claiborne, was sufficient, though McKenna implored the Sportsmen's Club to invest in VMI football so the Keydets could keep pace in the future, and enjoy more moments like this one.

"The win was gratifying as only a win over Tech can be," he wrote. "And all evidence to the contrary as far as rain drenched and mud caked clothes were concerned, for me the sun shone brightly as I am sure it did for many VMI folk who were present."

"That was really the highlight, to finish your career with a win over Tech," said Mitchell, named the game's outstanding player.

1961 (6-4)

DATE	VMI	LOCATION	OPP
S 16	33	at Marshall	6
S 23	0	at Villanova	22
S 29	8	at Richmond	6
O 7	6	at George Washington	30
O 14	7	Virginia (Norfolk)	14
O 21	13	at Davidson	0
O 28	14	at William & Mary	7
N 4	8	The Citadel	14
N 11	39	at Buffalo	6
N 23	6	Virginia Tech (Roanoke)	0

Now, McKenna faced another reclamation project with 17 lettermen graduated and just three regulars returning in 1962. Only five lettered seniors were back and while the Keydets lacked beef up front on the line, the schedule had been beefed up to include Boston College and Holy Cross instead of Marshall and Buffalo.

More media and football fans were recognizing the consistently solid teams that McKenna was producing in the foothills of Southwest Virginia, and they weren't the only ones. Boston College had pursued McKenna in 1961, hoping to bring him north, but he stayed on post, speculation said the cost of living in Boston and his friendly relations with the Virginia media helped keep him in the south. Of course, it was the Virginia media making such speculation. They were indeed enamored of McKenna's stylish coaching and quotable nature in a difficult, disadvantaged circumstance.

Fred Russell, a columnist for *The Nashville Banner* for 68 years, profiled VMI's success and adherence to time-honored traditions on the eve of the 1962 season, offering this portrait of life on post:

(A VMI football player) lives in the barracks, eats in the mess hall and goes to the same classes. The entire cadet corps is up and out for breakfast at 7 a.m. every morning. Following breakfast, there are 20 minutes in which cadets must clean their rooms and have them ready for room inspection later in the morning.

Classes begin at 8 a.m., and run through 1 p.m. – five one-hour class periods. Usually 3 classes during this period, study (during) others. Lunch is at 1:00, mandatory check formation for all cadets. At 2:00, there's a 2-hour class period for lab or field work. At 4:00, every day except Wednesday, Saturday and Sunday, there's military instruction. One afternoon each week there is formal military inspection of all cadets and equipment. On Sunday, all cadets go to church. Saturdays are free for all cadets except football players. Of 33 football players last season, ten majored in civil engineering, nine in history, five each in English and biology (pre-med), two in electrical engineering, and one each in physics and mathematics.

As construction continued on a major Alumni Field expansion and summer practices opened, it looked like junior Butch Nunnally would take over as first team quarterback and handle the punting. Chuck Beale, Andy Tucker and Bill Davis, back at fullback after the brief move to guard, would join Nunnally in the backfield. Ken Reeder, a co-captain, and up-and-coming sophomore Joe Bush lined up at the ends.

Both Bill Welsh and Conrad Davis, who barely tipped the scales at 200 pounds, looked like the tackles. Bill Black and Gil Minor, also a co-captain, were back at the guard slots, and Charlie Cole and Bill Tornabene were at center, considered the strongest position on the team.

Minor, sophomore tackle Bob Lee, and guard Bill Hughes were the largest players on the team, each at 215 pounds. The first line averaged just 197 pounds and would be among the lightest in the Southern Conference.

Sophomores Charlie Snead at quarterback and Donny White at halfback looked like they could provide some immediate help. And the Keydets could use as much help as possible, as college football was again changing.More and more substitutions were allowed, and many teams were now playing "three-platoon" football, the best 11 players on a first unit, but the next 22 broken into separate offensive and defensive units.

The Keydets didn't have that kind of manpower nor, now, much name recognition. McKenna said this was a team without stars, and that was just fine with him. "That's the way we like it. Were I given a choice, I'd take the Southern Conference title over four players on the All-Southern every time."

So how did McKenna keep cobbling together winning teams? In a preseason interview with *Roanoke World News* sports editor Bob McClellan, he laid out some basics:

I think I would have to say that I am a good fundamentalist. There's no such thing as a miracle worker in football. You only succeed through hard work.

I believe it's much better to do a few things well than it is to try a lot of different things. We probably have fewer plays than any team on our schedule. But we change plays at the line about 60 percent of the time. There are a lot of reasons for this. First of all, we have been blessed with a group of smart boys. Then, since we have so few plays, they are able to master them better. Sometimes we see that we can do a certain thing during a game. But we won't try it unless we have worked on it that week.

The Keydets must have worked on special teams leading up to the season opener against George Washington, a couple of big plays in that realm sparking a 22-6 win in the Jaycee Bowl in Lynchburg. It was memorable not only for the surprisingly strong start for the young team, but it was also McKenna's 50th career win.

VMI scored to open the game, driving 52 yards, with Nunnally hitting Bush for a 7-yard score on a hook route. The Colonials tied the game in the second quarter, but VMI took control when Andy Tucker took the ensuing kickoff 86 yards for a touchdown. Tornabene had a big block (keeping Tucker "free from any molestation," McKenna wrote) on the big play, and Nunnally's two-point conversion made it 14-6.

Doug Walker came up with another important special teams play, blocking a punt that Bruce Leve recovered at the GW 45. Mark Mulrooney, now in at quarterback, hit Chuck Beale for 18 yards and then found Reeder for a three-yard score.

Bush, who had scored in his first varsity game, thought it was a precursor of things to come, but though he would lead the Keydets in receiving his junior and senior years, that amounted to just 38 total catches.

"That first game I caught a touchdown and thought, 'this is going to be great," he laughed. "But it wasn't to be. Coach McKenna's style wasn't to throw the ball much."

Bush and some of his fellow second-year men were also learning other things about their intimidating coach.

"He had a name for everybody," recalled Bush. "He called Donny White 'Whitey', he'd go, 'Yo, Whitey!' and if he said that you better hop to it and get over there. He always called me 'Joe Bush,' he never said 'Joe' or anything else."

McKenna may have wanted to use a few other choice names for players after the next game, a brutal loss to his alma mater. A powerful Villanova squad brought the Keydets down to earth with a convincing 24-0 win on a cloudy September 22, before 8,500 in Philadelphia. The defending Sun Bowl champions scored midway through the first quarter and led 10-0 at the half. They were never headed, as VMI couldn't match Villanova's size (a 26-pound average advantage per man on the line) or the Wildcats' polished attack.

A powerful line fueled the Wildcats' dominance, and VMI's lack of size was exposed. "Villanova did nothing offensively or defensively that we did not expect," wrote McKenna to the Sportsmen's Club. "Against us, they were not a fancy dan club, using no reverses or formations that we were not prepared to meet. The Wildcats' use of their plus factors, however, was perfect. Much of their yardage was gained on straight power plays off tackle and sweeping runs around end which, in effect, enabled them to blow us out of the stadium."

The Keydets had just two first downs, one in each half, amassing only 61 yards of total offense, the lowest output in school history. VMI punted a record 11 times. Despite the lopsided loss at his alma mater, McKenna didn't raise his voice after the game and concentrated on showing the Keydets their correctable mistakes in a long film session the following Monday.

McKenna's gentle motivation worked, as VMI bounced back with a 21-0 win at Richmond. After a scoreless first quarter, the Keydets began to assert themselves on the road as Bush and the defense dominated. VMI was playing a new "monster" defense this season, utilizing line stunts and a linebacker deployed to the wide side of the field. The gambling, blitzing scheme made for some exciting moments, mostly positive for the Big Red, particularly on this day.

Nunnally capped a 41-yard drive with a two-yard scoring run in the second quarter. Tackle Dave Kiger recovered a fumble deep in Spider territory, setting up speedy Donny White's 7-yard scamper in the third period.

White wasn't through. He gathered in an interception and zipped 63 yards to put the game away. That play was the cap on a superb defensive effort, with VMI holding Richmond to just 52 total yards while intercepting three passes and recovering three fumbles.

"The game films indicated our rangy linemen are becoming more adept in using the new penetrating defense we installed last summer," wrote McKenna. "End Joe Bush, tackles John Boyda and Bill Welsh, and centers Charlie Cole and Bill Tornabene were stand-out players."

That defense also helped the Keydets hang tough in a game at Boston College the following week, before VMI succumbed 18-0 to a big, undefeated BC squad. The game, but undersized, Keydets kept the contest close, trailing by just one score into the fourth quarter, the stunting defense often guessing right and plugging holes to contain the Eagles' rushing attack.

A wet, muddy track hurt the Keydet cause, their speed nullified against the Eagles' superior size. BC's quarterback Jack Concannon's second period 62-yard touchdown pass to Pete Shaughnessy was the only score until the fourth quarter. Concannon was the first selection in the 1963 AFL Draft by the Boston Patriots but chose the sign with the Philadelphia Eagles in the 1964 NFL Draft. He played three seasons with the Eagles and five with the Chicago Bears, ending his NFL career as a back-up with the Detroit Lions.

Leading 6-0, the Eagles got a 50-yard run from Harry "The Thump" Crump to change field position and set up a second touchdown. The VMI offense never shifted into gear, mustering just 110 yards, never penetrating the 35-yard line and losing two fumbles and two interceptions.

McKenna thought his team's immaturity played a factor. In particular, he said that defensive backs relaxed at inopportune moments, and the Keydets just missed a couple of opportunities to block punts and change the game's momentum. He hoped the maturation process would come quickly.

But it was more bad news on October 13, Virginia vanquishing VMI 28-6, thanks to a big day from quarterback Gary Cuozzo in Charlottesville.

Another future NFL signal-caller, Cuozzo was 11-of-18 for 180 yards. His quarterback sneak put the Cavaliers ahead early, and he passed for another score to make it 13-6 at the half. Cuozzo played ten years in the NFL, first as a back-up for Johnny Unitas and later as the inaugural starting quarterback for the expansion New Orleans Saints. He also played for the Minnesota Vikings and the Saint Louis Cardinals.

VMI's score came on a 20-yard Mark Mulrooney missile to Reeder. Mulrooney was 7-of-17 passing for 104 yards. Reeder had four receptions for 66 yards. Terry Sieg ran 33 yards for a third quarter Virginia touchdown, and the Cavaliers tacked on one more score in the fourth quarter for their second win of the year. VMI, which was flagged six times for 88 penalty yards, dropped to 2-3.

"As the interceptions stalled us and the penalties nullified several of our good gains, they in turn set up all four Virginia TDs," wrote McKenna. "Christmas came early at Charlottesville, and we played Santa Claus."

Hoping to snap a two-game losing streak, the Keydets returned to Lexington for the opening of their new $230,000 stadium at Alumni Field. The improvement was funded by an allocation from the Virginia General Assembly, designed by the Lynchburg engineering firm of Wiley & Wilson, and constructed in three months though not entirely complete on this opening date. Dressing rooms, a new press box and several ramps at the top still needed to be finished.

"It was pretty special," recalled Joe Bush. "It really was needed because we didn't have much of a stadium before those stands. It made it really nice to be able to play home games rather than go over to W&L."

The new stadium "home" side, 173 feet and 53 rows high, had seating for 7,286, and joined the existing 3,000 seats on the opposite side. The rock foundation grandstand was built into a sloped hillside and offered "spectator viewing unparalleled by any football stadium in the state."

From that view, VMI fans saw Bill Davis score three times, leading to a 20-7 win over Davidson. McKenna attacked the Davidson defense right up the middle, meaning a heavy workload for his 6-foot, 200-pound fullback, who rushed 18 times for 94 yards.

That was fine with Davis, whom *The Roanoke Times* described as "rugged (and) hitting harder than anyone on the team." McKenna sometimes struggled with how best to deploy this weapon, claiming Davis would be all-conference as a linebacker but "we cannot sacrifice him from the offense."

Davis would go down as one of the great fullbacks in school history, famous for his blocking and his bull-like runs up the gut of defenses that often knew he was coming and still couldn't stop him.

The Wildcats scored first, quarterback Kent Tucker sneaking in from a yard out, late in the first quarter. Mulrooney got the Keydets going, hitting Reeder for a couple of big gains on a 68-yard drive. Davis smashed over from the one, but the two-point pass failed, and VMI trailed 7-6 at the half.

Mulrooney found Reeder for 24 yards early in the third quarter, part of a quick 53-yard drive. Davis then bulled in from eight yards to put the Keydets ahead. The VMI defense put the game away, intercepting the Wildcats for the third time late in the contest. Tornabene came up with this pick at the Davidson 9-yard line, and three plays later, Davis again scored from the one. Nunnally and Rudy Amos also had interceptions to halt Davidson drives in VMI territory.

VMI also drew inspiration as trainer Herb Patchin returned to the sidelines for the first time this fall following his heart illness. The team gave him the game ball from the first contest in the new stadium.

Meanwhile, McKenna thought he could tweak the offense using Mulrooney more often, and he named him starting quarterback for the upcoming William & Mary game. "It's not so much of a demotion for Nunnally as a promotion for Mulrooney," McKenna told the media.

Playing at home for the second straight week, VMI was able to stay on top of the Southern Conference standings with a hard-fought 6-0 win over William & Mary before 4,000 fans.

VMI stopped the Indians and Dan Henning on downs in VMI territory in the first quarter. Early in the second quarter, a clip nullified Pete Mazik's 80-yard punt return for a score.

Bill Welsh recovered an Indian fumble at the 26, and Mazik got his score back, taking a pitch from Mulrooney and rambling for the game's only touchdown with eight minutes left in the half.

In a game that featured 17 punts, Henning drove William & Mary deep into VMI territory with just 50 seconds remaining but, McKenna's "Victory Defense" – with three men deep and one safety behind them to prevent the "home run" – held.

A couple of passes had moved the ball to the 11 yard-line, where the Keydets called timeout with 44 seconds left to settle themselves. The Indians were out of timeouts.

"Our kids are told to call time any time a team drives the ball like (the Indians) did," explained McKenna. "They had enough time to score anyway so the timeout didn't matter. We called time to regroup and it worked."

Tackle John Boyda and the VMI front got pressure on Henning. Charlie Cole batted down a pass, then Davis did the same. Henning was forced to run out of bounds on third down. On the deciding play, a W&M receiver broke open, but Nunnally appeared to come out of nowhere to bat the ball away.

Henning would go on to play quarterback for the AFL's San Diego Chargers and had a lengthy career in the NFL coaching ranks. He was offensive coordinator for six teams, including the Washington Redskins, winning two Super Bowl rings. He was head coach of the Atlanta Falcons (1983-86) and the San Diego Chargers (1989-91). His son Dan played quarterback for Bobby Ross at the University of Maryland.

McKenna said he was "pleased with the overall effort" but that this was "not the kind of game you get excited about."

What he was excited about was VMI's 4-0 mark in the Southern Conference.

"We are surprised like everyone else," he offered.

The Keydets took to the road for another conference contest, traveling to Charleston, South Carolina to meet the team that they usually had to go through to win a title, The Citadel. Davis was again a workhorse in a 16-7 win.

Reeder's 43-yard run early in the second quarter set up a Davis one-yard touchdown run. It took the Bulldogs just five plays to answer, though, and go on top 7-6. That lead held up into the fourth quarter. Nunnally missed VMI's first field goal attempt of the year, but his punting was changing the field position in the game. When VMI took over on The Citadel 46, it took just seven plays before Davis climaxed the drive with a 9-yard run. Davis carried six times for 23 yards on the march and added the two-point conversion, ramming into The Citadel's eight-man front.

After another Nunnally punt pinned the Bulldogs at their own two, Bush sacked Sid Mitchell for a safety that locked up the victory.

Mulrooney was livening up the offense with more passing, hitting 12 of 25 for 173 yards in the last two games. Reeder, his Wilmington, Delaware, prep school teammate, caught eight of those passes, and the Keydets had suddenly won three games in a row to improve to 5-3.

The winning streak ended in Worcester, Massachusetts though, as a strong Holy Cross team handed the Keydets a 20-14 defeat. VMI fell behind 20-0 but fought back, playing uphill all day. The Crusaders led 14-0 at the half, and recovered a fumble on the second half kickoff to set up another touchdown.

The Keydets got a spark from halfback Chuck Beale off the bench in the fourth quarter and mounted a 77-yard drive. Nunnally hit Granville Amos from five yards for the score. After a Holy Cross fumble, Reeder went 35 yards on a sweep for another touchdown. Charlie Snead's pass to Bush added two more points and pulled the Keydets within a score with seven minutes to play.

VMI had one more chance with the ball but couldn't advance and punted. The Crusaders were able to run out the clock and curtail the Keydets' streak.

The extra practices heading up to the season-ending meeting with Virginia Tech were as intense as always, perhaps more so, with the Keydets gunning for an undefeated Southern Conference slate and a fourth league title in six years, as improbable as that event had once seemed.

Over 25,000 fans turned out on Thanksgiving Day at Victory Stadium 1962, and they saw the Keydets score a 14-9 victory that fulfilled that destiny. VMI trailed 7-6 at the end of the first quarter despite an 80-yard touchdown run by Mazik. Rudy Amos, who had the big block to spring Mazik, set up the second Keydet touchdown, recovering a fumble on a punt at midfield. Davis ended up with a one-yard score and then added the two-point conversion. A reverse on a third-and-10 play was a signature moment, Reeder handing to Beale, who got a first down on a play McKenna added to the offense just for the Tech game.

With a precarious 14-7 lead, VMI was pinned deep by a Bob Schweikert punt. Nunnally stepped to the line on fourth down, took the snap and dashed into his own end zone for a safety. With room to punt on the free kick, though, Nunnally pushed the Gobblers back, and the Big Red defense held on.

"It just has to be the best championship of them all," said McKenna of the Keydets' charge to another title. McKenna was rewarded with a new five-year contract, the old deal scrapped with a year left. He was named Southern Conference Coach of the Year for the third time in six years.

Joe Bush, who grew up in Roanoke and first became enamored of the Keydets at these annual Thanksgiving clashes with VPI, recalled that taking the safety was actually a play the Keydets had practiced but had never used before.

"It was great strategy," Bush said. "At that time you hardly ever saw a team do something like that. Coach McKenna was ahead of his time. It was a great call, but it was because Coach McKenna had great faith in our defense."

McKenna was happy and succinct in the post-game. "I hope you enjoy your Thanksgiving turkey dinner as much as I enjoyed mine," he told the media.

Davis finished as the conference scoring champion and led the team with a modest 316 yards rushing on the season, earning honorable mention all-conference honors along the way. Reeder, who led the team with 12 receptions for 159 yards, was also honorable mention, as was Minor. The big stars of the balanced team were on the line, tackle Bill Welsh coming on to earn First Team all-conference honors, and Bill Tornabene was second team.

"All in all, it was one of the most rewarding campaigns of my tenure here," said McKenna. "I am sure that this is the feeling of the entire coaching staff, and I trust that you people who support the program and share the Keydets' success will concur."

Years later when this special team held a reunion, Gil Minor, who would go on to become Chairman and CEO of Owens-Minor, Inc., a Fortune 500 company, tells this personal story about McKenna:

Kenny Reeder and I were the co-captains and looked forward to celebrating perhaps one of Coach McKenna's greatest coaching jobs. A month before the reunion of the team, I weighed 265 pounds compared to my playing weight of 210. I knew Coach McKenna would take notice of that, so I decided to lose some weight. Well, I lost 4 pounds, but I felt better about facing Coach McKenna at the reunion. We all had a wonderful time, and Coach McKenna never commented on my weight. I was so relieved.

A week later I got a letter from him. The letter said how much he had enjoyed the reunion. He went on to say, "Gil, I'm worried about your health. If I were you, I would rather be looking down at the daisies than up at them. Take better care of yourself." Coach

My parents, my friends and just about everybody had been on my case to lose weight for all the obvious reasons. I had been to all the diet programs that were offered back in those days, made a little progress, but never sustained it. When Coach McKenna wrote his letter to me, for the first time, I took it seriously and wrote him back and said, "Okay, Coach, I will do this." Over the next ten years, I diligently lost 5 to 7 pounds each year, got to a place where I was exercising regularly again, and did what Coach McKenna told me to do, take better care of myself. His words, his wisdom, his caring, his passion for doing the right thing remain with me today.

Minor also served as president of the VMI Board of Visitors from 2005-2008.

With a 6-4 overall record, including 6-0 within conference, VMI claimed its fourth Southern Conference championship in six years. The string of winning seasons was stretched to six, and the Keydets won a second straight Virginia Big Five title, the fifth in the past 10 years.

"Outweighed, outmanned, but never outcoached, the Keydets plowed through a tough schedule," trumpeted *The V.M.I. Cadet*. "The Keydets were underdogs in eight games yet still managed the winning record and the conference title. The cagey McKenna's powers seemed limitless and the future bright for the Keydets."

But college football was continuing to change, and at VMI, things would never be the same.

1962 (6-4)

Southern Conference Champions

DATE	VMI	LOCATION	OPP
S 15	22	George Wash. (Lynchburg)	6
S 22	0	at Villanova	24
S 28	21	at Richmond	0
O 6	0	at Boston College	18
O 13	6	at Virginia	28
O 20	20	Davidson	7
O 27	6	William & Mary	0
N 3	16	at The Citadel	7
N 10	14	at Holy Cross	20
N 22	14	Virginia Tech (Roanoke)	9

Chapter Twelve

COMING DOWN
FROM THE CLOUD

In January of 1963, down in Dixie where the heart of college football beats most vigorously, the powers-that-be in the Southeastern Conference were engaged in a debate over how many football scholarships member schools could hand out. That number, in the SEC among Alabama, Mississippi, Louisiana State University and their brethren, went to 120 per school.

Or about 10 times as many as the Keydets were giving out each year.

"In our league four schools have twice as many scholarships as we do, and only Davidson has less," pointed out McKenna, who nonetheless was an advocate for what it meant to have so many players, two-platoon football. With McKenna it all came back to teaching the game.

"I prefer two-platoon football," he told the *Norfolk Virginian-Pilot*. "More boys can play and sophomores would play more quickly. We rarely use sophomores at VMI because there is so much to learn. Two platoons cut down the amount of learning needed. The one-platoon rule was adopted to help cut down the size of squads as much as anything. Then by constantly changing the rule they have made three platoons possible and increased the size of squads."

A new rule coming in the fall of '63 seemed aimed at ending some of the specialization that was becoming common in the sport. A substitute entering the game would have to play at least two plays. More importantly, it kept a player going to the bench out an extra play. For example, a quarterback replaced by a kicker or punter would have to miss another down. The rule set up some awkward situations, particularly on change of possessions.

Back in Lexington, late that summer, the Keydets were loaded with experience, 24 lettermen back, including nine starters. Co-captain Bill Welsh was returning at tackle along with Conrad Davis. Bruce Leve, Jim Shumaker, Butch Land, and Bill Mowli were in reserve.

Bill Black, Joe Straub, Doug Walker and Richard Phillips returned at guard but replacing Gil Minor was a major obstacle. Bill Tornabene was a co-captain, and he and Charlie Cole again made center one of the team's strongest positions.

"Charlie was an over-achiever; he was a tall guy out of Martinsville," remembered Joe Bush. "He played center and linebacker and he was very quick. He could go from sideline to sideline making tackles. He put on weight because he was really skinny when he got (to VMI)."

Bush said Tornabene was "the prototype linebacker, short and stocky and just tough." Bush and Tornabene would later coach together at VMI and then at Hampden Sydney.

Bush and Eric Hart were the top ends, holding off Don Giles, Dan Phlegar, and Carl Rhodes. Phlegar, out of Narrows, was a promising 6'-4", 225-pound target, but McKenna was telling everyone to keep an eye on Rhodes, who "inhales footballs."

Big Bill Davis was back at fullback, flanked by a lot of depth at halfback, including Granville Amos, Donny White, Pete Mazik, Chuck Beale, Andy Tucker, converted flanker Kenny Reeder and spring game sensation Butch Whitt, a non-lettered junior.

Mark Mulrooney and Charlie Snead were slated to handle the quarter-backing duties, with Butch Nunnally expected to concentrate on defense and punting. The passing attack was still a concern. The Keydets wound up last in the Southern Conference in 1962 in that category with a paltry 47 yards per game passing. Nunnally was just 17 of 47 through the air on the year.

McKenna went back to the basics to improve the aerial attack, more throwing and catching among the particulars in practices and more work without the ball on route-running and timing.

"Like most McKenna teams, this year's edition will be light and fast afoot," *The Roanoke Times* said. "The emphasis again will be on defense, out of necessity as much as anything, with Davis and Tornabene ranking among the league's best at stopping people."

Bush said McKenna was expert at scheming to utilize the team's quickness to combat larger teams. "Our tackles, Bill Welsh and Conrad Davis were maybe 215 pounds, so we had to play that way," he said. "On defense, we sort of slanted up front, always moving to take advantage of our quickness."

That summer, West Virginia, Virginia Tech, and VMI were consistently listed as the teams to beat in the Southern Conference, though a nasty rash of injuries was starting to cut into the Keydets. Sophomore guard Ricky Parker, who looked like the best kicker in camp since Sam Horner in 1959, went down with a hip injury, and other nagging injuries hurt the depth in the line. McKenna moved 5'10", 182-pound halfback Eddie Willis and 6-foot, 190-pound fullback Marshall Taylor to guard.

Another surprise was Nunnally, the senior from Richmond, coming on strong to win the quarterback position. McKenna explained, "No, I'm not surprised that Nunnally is doing the job. We just think that he is finally realizing the potential he always had. Now Butch is throwing the ball better than any of our quarterbacks, and he's doing more things well. That's what we're for – consistency. Nunnally, Snead, and Mulrooney have all had flashes of brilliance, but we want someone on whom we can depend for a good job all the time."

VMI lost a man they could always depend on when long-time trainer Herb Patchin passed away on September 4, 1963. Patchin had come to the Institute in 1929, and he served as VMI's Director of Physical Training and as the school's athletic trainer for 34 years, presiding as "philosopher, pain killer and father confessor," according to *The Norfolk Virginian-Pilot*.

Bill Brill of *The Roanoke Times* wrote that Patchin was a "giant of a man – a large hulking figure, who up until that first heart attack last year paraded around the VMI campus with that ever-present cigar a part of his moon face…Herb Patchin was VMI."

McKenna had lost a dear friend, one with whom he shared many a laugh and many a frank assessment. Shortly after his death, the VMI Board of Visitors passed a resolution renaming VMI's two baseball diamonds, Patchin Field. Today, VMI's soccer practice and playing area is named Patchin Field, the same site the baseball fields once occupied.

The football season opened at home on September 21 with George Washington. Nunnally started and helped VMI overcome an early 6-0 deficit. His pass from the 10-yard line midway through the second quarter hit Joe Bush's fingertips and popped in the air. Three Colonial defenders had a chance to make an interception, but the ball bounced to Chuck Beale for a touchdown. Parker's point after put the Keydets ahead.

After GW turned the ball over on downs near midfield in the fourth quarter, Snead came on to lead a six-play drive. He hit Phlegar for 10 yards, then Beale for 23. His eight-yard pass to Mike Patterson provided a 14-6 victory. It was Snead's first touchdown toss ever and after one game, VMI already had half as many touchdown passes (two) as the Keydets did all of the previous season. The "loosey-goosey" Snead was 8-of-14 for 123 yards, and VMI totaled 172 yards passing, part of 336 total yards.

However, McKenna wasn't pleased with the mistakes his men made, including two fumbled punts and a bad snap that led to GW's score. "There was no excuse for those kinds of mistakes," he said. "Those are the ones that will beat you. They simply have to be eliminated."

VMI and George Washington both got delay of the game penalties after touchdowns involving the substitution rule. "The new rule is a pain in the neck," McKenna fussed.

The next weekend, the Keydets traveled all the way to Ames, Iowa, (a three hour and 15 minute flight from Lynchburg, McKenna noted in his newsletter) and went toe-to-toe with Iowa State of the Big Eight Conference. They outgained the Cyclones 228 yards to 213, before falling 21-6.

Just after the Keydets scored their lone touchdown to cut the Iowa State lead to a point in the second quarter, the hosts ran the ensuing kickoff 90 yards for a touchdown and a 14-6 lead late at the half.

VMI's score came on Nunnally's nine-yard pass to Eric Hart in the second quarter. "We're naturally unhappy about losing, but the boys proved to themselves they can hold their own at a high level of competition," said McKenna. "Their size told on us. In the second half we just couldn't move against them."

Charlie Cole had 10 tackles, perhaps inspired by his father flying to Ames to see the game.

VMI couldn't duplicate the gallant effort the following week at Davidson. Five lost fumbles, three of them inside the 15-yard line when it looked like VMI might score, cost the Keydets dearly.

Davidson drove for a field goal on the Wildcats' opening possession and made that 3-0 lead stand up through the half. Davis fumbled early in the third quarter, and Davidson went 27 yards in nine plays to take a 10-0 lead on Lyle Blalock's three-yard run. After Nunnally pinned the Wildcats back with a deep punt, VMI got good field position, and Granny Amos scooted 25 yards to set up his one-yard scoring run with about five minutes left.

The VMI defense stiffened, pushed the Wildcats back, and then recovered an ill-fated quick kick attempt at the 10, where Bush fell on the ball. Davis went seven yards but was hit and fumbled again. In the fourth quarter, Doug Walker's interception set up a Rick Parker field goal from the 11, as VMI tied it up late.

With time running down, Butch Whitt intercepted a pass and went 43 yards, looking like he might score, before running into teammate Dan Phlegar and falling down at the Wildcat 27. Cole was again a standout on defense, but the Keydets knew they had let one slip away. The game ended in a 10-10 tie.

"This was the sloppiest game a team ever played for me in 11 years," said McKenna. "I wouldn't say we beat ourselves. Davidson played a good game, but I must say we prevented ourselves from winning."

McKenna was even blunter in his newsletter. "I must say that in the 11 years I have coached at VMI, this is the low point. The Davidson debacle should not be the labeling of this football team. The meat of our schedule is forthcoming, and it will be there that the die will be cast."

The Keydets suffered another setback that week in practice when Donny White dislocated his elbow and was expected to miss three or four weeks.

VMI apparently couldn't afford to be without any offensive weapons. Virginia shut out the Keydets 6-0 the following Saturday in Lynchburg's City Stadium. The Cavaliers scored early and held on, stymieing VMI with their large defensive front wall.

Charlie Cole, Conrad Davis, Bill Black, and Bill Davis led a defense that stopped the Cavaliers most of the afternoon. In the second quarter, VMI partially blocked a punt and Snead moved the Keydets on their best opportunity. Amos had an 18-yard run, but the drive stalled at the 26, and Parker missed a field goal attempt.

Cavalier quarterback Tom Hodges scored from the six-inch line with 50 seconds left in the half for the game's only score. He picked up short yardage in key situations all day to the frustration of Keydet defenders. Virginia out-rushed VMI 203-83 and moved the chains on several fourth downs, opting to avoid punting to speedy VMI.

Snead had a rough day with just five completions in 18 attempts for 43 yards and was under duress all afternoon. Nunnally, who had hurt his arm the previous week, couldn't throw.

At this precarious juncture in McKenna's tenure, it came time for his Keydets to meet a legend in the making. VMI was headed to Norfolk to host Navy and Heisman Trophy candidate Roger Staubach in the Oyster Bowl, at Foreman Field in Norfolk, Virginia, on October 19. Staubach was on the cover of *Time* magazine that week and led the nation in total offense.

The Keydets turned in another great effort against a top opponent and were tied late in the second quarter before Staubach moved heavily favored (between 23 and 34 points) Navy on a drive to the 16-yard line. There, Staubach was trapped for losses twice, and the Midshipmen missed a field goal attempt. It was short, and safety Mark Mulrooney batted down the ball thinking the play was over. Alert Navy kicker Fred Marlin ran in and pounced on the live ball in the end zone for the game's first score.

"It was an unusual play," said McKenna. "I never saw it before, and I hope I never see it again."

Nunnally took the ensuing kickoff back 59 yards, almost breaking it, but VMI had to settle for a field goal attempt, which Emmy Shedlock missed from 45 yards. Navy got two quick touchdowns in the third quarter over a four-minute span, one set up by a fumble and pass interference penalty resulting in Staubach's one-yard sneak that made it 21-0.

VMI's offense came to life with a 33-yard Andy Tucker gallop. Nunnally hit Bush for 10 yards, then Beale dashed 42 yards for the score. The defense stopped Staubach at the one yard line to get the ball back midway through the final quarter, and the Keydets went 99 yards. Nunnally's 46-yard strike to Bush was the big play, which set up Nunnally's eight-yard scoring pass to Mike Talley with one second left for a 21-12 final.

The 31,500 fans on hand saw the heavy underdog Keydets scare Navy, which would finish the regular season ranked second in the nation. VMI, led by lanky linebacker Charlie Cole's 13 tackles, also kept the clamps on Staubach, limiting him to just 147 total yards, including minus-one rushing. He was in Cole's sights all day, and the 6'-4" Martinsville native had several big hits on him.

Years later after Staubach retired from his all-star career with the Dallas Cowboys, Bush met up with him, and was amazed that "Roger the Dodger" seemed to recall every detail from that 1963 game. "I thought that was pretty neat that he remembered that game," said Bush. "We had a great game-plan. Weenie Miller did our scouting, and the coaches came up with this plan where the ends kept him in the pocket and didn't let him get up the field."

The Keydets hopes for a seventh consecutive winning season weren't advancing, however. Now 1-3-1, VMI was off to its slowest start since losing eight straight games in McKenna's third season in 1955. Hoping to shake up the offense, McKenna moved quarterback Bill Gedris up to the second unit with Mulrooney. He hoped Gedris' running ability might help in certain situations.

But the offense struggled again at Richmond in a 7-7 Friday night tie. Phlegar came up with an end zone interception in the closing seconds to stave off another defeat. Before 9,500 fans, Tucker's 51-yard punt return in the third quarter set up Bill Davis' one-yard score. The Spiders tied the game with 11 minutes left and drove to the VMI eight later in the quarter, before Phlegar's big play on a pass deflected by Cole. The interception saved a short field goal attempt by Bruce Gossett, who would go on to a long NFL kicking career.

Now at 1-0-2 in the Southern Conference, VMI appeared to have a tough road to defending its title. There was other bad news. Tailback Pete Mazik was out for the year with a knee injury, and McKenna was juggling his lineup, now starting Phlegar and returning Bill Davis back to first team after a one-game demotion. He was also talking about using Mulrooney at quarterback the following week against William & Mary. Mulrooney had been hampered by a dislocated finger but looked good in practices with the second team.

"Our passing is such a hazardous thing that we can't throw unless we have excellent field position," lamented McKenna, who may have been sandbagging a bit.

VMI threw 41 times that Saturday in Williamsburg, opening things up in a 26-6 win at Carey Field. The victory moved VMI into third place in the Southern Conference standings and kept the team's slim title hopes alive.

The Indians had led 6-0 in the first quarter, but McKenna inserted Mulrooney at quarterback, and the team roared 80 yards in seven plays for a tying score. Mulrooney hit Hart for a 24-yard touchdown. Mulrooney was 4-of-10 passing for 69 yards, and Nunnally hit on 10 of 27 throws for 103. Phlegar, in his first varsity start, caught five passes for 60 yards.

"At the present, plans call for us to keep throwing, although not at the rate of 41 a game," wrote McKenna to the Sportsmen's Club. "The receiving of Don Phlegar (5), Joe Bush (4) and Don Giles (3) as well as the others enabled us to loosen up the stacked William and Mary defenses against our running game giving us the well-rounded attack needed all season."

An Andy Tucker interception set the offense up at the W&M 21 in the third quarter, and Nunnally hit Beale for a six-yard go-ahead touchdown. Amos, in for an injured Davis, added two short touchdown runs in the fourth quarter.

"I don't remember when we last got four touchdowns," said McKenna. (It had been 19 games since a 1961 contest against Buffalo.)

Things wouldn't get any easier with All-Southern Conference right tackle Bill Welsh now out with a leg injury.

VMI's losing streak against non-conference foes reached eight games with a 14-12 setback at previously winless Holy Cross (0-5-1). The Crusaders were in their first losing season in nine years and the worst campaign ever under veteran coach Dr. Eddie Anderson, a 38-year veteran.

However, Holy Cross dominated this game, running 82 plays to VMI's 40. With the loss, VMI hadn't won outside the Southern Conference since that 1961 victory at Buffalo.

The Keydets had no steady offense against the Crusaders but did hit two big plays to keep things interesting. Nunnally connected with Bush for a 54-yard score to make it 8-6, with VMI failing to convert a two-point attempt after a Holy Cross penalty moved the ball to the 1 ½ yard line. In the second half following a Holy Cross touchdown, Nunnally found Beale for 57 yards, but VMI couldn't convert the two point attempt on a cold bleak day at Fitton Field before 7,500.

Snead was driving the team late for perhaps a winning field goal attempt. He completed three straight sideline passes to Bush, but his fourth such attempt was intercepted to end the threat.

It had been a disjointed weekend for the Keydets. One of the two chartered planes to Worcester was unable to land due to a driving rain storm, and half the squad and staff were forced to set down in Connecticut. Three hours elapsed before the two groups could join in Worcester.

Welsh was back at tackle the following week and the offense perked up in a 33-8 win over The Citadel that kept VMI's Southern Conference hopes afloat. Nunnally was 10-for-15 for 200 yards passing and two touchdowns. Amos had a one-yard scoring run in the first quarter, and Nunnally's 19-yard touchdown pass to Phlegar made it 14-8 at the half.

"I felt real good," said Nunnally. "I thought I threw the ball as well as I ever have. The blocking was tremendous. I had all the time in the world. The way the ends and backs ran the patterns, well, it made it a very easy job."

McKenna thought Welsh's return was a key. "Bill Welsh was outstanding for us in the line. He is really one of the South's top tackles, and Bill Black was another one who did a great defensive job."

The Bulldogs picked up just 35 yards rushing. VMI racked up a school record 550 yards, breaking a 1956 record of 514 set against Stetson. Twenty-three first downs tied a VMI mark.

How well did things go for the Keydets? Four different quarterbacks completed passes and another unlikely quarterback, lineman Doug Walker, took a snap and gained five yards on a sneak late in the game. Caught in a pickle by the substitution rule, rather than take a delay penalty, Walker went under center for one play.

Suddenly, despite that overall 3-4-2 record, VMI was still undefeated in the Southern Conference and could take another title by beating Virginia Tech, now 4-0 in conference play. The prospect made even the most stoic of Keydets practically giddy.

"That one is for all the marbles…I mean the chips are up for grabs…what I really mean is that I have my metaphors all mixed up," joked McKenna.

Over 27,700 fans turned out in Victory Stadium for the big game, and they saw a doozy of a first half, tied 14 all. For all practical purposes, the contest was decided early in the third quarter when VMI couldn't punch in a go-ahead score.

The Keydets had driven 68 yards after receiving the second half kickoff and reached the one-yard line on third down. Nunnally was stopped short, and then on fourth down, two Tech tacklers nailed Amos short of the goal line.

"I thought Nunnally had scored on the sneak," said McKenna. "That really hurt us. When you get down there you have to collect the points. You may not be back."

After Tech punted out, Beale fumbled. and the Gobblers took over on the 48. Nimble quarterback Bob Schweikert escaped a sack and shook loose for a 41-yard gain. Jake Adams then scored to put Tech ahead on the next play.

In the fourth quarter, Schweikert went back for his first punt return of the season. He took it 82 yards for a touchdown. Tech would win 35-20 and be crowned Southern Conference champions for the first time in 31 years. It would be the Hokies only Southern Conference title.

The Keydets had dominated statistically, out-gaining the Gobblers 417-176, a 22-6 edge in first downs and running 81 plays to VPI's 39. Tech had the big plays, though, including a 99-yard kickoff return to tie the score at 14.

Donny White gained 105 yards and scored the Keydets' first touchdown, but that was little consolation in a 3-5-2 finish, VMI's first losing season in seven years.

Seniors, tackle Bill Welsh and center Charlie Cole earned All-Conference honors, Welsh on the first team, and Cole on the second. End Joe Bush, who led the team with 20 catches for 333 yards, and back Andy Tucker were both honorable mention choices. Chuck Beale had a team-high 312 yards rushing on 68 carries, and Nunnally was the leading passer with 53 completions in 124 attempts for 744 yards.

McKenna said tackle John Turner was the team's most improved player. "He was tall and initially weighed only 207 pounds, but he could run like a deer," recalled Bush.

The injuries, especially to White, sidetracked the offense for much of the season, but the defense was stellar, yielding only 134 points in 10 games. Only Iowa State, Navy, and Tech scored as many as three touchdowns in a game against the Big Red.

"The discouraging events of the afternoon (against VPI) were typical of many of the games this season," wrote McKenna. "Solid, even sometimes brilliant, play was rewarded by too infrequent victories. This season's squad was truly a fine bunch of youngsters from every standpoint, youngsters who deserved much better than they received."

1963 (3-5-2)

DATE	VMI	LOCATION	OPP
S 21	14	George Washington	6
S 28	6	at Iowa State	21
O 5	10	at Davidson	10
O 12	0	Virginia (Richmond)	6
O 19	12	*Navy	21
O 25	7	at Richmond	7
N 2	26	at William & Mary	6
N 9	12	at Holy Cross	14
N 16	33	The Citadel	8
N 28	20	Virginia Tech (Roanoke)	35

* Oyster Bowl – Norfolk

THE DECISION

Clearly, John McKenna's efforts on behalf of VMI football had been extraordinary, but even at the time, with all of the approval of his coaching, it wasn't clear just how majestic they had been. Nor had it been entirely clear the degree of difficulty of the challenges he had faced season after season.

Only the passage of time would bring full clarity on the odds that he had overcome. Those odds steepened with the graduation of a fine group of seniors that spring and with further modification of the substitution rule for 1964. Now teams could make unlimited substitutions when the clock was stopped, such as on a change of possession and could make two substitutions even when the clock was running.

McKenna would alternate players at a handful of positions, but more than ever, VMI's lack of depth would hurt this season. More and more opponents began playing two-platoon football and taking advantage of superior numbers.

He had just 14 lettermen back from the '63 squad, and expectations weren't exceedingly high for VMI football that fall. *The Richmond Times-Dispatch* said that the Keydets were coming off their first non-winning season in seven years under McKenna, "and no one in Lexington would be surprised if it happens in '64."

As if to prove the point, the Keydets dropped their opener for the first time since 1955. William & Mary, under new coach Marv Levy, scored a 14-12 win on a muddy Alumni Field. After a scoreless first quarter, talented Tribe sophomore Chuck Albertson scored to put William & Mary on top. Both teams eschewed the pass in the wet conditions, but VMI got a long strike in the third quarter with Granny Amos setting sail on a school-and-conference record 98-yard scoring run. The Keydets went for two points, but Mike Patterson was stopped short.

The Indians rolled right down the field and used a quarterback sneak for a score and a 14-6 lead. Amos and Donny White led a late VMI drive, with White notching the touchdown with 35 seconds remaining. But Snead's conversion pass to Patterson failed. VMI had lost to William & Mary for just the second time in 12 years.

Amos had 132 of VMI's 189 yards rushing, but William & Mary's new defense kept seven players back in pass coverage, which left VMI attempting just two passes.

"We have stated in the pre-season that this would be a rougher season than most," McKenna wrote to the Sportsmen's Club that week. "However, we felt that William and Mary was one we could beat."

The following week Richmond recorded its first win over VMI since 1955 by staging a comeback before 8,500 fans at Richmond's City Stadium. The Keydets had gone ahead of the Spiders, 14-12, in the third quarter, with Amos zipping 3 yards for a score after VMI held Richmond on downs at the Spider 30. Behind a strong passing attack, Richmond roared right back, going 63 yards in 12 plays to regain the lead on a six-yard pass.

The Spiders missed a field goal late in the fourth quarter, and VMI was on the move when Snead was intercepted at the Richmond 36. The Spiders held on, 20-14, and just like that, the Keydets had already lost two games in the Southern Conference, something that hadn't happened in the last five seasons.

McKenna thought woes in the kicking game led to poor field position in the first two games, but he also cited poor decisions by the team – penalties and ill-advised kick returns, among them. "In the lean years of the football cycle, we expect to be beaten physically," he explained. "This is natural. However, we cannot accept an excuse for being beaten mentally."

The Keydets next faced their biggest test of the season at powerful and unbeaten Villanova. VMI was able to slow the Wildcats' vaunted running game early, but that only forced quarterback Dave Connell to throw two touchdowns – the Wildcats' only pass completions on the day – and open a 14-0 halftime advantage on the way to a 27-7 win.

The Keydets had one strong drive in the opening half as quarterback Hill Ellett led the second unit 53 yards inside the Villanova 10, but Connell picked off Ellett's pass intended for Eric Hart. The Wildcats' big line, led by All-American Al Atkinson, controlled the game all day. Donny White had five catches for 72 yards, including a 33-yarder on the scoring drive. White's play and the quarterbacking of Snead encouraged McKenna. He also found a punter in junior Carl Rhodes, who had boots of 52, 51 and 47 yards.

Then VMI fell to 0-4 after losing another tough one to Virginia in the 16th annual Tobacco Bowl at Richmond's City Stadium. The lead changed hands four times before Tom Hodges connected on a 31 yard touchdown pass to Larry Molinari for the winning score with just over four minutes left.

A bizarre event in the first quarter was an omen for VMI fortunes that day. Ellett, sharing time at quarterback, hit Hart for a 52-yard score to start the wild game. Virginia came right back after the kickoff to score. They converted the extra point, but a holding penalty pushed the ball back 15 yards. The kick was again good, but Virginia was called for illegal procedure taking the ball back to the 23 yard line. The Cavaliers, faced with a 40-yard attempt for the extra point, decided to go for two and converted on a pass over the middle for one of the longest two point conversions in college football history. Those two points were the difference in the game.

On the first possession of the third quarter, Donny White halted a Virginia drive at the six yard line. Two plays later, Mike Patterson put the Keydets back in front with an electrifying 81-yard run. Virginia regained the lead (14-13) in the third quarter, but Patterson's nine yard dash in the fourth quarter put the Keydets ahead 19-14, after the two-point conversion failed. "We had a good game plan, and the quarterbacks did a good job of calling plays," said McKenna. "We sent in very few from the bench. We figured Virginia would be vulnerable to quick toss pitches and that we could pass. We had good application."

McKenna used many of those pitches and some unbalanced line to create mismatches. The results were a balanced offense of 161 yards rushing and 143 passing. It wasn't enough to offset the Cavaliers' power ground game. Virginia rolled up 237 yards rushing, 140 by Carroll Jarvis and took a 20-19 victory.

"If we played in our first three games the way we played today, we wouldn't be 0-4," offered McKenna, who said the secret to playing better had been "work, work, and more work."

The Keydets were improved, and only a handful of mistakes had kept them out of the win column. For instance, a facemask penalty kept Virginia's final scoring drive alive. Phlegar "came of age defensively," according to McKenna, who also lauded Patterson's play and Rhodes' punting.

The next week's opponent, Buffalo, played Marshall that night so McKenna and his assistants flew to Huntington, West Virginia on a plane owned by an alumnus. "Coaching is getting more and more complicated," the coach lamented.

The scouting trip didn't help VMI. It was another heartbreaker the following week for the winless Keydets at War Memorial Stadium in Buffalo in front of 21,255. VMI led 10-0 into the third quarter and victory seemed imminent. But Buffalo's Jim Duprey intercepted a pass and rambled 56 yards to set up the Bulls' first score. Buffalo later added the game-winning score with just 3:12 remaining to prevail 14-10.

The Keydets had battled the bigger Bulls all day, gaining 309 total yards, and Snead was particularly impressive with 12 completions in 19 passing attempts for 128 yards.

It was Ellett, though, who produced the touchdown, hitting Tom Rhodes for a score on a play where the ball was deflected and Rhodes came up with a great catch for a nine-yard touchdown. Rhodes' 44-yard reception had set up the score.

The hallmark of a 0-5 football team is seldom the problem of holding on to the lead in close games week after week," McKenna pointed out in his newsletter. "Due to fine efforts by an undermanned club, we have led in almost all our games and never been beaten badly yet. Only 13 points separate us from a 4-1 record thus far."

VMI broke through the following week and blasted Davidson 35-0 for Homecoming before 5,500 fans. After six consecutive losses, extending to the previous season, the Keydets had finally notched a victory. Granny Amos, who had been out with a back injury, ran for two scores, and VMI capitalized on Davidson errors by recovering five fumbles.

The Keydets drove for three first-half touchdowns and went 85 yards with the second half kickoff.

The coach pulled his first two units at the end of the third quarter, though the Keydets did add one more score, rolling up a season-high 315 yards. VMI, for a change, had overwhelmed an opponent with size up front, by racking up 222 yards rushing.

McKenna played 46 players and enjoyed the proceedings, particularly Charlie Snead's hot hand passing. "Our senior quarterback has developed into one of the Southern Conference's best as the season has progressed," the coach wrote to the boosters. "Snead has continued his fine pinpoint passing. A brief note on Charlie, the forgotten man in the Southern Conference quarterback picture at the present time; after six games, he is throwing at a .526 completion clip. What pleases us most is that he has hit on 18 of his last 27 tries, almost 70 percent."

Bush's standout effort both ways won him Southern Conference Lineman of the Week honors. McKenna also praised junior linebacker Billy Currence, back at full speed at right linebacker, coming off an injury. The pass defense, ranked among the Top 10 in the nation, was another area McKenna lauded, noting the job new assistant Sam Timer had done with the unit.

"The difference between losing and winning – I almost forgot how good it felt," said the coach.

Unfortunately, McKenna wouldn't have that feeling again on the season. The next Saturday, VMI fell 25-6 in New Orleans at the Sugar Bowl, a victim of more untimely turnovers in sweltering late-season heat.

Just minutes after Tulane had gone ahead, their "Posse" defense came up with a big play. Jim Davis made a one-hand interception of Snead's pass and raced 50 yards to the Keydet 12. Four plays later, a quarterback sneak gave Tulane the score. Another interception set up Tulane's next score in the fourth quarter.

Currence, the 6'-1", 195-pound defensive specialist, had a titanic game against Tulane with 17 tackles, 12 unassisted. Currence had missed the first four games of the season with a broken hand suffered in a scrimmage.

John Turner also played well with 11 tackles, but the blowout loss had sent the season down an ugly route. The Green Wave had won just one other game since 1961, a span of 27 games. However, they had just missed upset bids of Mississippi and Georgia Tech the previous two weeks, and they were playing before a homecoming crowd of 18,000 in the Sugar Bowl. McKenna couldn't put his finger on a reason, but he felt his team played flat for the first time since the season opener against William and Mary.

"Of course, (flat performances) come to all teams, but some are lucky enough to get them against weaker clubs on the schedule," wrote McKenna. "We could not expect to play on the par with a Southeastern team with anything but our best showing."

The Keydets now had a short week to get back home and get ready for a Friday night game in Detroit against a large team. "We can't move them out of the way ourselves," said McKenna. "We're going to have to get them to move themselves…try to force them into a disadvantage."

VMI simply couldn't contain Detroit's power running game in a 28-7 setback. The Titans rolled up 412 yards and literally pounded McKenna's club.

Amos got VMI's score on a one-yard run in the second quarter. He also had an 85-yard kickoff return to open the game, but VMI couldn't cash in.

Despite the 1-7 record, some Keydets were starting to draw attention for their sterling individual efforts. Patterson was the ringleader of a secondary ranked among the top 10 in the nation defending the pass, and *The Richmond Times-Dispatch* said Joe Bush, a three-year stalwart, could be the best defensive end in the Southern Conference.

The following week at The Citadel brought yet another low point for the Keydets, who had hung tough against so many stronger opponents. VMI could muster just six first downs and 91 yards of total offense against a mediocre Bulldog squad. The Keydets moved into Citadel territory just twice the whole game and never seriously threatened to score.

The Citadel went on top with a field goal with just eight seconds left in the first half but struck for two touchdowns in a seven-minute span in the third quarter for a 17-0 victory.

McKenna had gone with a two-platoon plan (one offensive team and one defensive squad) for the first time, thinking that eight games in, he had enough experienced players. He did not, as the afternoon revealed.

The traditional season finale on Thanksgiving in Roanoke got off to a bleak start and headed south from there. VMI fell behind 21-0 in the first quarter to archrival Virginia Tech and succumbed 35-13 before 25,000 in Victory Stadium.

Snead rallied his team but couldn't match Bob Schweikert's three rushing touchdowns for the Gobblers. Still VMI had closed to within 28-13 in the third quarter and was driving. With a fourth down at the 2-yard line, Amos swept around end but was stopped cold.

Schweikert tacked on a fourth quarter touchdown with a 56-yard screen pass.

Snead was 16 of 27 for 256 yards and two touchdowns as VMI had to forego the run while trying to rally. VMI managed just 22 rushing yards while Tech rolled up 265 behind Schweikert and Southern Conference rushing leader Sonny Utz.

Despite the disappointing 1-9 finish—VMI's worst showing since going 1-9 in 1955 in McKenna's third season as head coach—tackle John Turner and defensive back Mike Patterson were named First Team All-Southern Conference. Bush garnered Honorable Mention honors after he led the Keydets with 18 receptions for 232 yards on the year and excelled on defense. Amos paced the squad with 68 carries for 312 yards. Snead was the top passer, hitting 65 of 133 passes for 899 yards.

"The Keydets had 13 seniors playing their last game," wrote McKenna to the Sportsmen's Club. "Among those who will be missed the most will be ends Eric Hart and Joe Bush, halfbacks Donny White and Mike Patterson, fullback Granville Amos and guards Joe Straub and Richard Phillips along with senior center Bill Reed."

As things turned out, that meeting with Virginia Tech in 1964 would be the last between VMI and VPI as Southern Conference rivals. Under youthful, aggressive university president T. Marshall Hahn, Virginia Tech left the Southern. The Hokies had hoped to move into the ACC soon but would operate for many years as an independent.

West Virginia would also leave the Southern before 1968, during another period of upheaval at the conference level.

DATE	VMI	LOCATION	OPP
S 19	12	William & Mary	14
S 26	14	at Richmond	20
O 3	7	at Villanova	27
O 10	19	*Virginia	20
O 17	10	at Buffalo	14
O 24	35	Davidson	0
O 31	6	at Tulane	25
N 6	7	at Detroit	28
N 13	0	at The Citadel	17
N 26	13	Virginia Tech (Roanoke)	35

1964 (1-9)

* Tobacco Bowl – Richmond

There was upheaval in VMI practices late that summer of '65 as well. McKenna, now in his 13th year at the school – the longest tenure of any Keydets' coach ever to that point – was looking for answers to changing the team's fortunes.

"From here it appears that we will be back to the drawing board and the recruiting wars," McKenna had written to the boosters at the close of the dreadful '64 campaign. "As stated before, every wheel has a top and bottom, and now we can look for an upswing following a rugged season such as this one."

The veteran coach never blamed the increasingly liberal substitution rules or the gradual return of "two-platoon football" for VMI's problems.

"The two-platoon system will be to our benefit," he said that summer. "You can take a mediocre kid and teach him proficiency in one aspect of the game. This can narrow the gap for you when you're not blessed with an abundance of talent."

VMI didn't have enough football scholarships to truly compete like it had just a couple of seasons ago, but that topic rarely emerged publicly. Instead, the Keydets set about readying for a grueling schedule that saw them on the road for the first seven weeks of the season.

The passing game was still a concern. Hill Ellett of Roanoke was a "gamer" but not blessed with great footwork. He was also a left-hander and threw a "heavy ball" that was hard to catch, though McKenna thought the receiving corps would be better. Sophomore Charlie Bishop of Staunton would back Ellett.

Tom Slater was moving in for Granville Amos at fullback. At 200 pounds, he was bigger but didn't have Amos' breakaway speed. Juniors Ted Mervosh and Tom Rhodes, along with sophomore Jim Burg, were the top candidates at halfback. The ends were deep and talented, starting with Dan Phlegar and Mike Talley, both over 6'-4", and 200 pounds. Sonny Fox, Carl Rhodes, and Jamie Browder were also dependable, particularly Rhodes and Browder on defense. Rick Irby, Eddie Willis, and Rusty Fitzgerald were solid in a defensive secondary that had been a bright spot the previous year.

On the line, John Turner was an all-conference tackle, and Larry Wertz, and Clay Minor also looked good. Sophomore guard Don Taylor of Vinton was a likely starter until he hurt his hand in the preseason. That left Ricky Parker, Dennis Telzrow, Bob Randolph, Jim Clarke and Bob LaPosta competing in the interior line and at linebacker. Bill Currence was back as the center. Randolph, who would co-captain the 1966 Keydet team, was academically distinguished English major, who, like Lee Badgett, would be selected a Rhodes Scholar.

McKenna thought his run defense would be better in 1965, along with improvements in the kicking game. The fact that most of his backs were bigger was also encouraging. VMI often had 150-pound halfbacks on the field in 1964, and that was small even by high school standards.

Mervosh and Parker were kicking the ball well, which brought McKenna to comment: "We feel like we can do some field goaling from 35 yards."

Unfortunately the hard luck Keydets picked up right where they left off the previous season. Leading into the fourth quarter before 10,000 fans in Williamsburg in the September 18th opener, VMI saw William & Mary battle back to take a lead and the game in sizzling 90-degree heat that wore on both teams.

Mike Madden swept around right end on an option play to put the Indians ahead 25-21 after VMI had led most of the way. Seven fumbles, including one that set up this score, undid the Keydets' chances in the 32-21 loss.

Chuck Albertson took a punt back 58 yards to open the scoring, but Ellett led a 61-yard drive to tie the game with Tom Rhodes carrying the final two yards. A 59-yard VMI march resulted in a six-yard Paul Hebert scoring run, and the Keydets led 14-13 at the half.

The first 30 minutes were played in such heat that the Keydets "made considerable use of the oxygen equipment purchased only last week," according to McKenna. The Big Red also changed jerseys and looked sharp in the third period.

Ellett hit Carl Rhodes on a 60-yard pass, and VMI had an eight-point lead. The Indians answered with an 80-yard drive to pull within 21-19 and scored two more second half touchdowns for the win. Ellett was 9 of 18 for 162 yards, and VMI moved well, though the Keydets didn't hang on to the sweaty ball enough. Each William & Mary score started with a Keydet turnover.

VMI played better the following Saturday, but Army pulled rank in a 21-7 victory at West Point. It was just the eighth meeting ever of the two schools and the first in nine years. The Keydets acquitted themselves well. After a scoreless first half, the Black Knights finally took a lead with a 75-yard march to open the third quarter.

Ellett passed the Keydets right back down the field and tied the score 7-7, when he hit Carl Rhodes from 16 yards. Ellett also had a 46-yard strike to Phlegar on the drive and generally gave the Army defense fits all afternoon.

Playing at home, before a crowd of over 21,000, Army scored twice more, and Army Coach Paul Dietzel kept his first team defense in the whole way to try to contain Ellett.

Army controlled the game up front, out-rushing the Keydets 292 yards to 58. Dietzel, a young, excitable coach, ran for the VMI dressing room as the game ended. He grabbed John Turner's hand, shook it firmly, and told the talented tackle, "You outfought and outplayed us. We were lucky as hell to win."

In his newsletter, McKenna said Dietzel "visited our dressing room after the game and told our squad that they 'had outfought his team and played magnificently.'"

It was the 14th consecutive non-conference loss for the Keydets, but it was noted that VMI rarely played these games at home. In 12 years just three "intersectional opponents" had come to Lexington – Catawba in 1953, and

Lehigh in 1953 and 1959.

The Keydets fell to 0-3 with a 14-0 loss at George Washington the following Saturday night. While the Keydet defense held All-America candidate Gary Lyle to just 28 yards on 16 carries, the VMI offense couldn't generate anything.

The Colonials scored with just over three minutes left in the fourth quarter to salt the game away. Paul Hebert led the Keydets with 48 yards on seven carries, and Ellett hit on 13 of 29 passes for 122 yards.

"All I hope is the kids don't get their hopes down and can forget about the losses," wrote McKenna. "I hope we never get the attitude that to play a good game, whether we win or lose, is enough."

McKenna desperately wanted a victory for his team's sagging confidence. October 9th the Keydets headed out on the road yet again, this time at Virginia on a gray, chilly afternoon in Charlottesville, where they went ahead early in the fourth quarter only to see Virginia battle back for a 14-10 win that handed VMI an eighth consecutive loss over two seasons.

McKenna's club had gone ahead 3-0 in the second quarter on a 35-yard field goal by Mervosh. Then Virginia recovered a fumble on a punt at the VMI 8-yard line, and two plays later Carroll Jarvis scored for a 7-3 lead at the half.

Ellett sneaked in for a score in the fourth quarter after a pass interference call in the end zone, and VMI went up 10-7. Turner led a strong defensive effort that produced three fumble recoveries and two interceptions. The Big Red held Virginia to 88 yards rushing, just 10 in the second half, as VMI dominated up front despite a Virginia line that averaged 246 pounds per man.

Cavalier quarterback Tom Hodges took Virginia 80 yards in the last 1:51 to beat VMI in the final minute for the second straight season. The Cavaliers converted a fourth down and 16 on that final march. Bob Davis scored with one second left, and Virginia students rushed the field.

"It was the toughest game I ever lost," said McKenna.

"Moral victories are wearing thin, and you cannot keep going to the well and never get a drink of water," he wrote to the Sportsmen's Club. "It was a maximum competitive effort by VMI only to fall victim to a couple of lapses in play."

Another blow came when halfback Jim Burg suffered a broken fibula that would end his season.

The Keydets traveled to Southern Mississippi the following week and lost another squeaker. Southern Mississippi's George Sumrall kicked a 35-yard field goal early in the first quarter, and that proved enough.

Carl Rhodes' punting, including a healthy 41.2-yard average per kick, helped keep the Golden Eagles at bay the rest of the day. Turner was again stellar, earning Southern Conference Lineman of the Week honors. Ellett left with a bruised shoulder he got while throwing a block for Mervosh on the last play of the first half. Backup Charlie Bishop was already out after breaking his hand in practice that week, so defensive back Rick Irby played quarterback for the second half in the 3-0 loss.

"We have placed most of our outstanding personnel on the defensive unit and the choice was dictated by the fact that even if they were on offense, we do not have the explosive power to outscore anyone," explained McKenna in his weekly newsletter. "We come up short in a couple of areas. We do not have enough strength to play ball control and, on the occasions when we do spring a back through, we don't have enough speed for him to go all the way. I don't say this in criticism just as an explanation of the way we are utilizing the present personnel."

An editorial in *The V.M.I. Cadet* that week pointed to VMI's problem on the gridiron where all of their foes were giving out more football scholarships now while VMI's scholarship numbers, between 11-13, had remained steady for seven years. The article cited that Virginia Tech had 52 scholarships, while Richmond, Virginia and William & Mary all offered between 25 and 30.

Those numbers were translating to the scoreboard for the Keydets. A week later, the VMI freshmen would lose to Virginia Tech 35-22, the Rats' fifth straight loss to the Gobblers "who have stepped up their recruiting program in an effort to get into the Atlantic Coast Conference," noted McKenna.

Besides Ellett's injury and the loss of Burg, backup quarterback Bishop, had broken his hand, and two of the best conditioned athletes on the team, key linemen Bob Randolph and Larry Wertz had battled heat exhaustion and missed time.

Ellett somehow managed to play the next game, October 23, at Davidson, by utilizing a special shoulder harness that trainer Fred Kelley had whipped up for him. Kelly, who came to VMI from Dartmouth in 1961 as a physical education instructor, became trainer in 1963 following the death of Herb Patchin. The Keydets snapped their losing streak with a 16-10 win on Davidson's Homecoming before 9,000 fans. The VMI defense kept the Keydets in it early by stopping the Wildcats in VMI territory a couple of times before a VMI fumble on the 14 allowed Davidson to score.

The Keydets fumbled on the ensuing kickoff to set up Davidson's field goal and a 10-0 deficit. The Wildcats had just 58 yards offense but led 10-3 at the half. Mervosh had banged home a 27-yard field goal for VMI's points.

A Davidson fumble set up VMI's first touchdown in the third quarter, and then Eddie Willis intercepted a deflected pass and returned the ball 25 yards to the Davidson five. Tom Slater scored his second short touchdown, this one from five yards, which put the Keydets on top for the first time.

After VMI lost its third fumble of the day, the Wildcats drove deep only to throw an incomplete pass on fourth down. VMI ran out the clock for the win, inspiring McKenna to say the victory was "the beginning of a new season for VMI," something he had talked about even before the contest.

"The redeeming feature of the game was our 223 yards gained rushing, by far VMI's best offensive performance of the year," the coach wrote. "We did not play one of our better games...but managed to win. I must admit it is a better feeling to play moderately and win than to have a great effort and lose."

Things had been so bad through the first five games that McKenna pointed out that the luckless Keydets had won just one pregame coin toss.

Boston College quickly ended the Keydets good thoughts the following week in a 41-12 rout in Chestnut Hill. VMI actually jumped to a 6-0 advantage but couldn't hold onto the lead or the ball. They fumbled seven times, including on five consecutive possessions to fall behind 21-6 by halftime.

Ellett's 25-yard touchdown strike to Carl Rhodes had put the Keydets ahead early, but then Boston College took advantage of the succession of VMI's turnovers. The Eagles pounced on a fumble at the VMI 2, and got a touchdown, and then repeated the process after another Keydet bobble on the ensuing possession.

Late in the first half, a fumbled punt turned into a 39-yard John Blair-to-Dick Leonardis touchdown. The Eagles scored twice more before Ellett hit Rhodes for a 64-yard score. Ellett was 12-of-18 for 215 yards and two touchdowns against a pass defense ranked fourth in the nation. VMI had little trouble moving the ball, just a lot of angst hanging on to it.

"Coaches feel that each fumble is a 35-yard loss, as it deprives you of a chance to punt," explained McKenna. "With seven lost fumbles that is 245 yards in losses. I also think that fumbling is a psychological rather than a physical thing. There is no reason that a physically fit player should fumble the ball when he has possession unless he is thinking about the fumble, rather than the gain."

By November 6, the Keydets were the only major college team in the nation that hadn't played a home game. Finally, Richmond brought an 11-game losing streak to Lexington where VMI managed a 21-14 victory before 3,800 fans at Homecoming.

In a familiar theme, Richmond scored first after a VMI fumble, but Ellett soon hit Tom Rhodes for a 10-yard score and a tie game.

Ellett was on his way to three touchdown passes, connecting on 19 of 29 passes for 194 yards. The 19 completions were just one shy of the school record and all with that special shoulder harness, which by now Ellett was only wearing out of superstition. He was throwing the ball better than he did before he hurt his left throwing shoulder.

McKenna, of course, had a theory beyond superstition. "The harness restricts Ellett to throwing short but aids his accuracy since it restricts lateral movement and makes Hill throw overhand," offered the coach.

Tom Rhodes would catch another touchdown, but Carl Rhodes set a school record with eight receptions, most of them on down-and-out passes or look-in routes. Slater dashed 37 yards early in the second quarter to set up Ellett's four-yard touchdown strike to Carl Rhodes. Slater finished with 98 yards on 17 carries.

The Spiders cut their deficit to a touchdown, but Eddie Willis preserved the hard-earned win with an interception on the game's final play. Richmond's losing streak was now a school-record 12 games.

"It's always good to win," said Ellett. "And we were happy to be at home. Home is like having 14 points right off."

In practice the following week, linebacker Ricky Parker stepped in a hole and hurt his knee. He would miss the upcoming Citadel game but had already had a pretty good week, receiving the ROTC medal from Virginia Governor Albertis S. Harrison. Parker called all the alignments on defense and was one of the brightest Keydets, a mathematics major from Arlington, Virginia.

The next weekend, the Keydets gave Coach McKenna two presents for his 51st birthday – a birthday cake on Friday night and then a 21-7 win over The Citadel on Saturday. The cake came after the Keydets had their traditional Friday night ritual of a movie and then milk and cookies with the coaches. They told McKenna they would win the game the next day for him.

All McKenna's players fondly remember "milk and cookies," late Friday before games. "At 10:30 or 11, he would have all the players back together," said Joe Bush, a '65 grad, of the Friday sessions. "I think it was part motivational and part because he didn't want the players to go to bed at 8:00 and sleep until the next morning. He'd have a very short meeting and then always milk and cookies."

This night was a special one, though, with the coach's birthday.

"We had written on the blackboard that we were going to get this one for him," said Tom Slater at the time. "We really thought very much of him and felt so badly for him, losing so many close games that year."

Ellett and Carl Rhodes hooked up for two touchdowns in the first nine minutes – the icing on that cake – and the VMI defense dominated as the Keydets won a second consecutive game for the first time since 1962. Turner again led the defensive charge, aided by end Jimmy Breckenridge and others, limiting The Citadel to just 164 total yards.

According to McKenna, Breckenridge "spent as much time it seemed in the game in Citadel's backfield than at his own defensive left end position."

Willis' 64-yard punt return to the Bulldog 20 set up the first Ellett-to-Rhodes score, and then Ellett took the team 54 yards in seven plays for the next Rhodes' reception score. After the quick start, though, the Keydets fumbled twice and threw an interception to thwart other potential scoring threats before an excited home crowd of 4,127.

In the third quarter, Mike Thacker recovered a Bulldog fumble and Slater ended up with a one-yard score. He had 82 yards on 19 carries. The Citadel got their lone score in the final two minutes.

The Keydets set several records. Ellett was 9-of-14 passing for 115 yards, and now with 173 attempts, passed Howard Dyer's 1960 record of 168. Eddie Willis' punt return broke Ken Reeder's mark of a 63-yard return in 1962. Carl Rhodes, who caught two touchdowns in a third straight game, moved within a score of the school record of nine touchdown receptions set in 1959.

McKenna gave his team a three-day furlough to heal and get ready for the big Thanksgiving game against Virginia Tech in 10 days. He said some new plays would be on display in the game, and he hoped they worked as well as the punt return that assistant coach Carmen Piccone had put in for Willis in The Citadel game for the "record romp." It was a favorite from Piccone's days as head coach at Southern Illinois University.

Meanwhile, there was now a lot of talk in the media about taking the

VMI-Virginia Tech game off the Thanksgiving Day menu, but 23,000 still turned out on a cold day in Roanoke. They saw a decisive 44-13 Virginia Tech victory, the most points the Keydets had allowed since 1956. In the last three games in the series, Tech had racked up 114 points.

Tommy Francisco galloped 93 yards with the opening kickoff, and it would be all down-hill from there. By past standards, it was a smallish crowd for the 61st renewal of the rivalry. Francisco dashed 36 yards from scrimmage for Tech's second score. Quarterback Bobby Owens would keep the Gobblers going, rushing for 169 yards in just 16 carries and scoring twice.

Slater scored on a one-yard thrust to make it 14-6 at the end of the first quarter, but Tech went 70 yards in just eight plays to answer.

A 70-yard Owens run on a quarterback draw – a play that worked all day – made it 27-6 at the half.

Undermanned VMI tried to play Turner, Willis and Rusty Fitzgerald both ways as McKenna hoped to keep his best players on the field, but Tech was just too big, too talented, and too deep for VMI.

Always proud of his record against Virginia Tech, McKenna found another loss most difficult. Bobby Ross, now a young assistant on the VMI staff, witnessed just how much of a toll the losing had taken. "I saw the wear on him during the season," Ross recalled. "When I first came there it was a lot of fun and enjoyment, but I think he became frustrated because we just started to wear down from competing so hard. You can only do so much with heart and effort. You reach a point where you want that talent, too, as a coach. I think coaching VMI is a very difficult job, and he started to feel that more after 13 years."

Despite the 3-7 record, VMI had a couple of standouts recognized at season's end. John Turner and linebacker Bob Schmalzriedt were named to the First Team All-Southern Conference defense, and Ellett was second team offense. Turner became just the eighth Keydet to earn the honor two straight years. Schmalzriedt became the first VMI sophomore so honored.

Slater led the '65 Keydets in rushing with 124 carries for 489 yards, and Ellett was the top passer with 92 completions in 210 attempts for 1,254 yards, all three totals school records for a single season. Ellett finished as the top Southern Conference passer, despite his poor footwork and heavy ball and playing the last three games in a harness. Carl Rhodes' 32 catches for 518 yards led all VMI receivers.

1965 (3-7)

DATE	VMI	LOCATION	OPP
S 18	21	at William & Mary	32
S 25	7	at Army	21
O 2	0	at George Washington	14
O 9	10	at Virginia	14
O 16	0	at Southern Mississippi	3
O 23	16	at Davidson	10
O 30	12	at Boston College	41
N 6	21	Richmond	14
N 13	21	The Citadel	7
N 25	13	Virginia Tech (Roanoke)	44

The golden age for the Big Red had seemingly passed. Ironically – or maybe not – McKenna went to see the Georgia-Georgia Tech game the Saturday after Thanksgiving to scout Georgia, the second VMI opponent on the 1966 schedule. He wrote about his thoughts to the Sportsmen's Club following observing two big-time programs:

"If VMI is to stay in business on the football field, we must approximate the programs of the schools on our schedule. Since Dr. Hahn came to Tech four years ago, there have been more than 150 full scholarships issued to football players. The teams in the Southeastern and Atlantic Coast Conference have as many as 45 per year and, in our own conference, the West Virginia program numbers 100 or more.

"This past season, VMI had 13 full scholarships and five partials, largest number ever issued here," he continued. "We are hopeful of getting 25 scholarships this coming fall, which will put us on even terms with conference schools, with the exception of West Virginia. If our program accelerates in the same fashion the next few years, I'm sure that the Keydets will once again be on the move. Even though Tech won 44-13 last Thanksgiving Day, it was no cause for us to panic. In the 13 years I have been head coach at VMI, we have won as many games from VPI as the other three state schools combined."

That February, McKenna resigned his post to accept an administrative job at Georgia Tech under Bobby Dodd, the Yellow Jackets' athletic director and head coach. McKenna was also slated to coach freshman football at

Georgia Tech. He had not confided in his staff about the move, Ross recalled. "We knew that there was something going on. We shared an office in those days, and I was the freshman coach. We all were in one office, and I can remember he was getting a lot of calls. He would ask us to leave so he could speak privately, which we would do and then come back in. I was young – I was new at it – I was naive. But I didn't think it was job seeking because he had been there so long, and he was a legend. My perspective was that he was going to be there until he retired. But that's not what happened. It was a shock to us. A real shock."

McKenna had never confided in him about his relationship with VMI's administration or his thoughts on his career. The coach was only 51. "My personal observation," Ross said, "is that he was just growing tired of issues at VMI, and he didn't see where it was going to get a lot better. That was my observation. I think the issues that were present at VMI were starting to wear him down."

Late in his own career, Ross took the head coaching job at Army, which provided him some insight into the difficulties McKenna faced. "It was a very similar thing," Ross explained, "because it is the type of job where you might plug one problem here, but then something else starts to leak. I think this stated to wear on him."

Late in his tenure at VMI, McKenna was told by a *Washington Post* columnist that he was going to be hired as the next head coach at the University of Maryland. But at the last minute, a powerful alumnus intervened to ensure that Maryland hired Lou Saban, who had coached the Boston Patriots and Buffalo Bills in the old American Football League. Saban lasted in the job one season, then bolted back to the AFL to coach the Denver Broncos. It was just enough to eclipse McKenna's sense of opportunity.

"I think that was a huge disappointment to him," Ross said of the missed opportunity at Maryland. "I think he might have taken that job. He probably needed to in retrospect. He had lifted VMI to a level that it could probably never get to again. Coaching at VMI is a very difficult job. I think he had started to feel that. I do."

Regardless, his legacy was intact. He had led the Keydets to four conference championships. Beyond the field, another great measure was the opportunity for success that his philosophy created for his players. General Binford Peay, who retired from the U.S. Army after attaining four-star rank, noted that of the 278 VMI football players coached by McKenna, 26 earned medical degrees, 22 earned law degrees, seven earned doctorates, and two were named Rhodes Scholars.

Yet it wasn't just the difficulty of VMI that had worn him down, so had the changing game, the increasing demands of the changing ethos of "amateur" competition. Several years later, *Sports Illustrated* took note of McKenna's response when asked why he would not coach again.

"I wouldn't go through the business of recruiting again, of fawning on teen-age athletes," he replied.

And so an era had ended, not just for VMI, but for all of college football. It was on to a new age with a new overhyped emphasis. There would be no turning back.

EPILOGUE

Two eras came to a close as John McKenna resigned as VMI's football coach in February 1966. In addition to his remarkable run at the school, the era of the one-platoon rules in college football officially ended. The NCAA once again authorized two-platoon play, and the larger schools soon busied themselves with adding scholarships and players as the age of specialization and commercialization took the game in a new direction.

In the eyes of many, the experiment in limiting substitutions and platooning had worked famously. Several great teams had found their power in that period from 1953 to 1965. In 1955-56, the University of Oklahoma, under Coach Bud Wilkinson, finished the season unbeaten and untied. Wilkinson's team would run off an NCAA record of 47 games without a loss, between 1953 and 1957. Other great one-platoon teams arose at Syracuse in 1959, UCLA in 1954, and LSU in 1958.

Former Missouri coach Dan Devine once recalled for *Sports Illustrated* that his Tigers were trying to come back against the Michigan Wolverines at Ann Arbor. But because he had messed up his substitution, Devine could not get his starting quarterback, Phil Snowden, back in the game. With two minutes to go, at their own 20 in a driving rainstorm, Devine and his staff feared it was over when they were forced to let backup quarterback Bobby Haas stay in the game. Haas drove the Tigers down the field to the win, one of the sorts of surprises that the one-platoon game could produce.

For VMI football, however, surprises, especially the good ones, were hard to come by.

McKenna was replaced by Vito Ragazzo, who had been his longtime assistant for five seasons, 1956-1960, and a good man, a former star as a tight end at William and Mary. The lack of scholarships and the immense difficulty of the schedule that had plagued McKenna in his final years provided Ragazzo with little chance of success, however. His team opened with a win on the road at Villanova but the next week faced the Georgia Bulldogs in Roanoke, a 43-7 loss. From there, the lineup brought trips to Boston College and Southern Mississippi plus the regular array of the usual opponents. Ragazzo's first season was capped by a 70-12 loss to Virginia Tech in Roanoke for Thanksgiving.

Somehow, VMI managed to finish 2-8. Worse, a pattern had been set. The schedule had begun to include destructive road losses to much bigger, much better-financed teams. These were "money games," that earned VMI substantial money to meet these opponents on their home turf. They helped the under-funded VMI athletic department make ends meet, but they were often devastating in terms of injuries.

In retrospect, 1967 was probably not a good season, although Ragazzo finished 6-4 with some truly impressive wins. But his accomplishment gave the administration and alumni base the false impression that somehow VMI could compete in a rapidly industrializing game. For example, there were no limits on scholarships in that period, and many schools were bringing better than 50 players a year.

VMI lost on the road to West Virginia and Georgia but then somehow managed to beat Virginia, Akron, and Boston College to stand 5-4 heading into the Thanksgiving meeting with Virginia Tech, having been humbled 70-12 the previous year. Once again, Ragazzo's team managed just 12 points for 1967, but in one of the best games in the history of the program, held Virginia Tech to 10 points that day.

Expectations soared in Lexington, but the opposite happened. Ragazzo's 1968 season played out with just one win (over Davidson) against nine losses, and 1969 brought the unthinkable, a winless season in which the Keydets were outscored 409 to 78.

In 1970, VMI had 20 freshmen scholarship players and dozens more walk-ons. By comparison, Virginia Tech was giving enough scholarships to fill three busses for its freshman football team (better than 90 in that age before NCAA restrictions on the number of scholarships schools could give.) Early September brought hope in the form of a win over Furman in the season opener, but that was followed by four straight road losses at Rice, West Virginia, Boston College, and Virginia.

At the end of that streak, Ragazzo's team had collapsed physically and mentally. The freshman team was handling them easily in practice each day. They lost at The Citadel, 56-9 and then to Davidson, 55-21. The first week of November they lost at North Carolina, 62-13. One practice was marked by a fight between Ragazzo and a senior offensive tackle, a team captain, as the freshman team watched in wide-eyed wonder. A star on the freshman roster, Gene Williams, who would go on to All America status at VMI, was struck that the fight was simply Ragazzo trying to get through to a group of seniors who had been hammered mentally and physically by facing superior numbers each week. The team lost 40-17 to Richmond the next week. The team somehow managed to rally for Thanksgiving, almost beating Virginia Tech before falling, 20-14 to finish 1 and 10.

Ragazzo, a longtime presence at the school, was furious and bitter upon his firing at season's end. In a smart move, the administration hired his top assistant, pesky little Bob Thalman, a former Marine who fought at Iwo Jima in World War II. It was a practice VMI would avoid in its future decades of misery, hiring one of its own assistant coaches from a woeful team. But it made sense. The school always proved immensely difficult for new coaches to fathom. By the time a coach learned how to function in VMI's rare environment, his record would be invariably bad enough to force his dismissal. Thus the cycle would start over again.

Thalman had been in residence at VMI, loved the place, and was, like McKenna, in some important ways explained Mike Strickler, who would serve as the school's director of athletic publicity for eight years during that era. "Like Coach McKenna, Bob Thalman took over the head coaching position after serving one year as an assistant. Thalman inherited a program near the end of the Vietnam era which had a 2-29 record over the previous three seasons, and the team was outscored by an average of 28 points per game over that period. He exuded enthusiasm and a can-do attitude."

After being hired, he and athletic director Tom Joynes crisscrossed the state and beyond spreading his message to alumni chapters that VMI could win again and injecting enthusiasm into a dejected alumni base while helping raise scholarship dollars.

Like McKenna, Thalman became a quick favorite of the VMI community, Strickler explained. "Almost every Saturday after home games, win or lose, Coach Thalman and his wife Mary would host many of these friends and some out-of-town alumni staying over Lexington for a party at their home.

And like McKenna, he was a hard-nosed disciplinarian, who was passionate about the positive aspects of the VMI military system and was tough on his players. He would never let them complain to him of their hardships through the unbending rules of the Institute."

"Also like McKenna, he was punctual. If a team bus was scheduled to leave at 1:00, he would stand on the bottom step of the entrance to the bus, looking at his watch. At 1:00 he would tell the driver to close the doors and go…a few of his players learned this lesson the hard way. "

However, Thalman was a strong advocate for his players and his program. The story goes that he once pounded his fist on the desk of the VMI Superintendent, a two-star Army General, to make a point regarding a particular need for his players.

"He was fiery, straight forward, and impassioned," Strickler recalled. "As an assistant coach, he entered the locker room at halftime in the middle of a brutal loss to The Citadel, picked up a chair and smashed a portable chalk board…also as an assistant, he stopped a defensive back, who had just allowed a first half ending touchdown pass in his area, and told him, 'If I had a gun right now, I might consider using it.'" This type of passion was not in Coach McKenna's make-up, but both men had the innate ability to get their players' attention.

As a head coach, Thalman twice during his tenure evoked the Battle of Iwo Jima to fire up his team for the game. These talks were fondly dubbed by his players, "The Iwo Jima speech." He broke it out for his very first game as VMI's head coach in 1971, recalled Melvin Clark, a reserve on that team. "When it was over, we were fighting to get out that locker room door to get on the field. I believe that day we could have beaten Michigan. He was always theatrical."

However, his players grew so emotional after he gave the speech to one of his later teams that they rushed out to play and promptly gave up three touchdowns in the first two minutes of a game against Richmond.

"Once he was at a coach's convention and a group of coaches were having conversation at cocktail hour," Strickler recalled. "A month or two earlier, one of them had failed to get back to Coach Thalman, who had left several messages. Coach Thalman interrupted the conversation, looked at the coach in question, and said, 'Hey, you're the guy who never returned my phone calls.'"

Even with such fiery propulsion, the turnaround was far from immediate. Thalman's first three teams were 1-10, 2-9, and 3-8, but the 1973 season closed with a victory over Virginia Tech in Blacksburg. Afterward, Thalman snatched a victory cigar from Melvin Clark and puffed away. The Thanksgiving Day affair in Roanoke had ended with Thalman's first year after decades as the central event of the football season in Western Virginia. However, Virginia Tech's fancy Lane Stadium held far more fans than Roanoke's decrepit Victory Stadium. Soon enough the rivalry would go away altogether.

True, Thalman lost 27 games in his first three seasons, but the administration sensed progress. The average loss per game fell to 16 points over the period.

Key to the turnaround was the play of defensive back "Mean Gene" Williams, according to Tommy Cole, who played on Thalman's teams. "Gene Williams was by far the greatest football player VMI ever recruited. Gene was a monster on the field, but a true brother off it." It was his "hit" in the closing seconds of that 1973 win over Tech which caused a fumble, preserving a 22-21 win. Williams would later serve on the VMI Board of Visitors.

After those first three seasons of transition, over the next nine years VMI's record was 45-49 with two Southern Conference Championships and four winning seasons. It was not the equal of McKenna's four Southern Conference titles or in terms of wins vs losses, but taken in the scope of the program's dismal later decades, the Thalman era would be remembered as a special, special time.

The 1974 campaign brought the breakthrough as VMI finished 7-4 and won the Southern Conference Championship with a victory over East Carolina in the final game of the season.

As with McKenna, so much of Thalman's success was personality-driven. "One of my favorite stories shows how impassioned Coach was and how totally engulfed he was in his profession," Strickler recalled. "The final game of the 1979 season, a good one for VMI (6-4-1), was against a highly favored Virginia Tech team in Blacksburg. The Keydets battled all day and gave themselves a chance to win on a late drive. Trailing 27-20 with about one minute left in the game, VMI had a first and goal at the Tech nine yard line. However, a corner blitz was not picked up, and VMI quarterback John Bangley was blindsided, fumbled and Tech recovered. As sports information director, it was my job to bring the coach out to talk to the media. After addressing the team, Coach Thalman went into his locker area, and I followed. He was so devastated, having been that close to the upset that he broke down and cried. The assistants tried to console him, but it took Coach over two minutes to stop and regain his composure."

The moment was remarkable, considering Thalman's relentlessly positive approach. "He was an acolyte of a book called *Success Through Positive Mental Attitude* written in 1960 by Napoleon Hill and W. Clement Stone," recalled Dan Smith, who covered VMI for *The Roanoke Times* in 1972. "Thalman was constantly referring to PMA. As I recall, PMA was even in the headline of the pre-season story I wrote. I went up there during his second year at VMI to write a preview of the upcoming season in August for the sports section. I was long-haired, sloppy, confrontational, and a little sullen over the assignment. This was during the Vietnam War, and I was not happy about going to a military school for a story. Thalman greeted me with enthusiasm, directness, and an optimism that you could almost touch. When I arrived back in Roanoke, I got a short haircut, cleaned up my clothing selections, and changed my whole outlook, though not my politics. It was Thalman's 'Positive Mental Attitude' mantra that affected even me. The man was a marvel."

"He said you couldn't win if you didn't believe you could win," Mel Clark recalled. VMI football had a "belief" problem that Thalman was determined to fix. "He was known as 'the eternal optimist,'" Strickler said, "and never entered a game thinking his teams could not win. Facing Georgia Tech in 1975, he had the staff bring in large loud speakers for practice and played 45 records on 78 speed (long before the days of fancy audio systems) to simulate crowd noise."

"He was incredibly gregarious but somehow managed to stir in a level of seriousness, intensity, and motivational virtuosity that one simply could not believe he would fail," Dan Smith remembered. "One of the most unusual coaches I ever saw."

Thalman shared McKenna's remarkable work ethic, Strickler recalled. "For the first ten years of his tenure, his office was on the top floor of the old and somewhat dilapidated Cocke Hall on VMI's post. There was a small shower in the office, and he had the building and grounds people bring him a VMI hay rack (bed frame) and hay (mattress). Often, during the season, he slept in his office three nights a week as he prepared for the next opponent."

And he always seemed to find a way for his teams to bounce back. In

1980 following a 55-10 drubbing in Lexington at the hands of Tennessee/Chattanooga, the Keydets faced a very good Richmond team on the road the next week and somehow came away with a 22-17 win. In 1976, VMI started the season 1-5, and the fan grumbling began. However, Thalman drove his Keydets to win their last four games of the season to finish at .500.

It also didn't hurt that, like McKenna, Thalman enjoyed the admiration of the press in Virginia.

"One of Coach Thalman's favorite TV sportscasters was Roy Stanley, with WDBJ-TV in Roanoke, who usually worked weekends and often during the week to do interviews for the upcoming game," Strickler recalled. "Roy was a happy-go-lucky guy who shot from the hip and was brutally honest. One Monday, after VMI had been soundly beaten on Saturday, Roy came to Lexington to interview Coach Thalman. Roy started the interview, 'Well Coach you really got clobbered on Saturday, what do you plan do about it this week?' Thalman got a big kick out of Roy's directness and honesty and proceeded to give him the interview he needed."

The coach wasn't quite as forgiving in the late 1970s when Bill Millsaps, sports editor of *The Richmond Times-Dispatch*, wrote a feature about him and described Thalman as "a five-foot-five bantam rooster."

Thalman, who <u>was</u> about 5-5, was known to be a little sensitive about his height. "He called me a five-foot-five bantam rooster," he told an associate. "Hell, that's a damn midget."

Thalman's 1981 season began with a 5-0-1 start, and many thought VMI had a shot at an undefeated season. But by the seventh game, two of his top players (a wide receiver leading the Southern Conference in receptions and a co-captain defensive tackle) were dismissed from school for honor violations. VMI lost its next three games to Virginia, Richmond, and Furman. The loss to Furman cost the Keydets the Southern Conference championship. However, Thalman again worked his magic as VMI stunned a Virginia Tech team, scheduled for a bowl game, 6-0 in Blacksburg to end the season 6-3-1.

An indication of just how dismal things would turn after Thalman was fired a few years later – No VMI coach has had a winning season since Thalman's 6-3-1 campaign in 1981. That would be 33 years without a winning record heading into the 2014 season.

That is why VMI treasures the success of the McKenna and Thalman years at VMI. The McKenna/Thalman legacy was buttressed when the McKenna's son, Steve, accepted a football scholarship to VMI playing defensive back for some of Coach Thalman's best teams in the mid-to-late 1970s. Steve graduated from VMI in 1979.

Thalman's teams had some monumental wins: Three victories over Virginia Tech in 1973, 1974, and 1981 and three consecutive wins over Virginia in 1976, 1977, and 1978, while losing to the Cavaliers by a single point in 1975 and by three points in 1981. VMI's only win in history over Army came in 1981. Over the nine-year stretch of his best seasons (1974-1982), the Keydets' combined record versus state rivals William & Mary and Richmond was 10-8.

"It's ironic that these coaches have the longest tenure of any in VMI history – Coach Thalman 14 years, Coach McKenna 13 years," Strickler pointed out. "Coaching at VMI is difficult and is arguably the toughest job in Division I football. Eddie Williamson, who succeeded Coach Thalman, was as principled a man as I have ever met. He set a goal for himself of turning the program around in four years. When he didn't do it, he resigned. One day in the middle of his third season, we were talking in his office, and he said, 'One day you and I are going to take off to Atlanta and find Coach Thalman and take him out for a big steak dinner, because anyone who can be the head coach at VMI for 14 years deserves a medal.'"

If Williamson had ever managed to make such a trip, he would have had to include Coach McKenna in the invitation.

LEGACY

Truth be known, there were more than a few players in the Thalman era that snickered behind his back at the coach's unbridled optimism. The same was true for John McKenna and his unbending discipline. Such cynicism is often the nature of young athletes, particularly in a place as difficult as VMI. But time had a way of curing even the staunchest non-believers. As the years passed, the era gained greater clarity in the eyes of the players. The more they came to understand what they had accomplished and what they had gained personally in the process, the greater the coach's esteem surged in their minds.

Thalman's success was an extension of John McKenna's legacy at VMI, and as the years passed that legacy evolved and matured, marked in time by reunions and gatherings with his players.

McKenna, of course, also made his mark at Georgia Tech, although the transition in Atlanta was not easy. In addition to assuming the role of associate director of athletics, he also ran the university's extensive intramural program. Plus he coached the Georgia Tech freshman team for Bobby Dodd, quite a step down from the duties of a Division I head coach. It was also difficult for his family, as his wife and children had grown fond of Lexington over the years.

However, the McKenna's made their way as did the coach in his various roles. Bobby Dodd held the title of athletic director/head football coach. But McKenna, in essence, was Georgia Tech's athletic director, Bobby Ross explained. "Coach was pretty much the AD. Basically, he ran everything. Coach Dodd had the title, but he was still coaching. He didn't have the time to do it."

Two decades later, McKenna also played a role in bringing Ross to Georgia Tech as head coach for five seasons, a tenure that culminated in Ross's 1990 team going undefeated and winning a share of the national championship, an accomplishment that crowned their relationship and their years at VMI together.

Despite such grand success, Ross in interviews always seemed to turn to his humbling moments in discussing his old coach. He often recalled the story of the opening game of his freshman year against Tulane at the Sugar Bowl, when he thought he might be going into the game at quarterback. Coach McKenna called him to the sidelines from the bench. Instead, McKenna asked him his shoe size, which was the same as the current quarterback Tom Dooley, whose right shoe was bothering him. Dooley, who would later become a prominent NFL official, returned to the game with Ross' right shoe, and Ross returned to the bench hiding his right foot.

Such tales came to dominate the numerous team reunions of VMI's McKenna teams in Lexington over the years. "He loved it up here," Ross said of Lexington, where the coach would sit and listen to the stories his former players would tell. "The guys would come up and talk to him, and they'd start telling stories, and he would laugh. He loved to hear those stories."

In the fall of 1987, as Ross was working his way through a tough first season at Georgia Tech, McKenna's undefeated team of 1957 held a special 30th reunion.

It was quite an affair, Julie Martin recalled. "Before the evening was formally underway, the alumni players were having a grand time over drinks and smokes at Moody Hall (VMI's alumni building), with lots of laughter and locker room tales – until Coach McKenna walked in. Suddenly, these grown men, now doctors, lawyers, and successful businessmen, looked like little boys with hands caught in the cookie jar. They grew silent, cigarettes were extinguished, beers and mixed drinks were shoved aside as if they belonged to someone else. Their old coach was still in full command."

McKenna would remain in command for three more decades, well into his nineties. Mark Berman, who began covering sports for *The Roanoke Times* in 1999, found himself with the duty of phoning Coach McKenna in search of an interview whenever one of VMI's former football greats passed away. A hard-nosed journalist, Berman was touched by McKenna's ability to recall great detail about his players. The reporter was also struck at the coach's great intellect.

No better example of that exists than McKenna's remarks in 2004 as a deathly ill John Morgan was inducted into the VMI Sports Hall of Fame.

When John Morgan was graduated from VMI in 1955, he was awarded a commission as a 2nd Lieutenant in the United States Air Force,' McKenna told the assemblage. 'After six months, he was called to active duty and was sent to flight school. He earned his wings in 1957 and was sent to Germany during the Cold War. Johnny flew countless missions and even broke the sound barrier a few times in a non-sonic aircraft…just for the fun-of-it and the hell-of-it. He paid his dues; he was now a golden boy, member of an elite team, the crème de la crème.

But when Morgan played on VMI's 1953 and 1954 football teams, he was an inside lineman, sometime and often known as a grunt. I don't say that disparagingly because I was a grunt myself, playing center in my college days.

Johnny made a major contribution because he blocked and tackled with ferocity and efficiency and most importantly with consistency. From the highlights of beating the University of Virginia and Virginia Tech and winning the State Championship, to the long afternoon against West Virginia and the abyss of the game with Cincinnati, John's attitude was like that of Welsh Poet Ethylwyn Wetherald…"I was not told to win or lose, my orders are to fight." In games against all opponents including those of superior teams like Boston College and Florida State, Morgan always played to the hilt. The 17th century poet John Dryden tells the story of John Morgan's career in football at VMI, quote, "play on my merry men all, I am a little wounded, but I am unslain; I will lay me down to bleed for a while, and I will rise, rise and fight with you again."

McKenna continued to enjoy that razor-sharp mind even as he encountered the other difficulties of age.

In 2001, he fell and broke his hip. Early in his rehabilitation, he received a floral arrangement and a get-well card from three members of the Class of 1960. The card read: "Dear Coach – sorry to learn about your accident… hope your recovery is quick and complete. PS - Move the drill ten yards."

He smiled at that one.

In 2005, VMI honored McKenna at a reunion of his teams. His words were, as always, succinct, well chosen, and at this venue poignant.

There are a few remarks that I wish to address to you former players who were young men when I made your fall and spring afternoons <u>miserable</u>, said McKenna.

*In the early 1900's, a great Yale football player asked that on his gravestone it would just state: "He played the game." Not that he was a star, or All-conference, or All-American, all of which he was. It simply said, 'He played the game.' All of you are entitled to say the same no matter how much or how long you played: Rat team, scout team or first team…**you played the game**.*

My strongest memories of VMI football are those games which we lost against teams with greater depth than we had, even though we held our own, outplayed them. There is a wry saying among coaches: Losing feels worse than winning feels good. The poet John Greenleaf Whittier perhaps said it better in a couplet in his poem <u>Maud Muller</u>…in a different context of course. – "For all sad words of tongue or pen, the saddest are these, It might have been."

But all the victories and all the disappointments fade almost from memory when I reflect upon what you have done with your lives since leaving the Institute to do battle in the so-called real world. You have achieved notable success in a diversity of fields: education, the law, medicine, dentistry, the military, business, industry and finance, ad infinitum. Your achievements dwarf what we accomplished together in the 50s and 60s. If I played even a minor role in that success, I am rewarded many fold.

Of the 278 players VMI football players McKenna coached, 89 percent received VMI degrees and several more obtained degrees elsewhere. Twenty-six received medical degrees, 22 received law degrees. Seven earned PhDs, and two were named Rhodes Scholars.

The 2005 event was also highlighted by the remarks of Dick Sessoms, former *Roanoke Times* sportswriter, who worked in athletic publicity at VMI with McKenna. He began by mentioning Stonewall Jackson and George C. Marshall and the leadership and personality traits they had in common. "They were iron-willed, merciless disciplinarians, stern as the Old Testament by which they fought, and vowed to the New Testament by which they lived, focused, in command of their battle plans down to the smallest logistical detail, respected by their troops if also hard on them...harder on their foes."

"And so we come to tonight...a night for remembering old gridiron glories, old dreams and legends...and we come to honor another in the company of the great men of VMI...John McKenna...a spiritual son of Jackson and Marshall, and so much more than a winning football coach...a teacher by the most exacting of standards...a life-long mentor not only to his players but to his fellow coaches and to all of us privileged by our association with him...a great and good man whose place among VMI heroes is assured.

So let's get right to the nickname...The Eagle. We may never know the player who first discovered Coach was all-seeing on the practice field. But we do know that whoever he was, he was amazed that Coach saw him skip that one lousy pushup."

"Of course, you guys all experienced his sense of humor, ever laced with devastating sarcasm. For example, the day things couldn't get worse at practice and one of our backs got a cleat on his left shoe tangled up with the shoestring on his right shoe coming out of the play call. He tripped so hard he was nearly knocked cold. 'Oh my God,' Coach exclaimed, 'We can't even get out of the huddle.'

"Such anecdotes flood Cameron Hall tonight as each of us recall personal exchanges with him. Outside of Eileen and possibly his family, I wonder how many know that for a spell his favorite country song was 'El Paso' by Marty Robbins. There became something real Freudian about that after the '57 team turned down the Sun Bowl to play in El Paso!

For many years Eileen got John to relax on Thursday evenings in season with a uncompetitive hand of bridge with their good friends, Tina and Bob Jeffrey. Of course, everything else John did during the week put the capital P into Preparation for the upcoming game. For example, I had three special jobs for him on road trips:

Find a blood and guts war movie for the team to see on Friday night... preferably John Wayne, but Gregory Peck in *Pork Chop Hill* would do!

Locate the nearest Catholic Church and find out times for Mass.

At breakfast, make sure that no one tried to serve us colon cloggers… (those are doughnuts for the benefit of you ladies.)"

And woe to the dining room manager who failed to follow John's advance menu instructions. I mean precisely. Quote: 'Our contract calls for a cup of soup…not a bowl of it. Take this back and serve it in a cup as specified.'"

"Attention to detail. That's what he taught us all. Perfection, or as close as we could come to it, on and off the field, was the slim margin he needed to win. Look at all those close scores in the winning years. It wasn't always talent. And he certainly never had depth…it was focus…commitment… it was skill…determination. And pre-game the dressing room wasn't for inspirational pep talks. Herb Patchin called that communion time. 'John communed with the team,' Herb would say. And Coach never forgot the text of the sermon…the last minute rules he drilled into you before you took the field. Quote, 'Be a 100 percenter all the time…on defense do your job – hit the man you are on…remember that a blocked punt can be advanced by either side…be alert for fumbles, get that loose ball…keep the blocker off your legs…huddle discipline is absolute, no one but the quarterback talks… cover kickoffs hard, stay in your lane…fire out on blocks, keep your feet moving…point out your man on punts, you must get the kick away.'"

"Well, it all comes back on a night like this doesn't it? John's dapper dress on game days…his businessman's hat…Herb's old black satchel and the smell of his training room…Henry Johnson, God bless him, washing your game uniforms…Tom Joynes laughing and telling the latest Doc Carroll story. And what a gift of perspective the great Herb Patchin had. Once, a Sportsman's Club supporter was distraught because coach refused to devote one of our precious few scholarships to this 6'-8" 240 pound prospect. He was a big kid but wasn't a player in John's book. So the alum goes to Patchin to complain. Herb set him straight in classic Patchin style. 'Let's put it this way,' Herb told him, 'I've got 10 fingers, but that doesn't mean I can play the piano.'"

"If I close my eyes, I can see the totally remarkable picture of the VMI sideline during most of Coach McKenna's 13 seasons. Army had a lonesome end, VMI had a lonesome coach. There wasn't an assistant coach in sight, much less a raft of offensive and defensive coordinators and position and special teams' coaches. During my time here, John had only two fulltime assistants. Clark King would be up in the press box on the phone to the bench, and Vito Ragazzo, succeeded in later years by Bo Sherman, would always be away scouting next week's opponent. Of course the Rats would be playing somewhere else for Colonel Sam Heflin, or later for Charley (Hi Fi) McGinnis...and Weenie Miller and Chuck Noe before him, would be scouting an opponent two weeks in advance, at least until they had to start coaching basketball. Thus we had to get to the final Thanksgiving Day game against the Hokies before the full staff could join Coach on the sidelines. Only in his final years was John awarded the luxury of a third full-time assistant...and coaches like Richard Bell and eventually Dick Harmison joined him. But mostly for nine games a year, the sideline was an unforgettable sight for me... the solitary figure of Coach McKenna standing in front of you. Standing, I can say in retrospect, like a stone wall."

"Sportswriters throughout the South exalted him as a coaching genius, and ever referred to him as 'scholarly,' 'articulate,' and as a 'consummate gentleman.' Indeed, I believe they admired him most for his integrity and because they understood what John McKenna meant to college football nationally in the '50s and '60s...The great writers 'get it' that he was nearly peerless in his profession...that his success with limited resources carried the very image of the gallant New Market charge...the very image of the Virginia Military Institute.

"And so we who are assembled here tonight, each of us bearing the McKenna imprint in our lives, and we grope for manly words to tell him how much he means to us...how much we and the Institute treasure him. John, surely it is one of the greatest honors of my life to be asked to reminisce tonight about your influence and about what it was like in an era of struggle, yes, but consistent triumph for VMI football. None of us would have articulated it this way 45 years ago, or perhaps even thought it, but, Coach, you earned the respect and this collective lump in our throats. There is only one word which sums up the feeling for you in this room tonight. It is love."

John McKenna died March 31, 2007. John Candler delivered an address at a memorial service held at VMI's Jackson Memorial Hall and Howard Dyer delivered the eulogy at his funeral in Atlanta. Here are excerpts from their addresses:

"So who was this special man," said Candler, "This McKenna whose life we celebrate today?

McKenna, like Churchill, Gandhi, Lombardi – He needed only one name.

McKenna said this, McKenna did that, McKenna's coming!

Coach combined character, integrity, and presence to lead. He understood leadership. He understood that leaders are highly visible and that they do the hard things. He understood that leadership is not rank, privilege, titles, or money; it is responsibility. He understood that leadership is not popularity, but it is about achieving results. He didn't try to be our friend; he didn't try to make us like him. I don't think we ever thought that liking him was our prerogative. But, we trusted him...we respected him...we feared him...we wanted to please him...we feared failure. We never took the field expecting anything but victory. We would have followed him anywhere."

"As 18, 19, 20-year old young men, we found him to be a strict, unbending disciplinarian," Dyer said. "He was the head coach in every sense of the word. Everything went through him. He was an intimidating figure to every player and was known secretly as 'The Eagle.' His mere presence in a room brought an element of fear with it. The challenges of the Ratline were miniscule in comparison to facing his disapproval. Little did we know or appreciate at the time that he was preparing us for the greater game of life for us to get the picture. Then it all became clear. It was not just about touchdowns, wins, championships, or whether you made the green, blue, or red team -- it was about facing life's journey, and the ups and downs associated include: a troubled marriage, loss of job, unexpected health problems, and the other myriad forms of adversity. Inexplicably, a little voice in our head would whisper, 'How would Coach McKenna handle the problem?' Always-always, that question was the litmus test. At those important times the comfort of his life's example sustained us, gave us strength, solace, and the confidence that we could handle the situation facing us. What a gift – what a treasure – what a man – what a legacy."

ACKNOWLEDGMENTS

It's my great honor to have been a part of a team helping to put together this retrospective on the tenure of coach John McKenna at the Virginia Military Institute.

He was a coach like no other, and I want to thank his family, his former players and co-workers, for all of the time they took to recall their time spent in his presence.

I'd also like to highlight the fine effort of my co-author, Mike Ashley, for his research and writing. I am extremely fortunate that Bobby Ross - VMI Class of 1959 - a name synonymous with college and professional football and whose roots are traced directly to Coach McKenna, agreed to write the Foreword for *Best Regrets*. Vital to this production were the design and editing efforts of longtime VMI staff member Burton Floyd. Julie Martin, retired assistant public relations officer, also provided a full edit of this book.

Many thanks as well to Greg Cavallaro '84, Donnie Ross '74 and the VMI Keydet Club for their assistance in publishing this work and preserving the legacy of John McKenna.

Diane Jacob and Mary Laura Kludy of the VMI Archives and Wade Branner '83 and the staff of the VMI Sports Information Office provided invaluable support. Thanks also to Sherry Teague in VMI's Preston Library.

Best Regrets is a direct function of the great love that Mike Strickler '71 has for the school and its athletic programs. He has been a man of keen insight, good humor, and uncommon persistence in the production of this book. Often such devotees can be over the top in their efforts, but Mike has always been so admirably measured and steady in his approach. His patience on this project has been so far beyond the pale, it's clearly Hall of Fame stuff.

Thanks, Mike, for all of your efforts on these pages here.

I'm also quite grateful for the opportunity this project has brought to work with General J.H. Binford Peay III '62 and to witness first hand his strong, steady leadership style and his dedication. I've worked with a variety of university presidents and officials, athletic directors, great coaches over my years. Clearly, General Peay is a cut above them all. His leadership and vision have allowed VMI to prosper in challenging times.

Like so many others who also played for McKenna, General Peay attributes much of his approach to the example set by "the Eagle."

Having attended Virginia Military Institute and graduated from the school in 1975, I had some idea of the great success of Coach McKenna when this project began.

I had even played a year in the football program beginning in August 1970, just five short seasons after he coached his last game there.

My experience playing there reminds me of just how focused college athletic programs are on "the now." There was never any discussion of coach McKenna that I recall as a freshman in the program, even though the varsity head coach was Vito Ragazzo, one of McKenna's longtime assistants. Everything was about each day's practice and preparation for the next game, as it should have been.

There was little or no time to talk about the past, especially at VMI, because the daily agenda was packed with all sorts of academic and military issues, which meant the football coaches had to make the best use of precious little time.

Obviously the circumstances have led to tremendous difficulty for VMI football over the years. A book like this finally allows the time to contemplate the values and singular approach of Coach McKenna.

Imagine what a strong, admirable competitive environment we'd have in college athletics today if coaches were more like John McKenna.

Sincerely,

Roland Lazenby '74
August 2014

INDEX

A